Views given for 'Alienation — — — 11

Alienation is ... understood int respect

Cline — p. 95

"How can alienation be overcome?"
98f.

The whole of world history is nothing but the creation of man through human labour

The changing of worker is not abolished but extended to all men. p103

# Marx and Alienation

*Also by Sean Sayers*

PLATO'S REPUBLIC
An Introduction

MARXISM AND HUMAN NATURE

SOCIALISM AND DEMOCRACY (*edited with David McLellan*)

SOCIALISM, FEMINISM AND PHILOSOPHY (*edited with Peter Osborne*)
A Radical Philosophy Reader

SOCIALISM AND MORALITY (*edited with David McLellan*)

REALITY AND REASON
Dialectic and the Theory of Knowledge

HEGEL, MARX AND DIALECTIC (*with Richard Norman*)
A Debate

# Marx and Alienation

## Essays on Hegelian Themes

Sean Sayers
*University of Kent, Canterbury, UK*

First published 2011 by
PALGRAVE MACMILLAN

Palgrave Macmillan in the UK is an imprint of Macmillan Publishers Limited, registered in England, company number 785998, of Houndmills, Basingstoke, Hampshire RG21 6XS.

Palgrave Macmillan in the US is a division of St Martin's Press LLC, 175 Fifth Avenue, New York, NY 10010.

Palgrave Macmillan is the global academic imprint of the above companies and has companies and representatives throughout the world.

Palgrave® and Macmillan® are registered trademarks in the United States, the United Kingdom, Europe and other countries

ISBN 978-0-230-27654-3      hardback

This book is printed on paper suitable for recycling and made from fully managed and sustained forest sources. Logging, pulping and manufacturing processes are expected to conform to the environmental regulations of the country of origin.

A catalogue record for this book is available from the British Library.

Library of Congress Cataloging-in-Publication Data

Sayers, Sean.
    Marx and alienation : essays on Hegelian themes / Sean Sayers.
        p. cm.
    Includes bibliographical references (p.      ) and index.
    ISBN 978–0–230–27654–3 (alk. paper)
        1. Marx, Karl, 1818–1883. 2. Alienation (Philosophy) 3. Hegel, Georg Wilhelm Friedrich, 1770–1831. I. Title.
    B3305.M74S315 2011
    193–dc22                                                          2011012467

10   9   8   7   6   5   4   3   2   1
20   19   18   17   16   15   14   13   12   11

Printed and bound in Great Britain by
CPI Antony Rowe, Chippenham and Eastbourne

*For Esmé and Neve*

# Contents

# Acknowledgements

I am grateful to the publishers of the following works for permission to re-use copyright material from them as the basis for the chapters indicated.

'Creative Activity and Alienation in Hegel and Marx', *Historical Materialism*, 2003, 11, 1, 107–28 (Chapter 2).

'Labour in Modern Industrial Society', in A. Chitty and M. McIvor (eds) *Karl Marx and Contemporary Philosophy* (Basingstoke: Palgrave Macmillan, 2009), pp. 143–58 (Chapter 3).

'Individual and Society in Marx and Hegel', *Science & Society*, 2007, 71, 1, 84–102 (Chapter 4).

'Freedom and the "Realm of Necessity"', in D. Moggach (ed.) *The New Hegelians: Politics and Philosophy in the Hegelian School* (Cambridge: Cambridge University Press, 2006), pp. 261–74 (Chapter 5).

'The "Uplifting Influence" of Work and Industry: The Philosophical Background to the Step of Steel', in *Serge Prokofiev, Le pas d'acier 1925*, DVD Set (Cheltenham: IDM Ltd and AHRC, 2006) (Appendix).

# A Note on the Term 'Alienation'

'Alienation' is one of the standard translations of both *Entfremdung* and *Entäußerung* in Marx's writings. The translations 'estrangement' for the former and 'externalisation' for the latter are also common, but 'alienation' is more familiar to most English speakers and I prefer it for that reason.[1]

According to Lukács (1975, 538), these terms were originally the German translations of the English eighteenth century word 'alienation' used in an economic or legal sense to mean the sale of a commodity or relinquishment of freedom. Marx sometimes uses *'Entäusserung'* to describe the way we relinquish ourselves in our products, and *'Entfremdung'* for the way in which these products become hostile forces working against us; but he also uses the terms interchangeably. These different usages can be seen in the following passage from the *1844 Manuscripts*.

> The object that labour produces, its product, stands opposed to it as *something alien [fremdes]*, as a power independent of the producer. The product of labour is labour embodied and made material in an object, it is the *objectification [Vergegenständlichung]* of labour.... In the sphere of political economy, this realization of labour appears as a *loss of reality* for the worker, objectification as loss of and bondage to the object, and appropriation as estrangement [*Entfremdung*], as *alienation [Entäußerung]*. (Marx, 1975e, 324)[2]

Some, like Kain (1982, 75–92), maintain that Marx uses these terms to denote distinct concepts. However, this is disputed (Bottomore in Marx, 1961b, xix) and I am not aware of any decisive evidence to show that it is true. In what follows I will not attempt to distinguish them or Marx's use of them.

---

[1]For summaries of issues of translation see Arthur (1986, 49–50, 147–9) and Marx (1975a, 429–30).

[2]'Der Gegenstand, den die Arbeit produziert, ihr Produkt, tritt ihr als ein fremdes Wesen, als eine von dem Produzenten unabhängige Macht gegenüber. Das Produkt der Arbeit ist die Arbeit, die sich in einem Gegenstand fixiert, sachlich gemacht hat, es ist die Vergegenständlichung der Arbeit.... Diese Verwirklichung der Arbeit erscheint in dem nationalökonomischen Zustand als Entwirklichung des Arbeiters, die Vergegenständlichung als Verlust und Knechtschaft des Gegenstandes, die Aneignung als Entfremdung, als Entäußerung.' (Marx and Engels, 1998, 656)

# Introduction

'Alienation' is one of the most familiar terms of Marxist philosophy. It is one of the few theoretical terms from Marxism that has entered into ordinary language, and yet it is one of the most misunderstood and misused terms in the whole of Marxism. In ordinary speech and even in academic contexts it is often taken to describe vague feelings of malaise or meaninglessness, particularly with respect to work. A similarly vague meaning is sometimes attributed to Marx as well. Whatever others may mean by it, Marx's use of the term cannot be understood in this way. Marx's meaning is precise and specific.

Alienation is a concept that Marx inherits from Hegel and the young Hegelians and it figures most prominently in Marx's early writings where the influences of these writers are most evident. I go out of my way in what follows to show in some detail how an understanding of Hegel's philosophy is essential for a proper understanding of Marx.

This might seem so obvious as to need no emphasis, but it has been widely disputed by the main tendencies of Marxist thought in recent times. Discussion of Marxism in the Western world since the 1960s has been dominated by a reaction against Hegelian ideas. This agenda has been shared equally by the analytical Marxism which has predominated in the English speaking world and by the structuralist Marxism which has been the major influence in the continental European tradition.

In the English speaking philosophical tradition, most analytical Marxists have simply shut their eyes to the Hegelian aspects of Marx's work and tried to re-write (or, as they say, 'reconstruct') his theories as though Hegel had never existed. On the other hand, many philosophers within the continental tradition, particularly those influenced by Althusser, have maintained that Marx made a sharp break with his youthful Hegelianism after his early period and that his later work is 'scientific' and free of this influence. Again the attempt is made to rewrite Marx's philosophy without referring to Hegel. In this book I show that this cannot be done without ignoring or doing violence to some of the most central and fundamental themes in Marx's thought.

One of the main things that Marx inherits from Hegel is the historical and dialectical approach. It is in the light of this that the concept of alienation must be understood. As I argue here, Marx is a thoroughgoing modernist. He maintains that there is a positive aspect to capitalism and the economic development it has brought about. This does not mean that Marx is not also profoundly critical of capitalism and its impact – indeed, it is a central purpose of the concept of alienation to express that criticism. However, it does affect the form that critique takes. This is historical in character. Alienation is not the simple moral notion it is often taken to be. The concept is used to understand capitalism and its development, not merely to condemn it.

After his early period, Marx does not often use the term 'alienation' – it and much other Hegelian language is for the most part abandoned.[1] Nevertheless, the *concept* of alienation is implicit throughout Marx's work, and it continues to provide a major basis for his understanding of capitalism and for his critique of the impact of the market. The view that he rejects the concept as well as the term and makes a total theoretical break with it was put forward by Althusser. However, this view is now discredited and has few proponents; even Althusser himself came to abandon it (Althusser, 2006). There are significant changes and developments in Marx's thought but no sharp philosophical break between his early and later works in this respect. I shall not spend time defending this view here. I shall, however, argue for it implicitly by discussing many passages from Marx's later works in which the concept of alienation is clearly being used.

Of course, it is also true that there are some major respects in which Marx differs philosophically from Hegel and rejects his ideas. In particular, Marx rejects Hegel's idealistic and teleological account of history. However, I do not dwell on this theme. My purpose here is the more limited one of exploring Marx's account of alienation and its overcoming and showing how a knowledge of Hegel's philosophy can contribute towards an understanding of this aspect of Marx's thought.

In Chapter 1, I give a broad outline of Hegel's legacy with respect to the concept of alienation in order to locate Marx's work in its wider philosophical context. According to the usual story, in the aftermath of Hegel's death, his followers split into 'left' and 'right' tendencies. While this is correct as far as it goes, it omits another important strand of post-Hegelian thought: the radical reaction against the Hegelian and historicist approach of individualist and 'existential' philosophers starting with Kierkegaard. This leads to an 'existentialist' tradition of thought about alienation which is often confused with Marxism and which needs

---

[1]With the important exception of the *Grundrisse* of 1857–8, an early draft of *Capital*.

to be distinguished from it in order to form a clear picture of the Marxist account.

The next two chapters focus on Marx's notion of alienated labour. In Chapter 2, I show that the keys to understanding the assumptions about human nature involved in it lie in Hegel's philosophy. In my previous work on this topic (Sayers, 1998, Part I), I was only dimly aware of the philosophical basis of Marx's concept of alienated labour and its Hegelian roots. I was surprised to find that is this most clearly articulated in Hegel's *Aesthetics*. As I show, knowledge of this work is enormously helpful for understanding Marx's philosophy.

Marx's concept of labour is often thought to assume a 'productivist' model of work, and it is widely criticised for being dated and irrelevant in contemporary postindustrial conditions. New notions, such as 'immaterial' and 'biopolitical' production, are needed, it is argued. In Chapter 3, I show that an understanding of the Hegelian roots of Marx's philosophy reveals a very different picture of Marx's account of labour that refutes these arguments and provides the basis for an illuminating understanding of postindustrial work.

Although discussion of Marx's notion of alienation has focused largely on the topic of labour, this notion plays a much wider role in his thought. Chapter 4 deals with alienation in social and economic relations. It shows how Marx's theory develops from Hegel's account of 'civil society' and uses a framework of historical development similar to Hegel's. However, I argue that Marx uses the concept of alienation to criticise the liberal, communitarian and Hegelian conceptions of modern society and to envisage forms of individuality and community that lie beyond them. Chapter 5 goes on to discuss Marx's notion of freedom in connection with his account of labour and to criticise some widespread and influential misconceptions.

The concept of alienation is almost invariably taken to be a purely negative moral notion based on a concept of universal human nature. This sort of account is criticised in Chapter 6. The concept of alienation, I show, must rather be interpreted in the light of the Hegelian historical ideas from which it derives. In Hegel, alienation is not a purely negative phenomenon, it is a stage in the process of human development. Marx's account of alienation must be understood in similar terms. Alienation is not a merely subjective discontent with work, it is an objective and historically specific condition, and a necessary phase of historical development. The criticism of capitalism implied in the concept of alienation does not appeal to universal moral standards, I argue, it is historical and relative. Overcoming alienation must also be conceived in historical terms, not as the realisation of a timeless, universal moral ideal, but as the dialectical supersession of capitalist conditions achieved in communism.

In the last group of chapters I explore Marx's concept of communism as an unalienated and free society in which the division of labour is eliminated, and private property and the market are abolished. Chapter 7 explains and defends the idea of the overcoming of the division of labour in communism. Chapter 8 deals with Marx's account of private property and its supersession, and Chapter 9 gives an overall account and justification of Marx's idea of communism in more popular terms.

Finally, the Appendix contains a brief article that was originally written to accompany a reconstruction of Prokofiev's Soviet ballet, *Le pas d'acier*, which deals with many of the themes covered in this book. The ballet was directed by Lesley-Anne Sayers, my sister-in-law, who sadly died suddenly this year while still in her prime.

This book is composed of a series of papers written during the last seven years. All focus on the topic of Marx's theory of alienation and its overcoming. They develop a single account and form a logical sequence. Originally I planned to write this material up as a book but I feared that I would not be able to complete it in time for the RAE deadline, so I wrote it as a series of papers instead.[2] Some of these have been published previously, but the majority appear here for the first time. The previously published material has been revised for the present volume to bring it into line with my present views where necessary and to remove repetition where possible.

The origin of the chapters as separate papers has meant that I focus on a number of controversial aspects of Marx's account of alienation rather than giving a systematic and comprehensive treatment. Some topics are passed over altogether, such as political and religious alienation, whereas others are discussed in considerable detail. Moreover, because some of the chapters were written as papers for particular occasions, the book lacks something of the unity of style and continuity of a book written as such; and, inevitably, some repetition remains. The

---

[2]The RAE (superseded by the REF since 2008) is a mechanism that has been used since 1992 for the distribution of state funding to British universities. Publications and research activities are graded on a quantitative scale in order to provide criteria for allocating funds. Scholarly work in British universities has been dominated, and seriously distorted, by the need to conform to these requirements in order to obtain funding (Sayers, 1997).

advantage, however, is that the chapters that go to make it up are self-contained pieces that can be read separately and in any order.

In writing this book I have been helped by a large number of people. I am particularly grateful for their knowledgeable and detailed comments on earlier drafts of many of these pieces to David McLellan and to the members of the Marx and Philosophy Society 'Work in Progress' seminars at which some of this material was first presented, including Christopher Arthur, Andrew Chitty, Jan Derry, Nick Gray, Geoff Kay, David Marjoribanks, and Meade McCloughan. I am also grateful to Edward Greenwood, Edmund Jephcott, Martin Scofield, and other members of the Philosophy Reading Group in Canterbury for their stimulus over many years. I have developed many of these ideas in courses on 'Hegel and Marx' that I have taught at the University of Kent, Mount Holyoke College, Massachusetts, Boğaziçi University, Istanbul and Fudan University, Shanghai. I am greatly indebted to many students in all these places for their questioning and critical responses. Finally, I am particularly grateful to Janet my wife for her continuing love and support.

Sean Sayers
Canterbury
December 2010

# 1
# The Concept of Alienation: Hegelian Themes in Modern Social Thought

The concept of alienation is one of the most important and fruitful  legacies of Hegel's social philosophy. It is strange therefore that Hegel's own account is widely rejected, not least by writers in those traditions which have taken up and developed the concept in the most influential ways: Marxism and existentialism.

Generalisation in this area is particularly difficult. The very claim that Marxism has a theory of alienation is controversial. The term has a shifting meaning in Marx's early writings and it plays only an occasional role in his later work. Generalising about existentialism is even more problematic: it is not a definite philosophical school at all. At best it is a loose tradition, and many of the writers associated with it do not explicitly use the concept of alienation.

Nevertheless, there is important common ground in the way philosophers in both these traditions respond to Hegel's philosophy and in their concerns about the self and society. These concerns, which play a central role in both traditions, are generally referred to by means of the term 'alienation'. So despite the problems, the concept of alienation provides a useful focus by means of which to explore these Hegelian themes in contemporary social thought.

Partly for the reasons just mentioned, much of the discussion of alienation is murky and confused. At times it appears that two quite different concepts have been mixed up in it which have little real connection with each other. In the Marxist literature, alienation is often taken to be a concept that describes and criticises the social and economic conditions of capitalism. In existentialist writing, by contrast, the concept is used primarily to refer to a psychological, perhaps even spiritual, kind of malaise which is pervasive in modern society but not specific to it. Rather it is symptomatic of the human condition as such.

Some writers try to merge these two strands of thought together (Pappenheim, 1959; Schacht, 1971), but that is unsatisfactory. It is tempting simply to distinguish two quite separate and distinct notions of alienation, a Marxist and an existentialist one; but that too is problematic. Even within these two traditions, both strands are present. Thus it would be wrong to suggest that Marx uses the term 'alienation' exclusively to describe a social or economic condition. On contrary, as Plamenatz (1975, 141ff) argues, two 'kinds of alienation' can be distinguished in Marx's work, 'social' and 'spiritual'.[1] Conversely, it is also a mistake to think that philosophers in the existentialist tradition are concerned solely with psychological or spiritual matters. A critique of the alienating conditions of modern society is a prominent feature of much existentialist thought.[2] In short, both aspects are a part of both traditions. To understand how they are related and how they differ we need to go back to Hegel.

## Two responses

The concept of alienation is central to Hegel's account of the development of spirit (*Geist*), and thus of the process of human self-development. In contrast to the enlightenment philosophers who came before him, Hegel does not treat individual self-consciousness as an immediate, unchanging given. The self is a historical and social creation. It develops through a process of alienation and its overcoming, self-estrangement and self-recognition, a 'fall' into division and reconciliation.

The story is often told of how, in the years immediately following Hegel's death, the Hegelian movement split. A number of 'right' or 'old' Hegelians remained loyal to what had become the conservative views of Hegel's later years. A larger and more influential group (which included Marx and Engels) rejected Hegel's account of contemporary society and developed a more radical approach.

For these 'left' Hegelians, Hegel's claim that reason had been realised and reconciliation achieved in modern society was absurd and untenable. Division and disharmony were all too evident in the unideal conditions

---

[1] Cf. Elster, 1985; Wood, 1981a. These writers do little to explain the connection and relation of these different kinds of alienation.

[2] I go on to discuss this presently. See for example Kierkegaard (1962) on the 'present age', Heidegger's (1962) descriptions of 'average everydayness', Nietzsche (1994) on 'herd' and 'slave' morality.

of Europe at the time, then undergoing the traumatic impact of indus-trialisation. Alienation had clearly not been overcome. Nevertheless, the left Hegelians maintained, the realisation of reason and social reconcilia-tion remained valid as ideals. What Hegel treated as an established reality, should be taken rather as an end, still to be achieved. Reason had not been realised, but it ought to be. These ideas were taken up by Marx in his early work, from which has grown one of the main strands of con-temporary thought about alienation.[3]

This story is familiar enough. Accounts of the aftermath of Hegel's philosophy often go no further. For a full understanding of Hegel's legacy, however, it is important to take a wider view (cf. Marcuse, 1955; Löwith, 1967). For Hegel's philosophy also provoked a quite different critical response of a kind apparent first in Kierkegaard's work. Kierkegaard was a close contemporary of Marx and Engels.[4] His philosophy was also formed in the Hegelian aftermath, but his rejection of Hegel is more thorough-going, he does not regard himself as a 'Hegelian' of any kind. Never-theless, his philosophy is formed in reaction to Hegel's and directly under its influence. It is the first example of a quite different, 'existentialist', way of thinking about issues of the self and alienation bequeathed by Hegel.

## Hegel and Marx on alienation

By 'alienation' Hegel refers to the process by which 'finite spirit', the human self, 'doubles' itself, externalises itself, and then confronts its own other being as something separate, distinct and opposed to it.

Hegel rejects the atomistic individualism of the enlightenment, and its view that the self has a nature which is prior to society and which flourishes best when unrestricted by it. Spirit, for Hegel, is social and historical. It develops through a process of self-division, self-alienation and its overcoming. This occurs in both the theoretical and practical spheres. 'Finite' human spirit, in contrast to infinite spirit (God),

> is bounded and restricted by its opposite, namely nature. This res-triction ... the human spirit in its existence ... overcomes, and thereby raises itself to infinity, by grasping nature in thought through theoret-ical activity, and through practical activity bringing about a harmony

---

[3]Marx, 1975b. See also the illuminating retrospective account in Engels, 1958d.
[4]Kierkegaard and Engels attended the same lectures by Schelling in Berlin in 1841 (Hunt, 2010, 47).

between nature and the spiritual Idea, reason, and the good. (Hegel, 1975, 454)

In practical life, this occurs through work on the natural world and through relations with others in society. In this chapter I will focus particularly on the social aspect of alienation.[5]

According to Hegel, self-conscious spirit evolves through a series of different historical and social forms. Subjectivity, individuality, and freedom develop through a process in which the self is alienated from itself and then comes to recognise itself in its alienation, so that, at the end of the process, the self eventually comes to be at home with itself.

Contrary to the enlightenment individualist account, social relations and institutions do not necessarily constitute barriers to individual development and freedom. On the contrary, individuality and freedom involve the exercise of powers and capacities which can be acquired only in and through community with others. Alienation can be overcome and individuality developed and realised only through participation in a social world: by fulfilling, in Bradley's (1927, chapter 5) phrase, 'my station and duties' (cf. Hegel, 1991, §149).

The self is also historical. It evolves by passing through a series of historical forms. Hegel (1956) portrays human history as a progressive development which starts from the immediate unity and harmony of the earliest communities. This initial phase culminates in the ancient Greek *polis*. With the breakup of the *polis*, humanity then passes through a long period of division, fragmentation and alienation. But the results of this are not purely negative. For in and through this process, individuality, subjectivity and freedom grow and develop. Finally, in the modern liberal state as it emerges after the French Revolution, free and self-conscious individuals at last find reconciliation with the natural and social world. Thus for Hegel, the two aspects of alienation, social and spiritual, are closely linked.

Hegel himself was well aware of the continued existence of social problems and divisions in modern liberal (i.e., capitalist) society. He describes them in remarkably clear and uncompromising terms (see Chapter 2 below). Nevertheless, he sees them only as 'anomalies' (Kuhn, 1970) which do not ultimately refute his idealised picture of the present. To many subsequent thinkers, however, it has seemed absurd to suggest that alienation has been overcome and reason realised in the modern world.

---

[5]I shall discuss alienation in labour at length in some of the chapters that follow.

Both Marxism and existentialism take this view. They agree in rejecting Hegel's picture of modern society in this respect, but they do so in very different ways. Contemporary theories of alienation spring from these different responses.

Marx's account of alienation draws explicitly and directly on Hegel's work. He uses the term to refer to a situation in which our own activities and products take on an independent existence and become hostile powers working against us (Marx, 1975e; cf. Elster, 1985, 100). Marx's main use of the concept is in reference to the form of labour in capitalist society, but he also talks of 'alienation' in the spheres of social and economic relations (division of labour, 'fetishism of commodities'), the state and religion (Marx, 1975e; Marx and Engels, 1978b; Marx, 1961a).

Marx's ideas in this area are directly inherited from Hegel, and there is a considerable congruence between their social theories. Marx agrees with Hegel in regarding the self as a social and historical creation. He regards self-alienation as a social and historical phenomenon which is destined to be overcome with historical development and progress. Thus in Marx, as in Hegel, the social and spiritual aspects of alienation and its overcoming are united.

However, as mentioned already, Marx rejects the Hegelian view that alienation has already been overcome in present society. He also criticises Hegel's account of history as the self-development of spirit for its idealism and instead propounds a materialist theory. Present capitalist society is characterised by alienation. This has an economic and social basis. Alienation will be overcome only when this is changed. Alienation thus serves as a critical concept pointing towards the material transformation of the existing order.

## Existential ideas of alienation

Kierkegaard's philosophy is also formed in response to Hegel. Though he does not use the language of alienation, his ideas about the self in modern society are in some important respects similar to those of Marx. Like Marx, he rejects the Hegelian idea that in the modern world the individual can find reconciliation and alienation is overcome. On the contrary, in the 'present age' individuals are estranged from themselves and from the world, which is experienced as hostile to subjectivity and individuality.

Such estrangement takes the form of 'inauthenticity': of not 'being oneself' or 'true to oneself'. For Kierkegaard such estrangement is characteristic not only of modern life but of the human situation generally.

Similarly, for Heidegger 'inauthenticity' is our normal, 'everyday' state.[6] It is not specific to modern society or to any particular social or historical conditions. On the contrary, for Heidegger (1962, 220), inauthenticity is 'that kind of Being which is closest to Dasein and in which Dasein maintains itself for the most part'.

Neither Kierkegaard nor Heidegger accept the idea that the self has a pregiven nature which will flourish if left alone, uninfluenced by society. Like Hegel and Marx, both believe that the self is necessarily engaged in the world and with others. Authenticity is a mode of being-in-the-world and being-with-others. However, this must not be confused with Hegelian or Marxist notions of self-realisation. In the first place, the existential self has no predetermined 'essence' to be realised, rather it must determine and create itself (Golomb, 1995, 53–4). Second, both Kierkegaard and Heidegger reject the Hegelian view that the way we find or realise ourselves is in and through our social roles. On the contrary, we tend to lose ourselves in them.

Kierkegaard identifies authentic selfhood with true Christianity. 'The speculative [i.e., Hegelian] philosopher views Christianity as an historical phenomenon. But suppose Christianity is nothing of the kind' (Kierkegaard, 1941, 52). Authenticity, he insists, cannot be achieved merely by doing one's duty or fulfilling an objective social role, it is essentially a subjective phenomenon. 'Christianity is spirit, spirit is inwardness, inwardness is subjectivity, subjectivity is essentially passion' (Kierkegaard, 1941, 33). For Kierkegaard, 'socialization must not be confused with salvation', as Westphal (1987, 33) puts it. He scornfully repudiates what he takes to be both the common and the Hegelian view, that being a Christian involves nothing more than carrying out 'my station and its duties'.

> If a man were to say quite simply and unassumingly, that he was concerned for himself, lest perhaps he had no right to call himself a Christian ... he would be smothered in angry glances, and people would say: 'How tiresome to make such a fuss about nothing at all; why can't he behave like the rest of us, who are all Christians?' ... And if he happened to be married, his wife would say to him: 'Dear husband of mine, how can you get such notions into your head? How can

---

[6]Heidegger (1962, 223) talks of 'the groundlessness and nullity of inauthentic everydayness'. Kierkegaard and Heidegger have similar ideas on the issues I am discussing. I shall take them as representative of the 'existentialist' position in what follows.

you doubt that you are a Christian? Are you not a Dane, and does not the geography say that the Lutheran form of the Christian religion is the ruling religion in Denmark? ... Do you not perform your duties ... are you not a good citizen of a ... Christian state? So then of course you must be a Christian!' (Kierkegaard, 1941, 50)

For Heidegger, too, normal social life is no guarantee of authenticity. On the contrary, in our everyday social existence we are estranged from ourselves and inauthentic. Heidegger, like Hegel, uses the Biblical metaphor of the Fall to describe this condition. In everyday social life we 'fall' away from ourselves, into the world and into relations with others (Heidegger, 1962, 220). We are 'dispersed' in our involvements, lost in the world, dominated by the 'they' (Heidegger, 1962, 166–7). Such 'fallenness' is not the product only of particular social or historical circumstances, it is the normal mode of human existence. Inauthenticity, self-estrangement, is an 'ontological' characteristic of 'Dasein'.[7] Philosophers like Hegel and Marx are guilty of unwarranted optimism. 'We would ... misunderstand the ontologico-existential structure of falling if we were to ascribe to it the sense of a bad and deplorable ontical property of which, perhaps, more advanced stages of human culture might be able to rid themselves' (Heidegger, 1962, 220).

This is not to say that alienation is inescapable. Authenticity is possible, but it is an individual rather than an historical achievement. To find myself and be authentic, I must stand back. I must detach myself from the 'they', from my social existence, and make contact with my authentic individual self. However, this is not our natural or normal way of being and it is complacent to believe that mere social change is going to bring it about. On the contrary, for Heidegger, as for Kierkegaard, the 'present age', the era of mass society, has only made the situation worse.

## Alienation as an objective phenomenon

There is an important measure of truth in the existentialist insistence on the significance of individuality and subjectivity for the modern

---

[7]Although Heidegger denies that his use the notion of 'fallenness' has a moral content and does not explicitly invoke its theological associations, he appears to conceive of it as a sort of 'original sin' which cannot be abolished by mere social action or social change. This is Tillich's explicitly theological account, quoted by Pappenheim, 1959, 110–12.

self. Despite the fact that the existentialist position is formed mainly as a critical response to Hegel, Hegel himself goes a long way towards recognising this. In the development of individuality, he too maintains, there must be a moment of separation and detachment, a subjective and negative moment. Modern individuality is not given simply through the performance of a social role. To be for-itself and free the individual must be able to reflect, to will and to choose. Hegel is well aware of this, his philosophy cannot be reduced to one of 'my station and its duties' alone. It is not sufficient simply to perform a social role, one's role must be inwardly willed and chosen if it is to be an authentic expression of individuality and selfhood in the modern world. The moment of subjectivity, of choice, of negative liberty, is essential too. This is stressed not only by existential philosophers, it is also a fundamental aspect of Hegel's (1991, §§5–7) account of the self and self development.

However, writers in the Marxist tradition have not always appreciated this point and, arguably, neither does Marx. Marxism often presents itself as a *purely* social philosophy. The self is portrayed as a merely social creation.[8] Marxists often seem to imply that social change alone will be sufficient to transform and realise the self – as though 'after the revolution' all conflicts between self and society will automatically be resolved without any action on the part of the individual being required. This is untenable, as the existential account quite rightly insists (Sartre, 1960).

In short, there is an individual, subjective dimension to alienation and its overcoming. Will and choice are necessary. But they are not sufficient. The self must also be able to express itself, to realise its will and objectify itself. In doing so it comes up against existing objective conditions,[9] and these may either facilitate its expression or hinder it. In this way there is an objective dimension to alienation, and its overcoming requires the existence of specific objective social conditions.

This holds true not only for the Hegelian and Marxist account in which the self has a determinate 'nature' to be realised, it applies equally to existential philosophies of self-creation. For even if the self does not begin with a determinate nature, in order to create itself it must acquire a definite content and be realised in the world. Thus

---

[8]Or in the extreme, as the mere 'bearer' of social relations (Althusser and Balibar, 1970).

[9]'Men make their own history, but not of their own free will, not under circumstances that they themselves have chosen' (Marx, 1973b, 146).

there is an objective social dimension to alienation and its overcoming. Some conditions of social and economic life are objectively alienating; some social roles and relations systematically require inauthenticity.

Existential philosophies, like those of Kierkegaard and Heidegger, do not consistently acknowledge this, at least at a theoretical level. They tend to regard authenticity as a subjective and individual affair which resides in the way in which one chooses oneself and lives one's situation, whatever that may be. The implication is that it is possible to respond more or less authentically in any situation, regardless of the specific social circumstances. There are no objective conditions that are in and of themselves alienating, or that prevent or engender authenticity. Any necessary link between the spiritual and the social aspects of alienation is thus severed. As a result, the existential account of the 'present age' loses any specific social or historical grounding, and its critique of modern mass society is undermined.

## Alienation as a historical phenomenon

The existential view that alienation and inauthenticity are universal features of the human condition, 'ontological' characteristics of the self, is questionable on historical grounds as well. For there are good reasons for the view that specific social and historical circumstances are needed for the development of a self-conscious self – a self that can and will choose, and for which alienation is an issue.

The abilities to reflect, to will and to choose are not natural human endowments. Rather they involve the capacity for self-consciousness and powers of reason that can be acquired only socially and that develop historically. The very existence of a self that can experience alienation and inauthenticity and seek to overcome them is a social and historical creation. Alienation and inauthenticity are historical conditions. Indeed, they are distinctively modern phenomena.

In a pre-modern community the self is defined primarily by its social 'place'. Identity is determined by social role. In such societies, as MacIntyre (1985, 160–1) says, 'the individual is identified and constituted in and through certain of his or her roles.... I confront the world as a member of this family, this household, this class, this tribe, this city, this nation, this kingdom. There is no "I" apart from these'.[10]

---

[10]See also Berger (1984, 154), 'the individual discovers his true identity in his roles, and to turn away from these roles is to turn away from himself'.

In the modern world, by contrast, the individual no longer has a fixed and given position in society. The very notion of a social 'place' or 'station' has all but ceased to have any application. The self has far greater independence from its roles. These are regarded as external to the self and contingent. Identity is no longer a social given. Individuals must now choose their social place and role and, in doing so, create their own identities. Only in this situation can issues of authenticity and self-realisation arise. For only now can the self stand back from its activity and ask itself whether it is realising itself and living authentically. The mere fact that the individual is fulfilling an allotted social role is no longer a guarantee of this.[11]

Hegel was one of the first authors to describe these changes.[12] The historical theory of the self is one of Hegel's great achievements as a philosopher. Marx follows and refines this historical account, adding a realistic, material dimension to it. By contrast, writers like Kierkegaard and Heidegger tend to take the self-conscious self as directly given. In Kierkegaard it is simply presupposed. 'Every human being must be assumed in essential possession of what essentially belongs to being a man' (Kierkegaard, 1941, 318–19). Heidegger takes more care to justify his initial assumptions. Nevertheless, the implications of his phenomenological approach are similar. 'Dasein' (self-conscious being) is taken as the immediately given starting point.

This is not to suggest that either of these philosophers reverts to the atomistic individualism of the enlightenment. On the contrary, Kierkegaard regards the self as essentially social (Westphal, 1987, 30–3); Heidegger insists that Dasein is always 'with-others' and 'historical' in that it is necessarily oriented to the past, present and future of its community. Nevertheless, neither of these writers regards the particular forms of 'Being-with' or 'historicality' that they describe as socially or

---

[11]Almost the reverse if anything. The view that seems to be implied in some existentialist writing on authenticity is that we can be true to ourselves *only* by emancipating ourselves from socially imposed roles (e.g., Camus, 1961), though this is not the view either of Kierkegaard or Heidegger as we have seen.

[12]It is not clear when these changes should be located. 'Self-alienated spirit', according to Hegel, begins to emerge with the breakup of the ancient *polis* (Hegel, 1977, 294–320). That is perhaps too simple. Even in earlier periods of rapid social change, traditional roles and identities are questioned. Thus the Sophists and Socrates, in 5th century BC Athens, discuss the identity of the self and many of the issues raised by the concept of authenticity, though not in these terms which are, indeed, distinctively modern (Trilling, 1972, chapter 2).

historically specific. Both treat sociality and historicality as universal, 'ontological' features of the human self, and neither regards alienation or inauthenticity as socially or historically specific. Thus for Heidegger, as we have seen, alienation is a pervasive feature of everyday life. 'Fallenness' is a normal part of the human condition.

For Hegel, by contrast, our 'fall' into social division and alienation is an historical process; and such 'fallenness' can be and is being redeemed through the course of human development and progress. Hegel's optimism on this score may, of course, be questioned. However, at least it is grounded in his historical theory of the development of the self; whereas Heidegger's pessimism is not grounded on any theory, historical or otherwise. It appears to be a mere artefact of his phenomenological method, and it is merely asserted.

## Alienation as a critical concept

I will conclude this discussion with some comments on the nature of alienation as a critical concept. Surprisingly, Hegel, Marx, and Heidegger all deny that their ideas in this area have any critical or evaluative purpose. All these claims are questionable.

Hegel says that he is giving a theoretical description of the self and its development. He explicitly repudiates the view that his purpose is social criticism (Hegel, 1991, 21). However, this is often disputed. Starting with the left Hegelians, many have taken Hegel to be giving, not so much a critical as an *uncritical* account of modern society. Part of his purpose appears to be the evaluative one of justifying the social order of his day. This is not to suggest that he was unaware of the problems and defects of the society of his time. As already mentioned, Hegel is remarkably acute about these, he is not a mere apologist. He was particularly aware of the persistence of poverty and social exclusion, which he saw as structural problems with no evident solution. Even so, he does not ultimately take such problems to refute his picture of the modern era as one of reconciliation and harmony.

Marx also denies that his purpose is evaluative, he maintains that his work has a 'scientific' character. Its main aim, he insists, is to understand and explain capitalism and its historical trajectory, not to criticise it. Even so, criticism is an unmistakable aspect of it, whatever he says (Sayers, 1998, chapters 7–9), and this is aimed partly at defenders of liberal society such as Hegel.

Heidegger, too, denies that his work has a moral purpose. 'Our interpretation is purely ontological in its aims, and is far removed from any moralizing critique of everyday Dasein, and from the aspirations of a "philosophy of culture"' (Heidegger, 1962, 211). As with Marx, however, the critical intent of his work is unmistakable; and, as with Marx, this is aimed partly at Hegel's uncritical celebration of modernity.

In short, as I have been arguing, both Marxism and existentialism are united in rejecting Hegel's uncritical picture of modern society. Both strands of thought see alienation and inauthenticity as endemic to modern society, and base their critiques of it on this. However, as we have seen, these critiques are very different.

Kierkegaard and Heidegger condemn 'the present age'. They give a thoroughly negative picture of modern social life. Kierkegaard's diagnosis is that individuals in modern 'mass society' lack 'passion' and individuality. Through increasing equality and 'levelling' they are reduced to conformity and uniformity.

> Just as desert travellers combine into great caravans from fear of robbers and wild beasts, so the individuals of the contemporary generation are fearful of existence, because it is God-forsaken; only in great masses do they dare to live, and they cluster together *en masse* in order to feel that they amount to something. (Kierkegaard, 1941, 318)

Similarly, Heidegger (1962, 164) describes the way in which modern social life imposes the 'dictatorship' of the 'they' upon the individual, Nietzsche (1994) talks of modern 'herd' and 'slave' morality, Sartre (1957) of the pervasiveness of 'bad faith'.[13]

What is the basis for these denunciations? In the existentialist account, as we have seen, authenticity and alienation are not historically specific phenomena. It is thus questionable whether they can provide valid grounds for judgements about 'the present age'. Nevertheless, these writers give a bleak and pessimistic picture of contemporary conditions. The destruction of local communities and the increasing equality and uniformity of social experience are erasing individuality and difference. Modern education and mass communications and other such developments are churning out of an undifferentiated mass without 'passion', personality

---

[13]Similar ideas as to be found outside the existentialist tradition. For example, Weber's (1958, 181) view that the individual in modern 'rationalized' society is increasingly confined in an 'iron cage', Mill's (1962) warnings against the power of 'public opinion' and the 'tyranny of the majority', Fromm's (1942) account of modern conformity and the 'fear of freedom', etc..

or character. Previously such tendencies operated only on a regional and national scale, now they are functioning at a global level.

Marx also describes the increasing scale of modern social relations which he sees as an inherent effect of the expansion of capital. However, Marx's estimation of the impact of this is entirely different, and so too is his critique of capitalism. He does not regard any of these developments towards 'mass society' as simply and solely negative in their human effects. Globalisation and the erasure of local differences, the equalisation of social experience, the growth of mass education and mass culture, even the all-pervasive cash-nexus and alienation brought about by capitalism – none of these tendencies is purely negative or destructive in its impact on human life. As much as these developments destroy local communities, and fragment, 'level', homogenise and alienate people, at the same time they also create new and wider relations and connections between people; and in so doing they open up opportunities for self-development and cultivation previously available only to a tiny elite. To be sure, these forms of activity often take commodified and commercial forms which limit their human value. Nevertheless, any adequate account of the character of modern society must register both sides of the case, the positive as well as the negative.[14]

Thus, the concept of alienation is not a purely critical one in Marx. For Marx, like Hegel, gives a historical account of the self and society. He does not regard the alienation and disharmony of modern society as a merely negative condition. Rather its impact is contradictory. Although it results in the division and fragmentation of people, at the same time it is also the means by which individuality, subjectivity, and freedom develop. It is a necessary stage in the process of self-development and self-realisation – necessary in that human development occurs only in and through it (Sayers, 1998, 138ff, 88f). Up to now these tendencies have appeared to be alien and hostile influences, operating as if they were uncontrollable forces of nature. With human historical development, however, people collectively can eventually come to understand them and bring them under their conscious control. Only then will they cease to be experienced as alien and hostile powers and be controlled and put to work for human good.[15]

---

[14]For an extended argument along these lines see Sayers, 2011.

[15]An earlier version of this Chapter was given at the annual conference of the Hegel Society of Great Britain, Oxford, September 2003. I am particularly grateful for helpful comments and criticisms to Joe Reynolds.

# 2
# Creative Activity and Alienation in Hegel and Marx

For Marx work is the fundamental and central activity in human life and, potentially at least, a fulfilling and liberating activity. Although this view is implicit throughout Marx's work, there is little explicit explanation or defence of it. The fullest treatment is in the account of 'estranged labour' [*entfremdete Arbeit*] in the *Economic and Philosophical Manuscripts* (Marx, 1975e)[1]; but even there Marx does not set out his philosophical assumptions at length. For an understanding of these one must turn to Hegel. Marx is quite explicit about his debt to Hegel in this respect.

> The importance of Hegel's *Phenomenology* ... lies in the fact that Hegel conceives the self-creation of man as a process, objectification as loss of object, as alienation and as supersession of this alienation; that he therefore grasps the nature of *labour* and conceives objective man – true, because real man – as the result of his *own labour*. (Marx, 1975e, 385–6)

Much of the discussion of this remark has concentrated on the 'master-servant' section of the *Phenomenology*, where Hegel explicitly considers the role of work in human life.[2] This focus is arbitrary and limiting. As Arthur argues, there is no explicit reference to the 'master-servant' section here or elsewhere in Marx, nor are there any good grounds to believe that it had any special influence on or significance for Marx.[3]

---

[1]See also Marx, 1973a.
[2]Hegel, 1977, chapter B.IV.A. See discussion in Arthur, 1986; Mészáros, 1970; Lukács, 1975; and the pieces collected in O'Neill, 1996.
[3]Arthur, 1983. As Arthur points out, the passage from which this quotation is taken is focused specifically on the final chapter of Hegel's *Phenomenology*.

Moreover, although many of the main themes of Hegel's account of work are present in it, it is a somewhat idiosyncratic passage in which the role of labour is by no means the central topic.

However, work *is* a major theme in Hegel's philosophy. It figures prominently in all his main writings, from the early Jena lectures on philosophy of spirit which preceded the *Phenomenology* right up to the final lecture series on the philosophy of religion and aesthetics. I shall focus particularly on the lectures on aesthetics. These are very helpful in understanding Hegel's account of work, and highly illuminating about Marx's views, but they have not so far been given the attention they deserve in this respect.[4]

One more preliminary point: for both Hegel and Marx work has both a social and a material aspect. Through work the worker relates not only to the object of work and hence to the natural world, but also – and through it – to other human beings.[5] In this chapter, however, I will focus on the labour process as such and on the relation of the worker to the object of labour.[6]

## Work as an essential human activity

In *Economic and Philosophical Manuscripts*, Marx (1975e, 328–9) describes work as man's 'vital activity', his 'species activity', 'man's spiritual essence, his human essence'.[7] The meaning of these phrases is much disputed. Similar ideas are also fundamental to Hegel's philosophy, where they are spelled out and clarified at length. According to Hegel, work plays an

---

[4]In what follows, I do not address the question of what actual influence Hegel's lectures on *Aesthetics* had on Marx. However, it is worth noting that Hegel's lectures were first published in 1835 (edited by H.G. Hotho). There is strong evidence that Marx studied them, probably in Summer 1837 in Berlin (Lifshitz, 1973, 12; Rose, 1984, 57–70) and that, initially at least, he was strongly influenced by them (Prawer, 1976, 22). In 1842, Marx planned to collaborate with Bruno Bauer on a 'left Hegelian' critique of Hegel's views on art and religion, and he drafted a lengthy manuscript on Hegel's 'hatred' of Christian art (Rose, 1984, 60). I also make reference below to Hegel's Jena lectures on the philosophy of spirit of 1805–6 (Hegel, 1983). These came to light and were published only in 1931–2 and could not have been known to Marx.

[5]This is Marx's main focus in the account of alienation in *Economic and Philosophical Manuscripts*; whereas in *The German Ideology* the main topic is the social organisation and division of labour.

[6]I deal with the topic of work as a social phenomenon in Chapter 4 below.

[7]Hegel and Marx both use 'man' in its general, species, sense to include also women. For stylistic reasons I shall follow them in this here.

essential role in distinguishing human beings from other animals. The (non-human) animal is a purely natural being, with a purely immediate relation to nature, both to the objects around it in its natural environment and to its own nature, its own appetites and instincts. Hegel calls this immediate relationship to nature 'desire' (Hegel, 1977, §§167ff, 105ff). The animal is driven by its desires and appetites to consume objects which are directly present to it in its natural environment. Furthermore, this consumption involves the immediate negation, the annihilation of the object (Hegel, 1983, §174, 109; Avineri, 1996).

The human being, by contrast, is not a purely natural being but rather a conscious, a self-conscious being, with 'being-for-self'. 'Man is a thinking consciousness.... Things in nature are only *immediate* and *single*, while man ... *duplicates* himself [*Sich verdoppelt*], in that (i) he is as things in nature are, but (ii) he is just as much for himself; he sees himself, represents himself to himself, thinks' (Hegel, 1975, 31; Hegel, 1971, 76).

The human being's ability to 'duplicate himself' and 'represent himself to himself' is most evident in thought, in self-consciousness. But it also takes a practical form. Work is a mode of this practical being-for-self and a means by which it develops. Work involves a break with the animal, immediate, natural relationship to nature. In work, the object is not immediately consumed and annihilated. Gratification is deferred. The object is preserved, worked upon, formed and transformed. In this way, a distinctively human relationship to nature is established.

It is these ideas that are at the basis of Marx's notion of work as man's 'species activity'. Like Hegel, Marx contrasts the relationship to nature established through work with the immediacy of the animal's relation to nature.

> The animal is immediately one with its life activity. It is not distinct from that activity; it *is* that activity. Man makes his life activity itself an object of his will and consciousness. He has conscious life activity. It is not a determination with which he directly merges. Conscious life activity directly distinguishes man from animal life activity. Only because of that is he a species being. (Marx, 1975e, 328)

## The development of being-for-self

Thus by working on the world, by shaping and forming it, human beings become separated from the natural world and established as self-conscious subjects, as beings-for-self, over against an objective world. This breach with nature is the negative aspect of work. At the same time, however, it is through work that human beings overcome this division from nature. This is the positive aspect. By shaping and forming the object, man transforms his environment and his relationship to it, and in the process he transforms himself.

Through work, says Hegel, the human being,

> imbues the external world with his will.[8] Thereby he humanizes his environment, by showing how it is capable of satisfying him and how it cannot preserve any power of independence against him. Only by means of this effectual activity is he no longer merely in general, but also in particular and in detail, actually aware of himself and at home in his environment. (Hegel, 1975, 256)

In the language Marx uses in *Economic and Philosophical Manuscripts* this is the process of 'objectification' [*Vergegenständlichung*].[9] There are two aspects to this process. In the first place, by objectifying ourselves in our products, we come to recognise our powers and capacities as real and objective. Thus we develop a consciousness of ourselves. Second, by humanising the world, we cease to feel that we are confronted by a foreign and hostile world. We overcome our alienation from the natural world and gradually, through a long process of social and economic development, come to feel at home in the world and in harmony with it. Hegel makes these points as follows.

> Man brings himself before himself by *practical* activity, since he has the impulse, in whatever is directly given to him, in what is present to him externally, to produce himself and therein equally to recognize himself. This aim he achieves by altering external things whereon he impresses the seal of his inner being and in which he now finds again his own characteristics. Man does this in order, as a

---

[8]'*die Außenwelt mit seinem Willen durchdringt*' (Hegel, 1971, 360). I have replaced Knox's 'impregnates' for '*durchdringt*' with 'imbues'. 'Impregnates' has unfortunate sexual associations which distract from the point that Hegel is making, 'imbues' is a better and less provocative translation (I am indebted to Edmund Jephcott for suggesting it).

[9]'The product of labour is labour embodied and made material in an object, it is the *objectification* of labour. The realization of labour is its objectification.' (Marx, 1975e, 324)

free subject, to strip the external world of its inflexible foreignness and to enjoy in the shape of things only an external realization of himself. (Hegel, 1971, 31)

Again these ideas are taken up by Marx, who repeats them almost exactly, even to the point of echoing Hegel's distinctive language of spirit's 'doubling' of itself.[10]

It is ... in his fashioning of the objective [world] that man really proves himself to be a *species-being*. Such production is his active species-life. Through it nature appear as *his* work and his reality. The object of labour is the *objectification of the species-life of man*: for man reproduces himself [*Sich verdoppelt*] not only intellectually, in his consciousness, but actively and actually, and he can therefore contemplate himself in a world he himself has created. (Marx, 1975e, 329; Marx and Engels, 1970a, 89)

## The story of the Fall

In this way, work involves both the separation, the alienation, of self from nature, but also the drive to overcome this separation and make ourselves at home in the world. For Hegel, this is a fundamental drive of human beings as 'spiritual' and self-conscious as contrasted with merely natural beings, and a basic human need.

Hegel makes these points in a graphic and illuminating way through his distinctive interpretation of the Biblical story of the Fall of Man, which he interprets as a metaphysical parable of the human condition.[11] Adam and Eve, the first human beings, were placed in a garden where God had forbidden them to eat the fruit of tree of knowledge of good and evil. But they eat the fruit and are expelled from the garden. Adam is condemned to 'labour in the sweat of his brow' and Eve to 'bring forth in sorrow'.

In the story, it is because of temptation by the serpent that we are led to eat the fruit and forced to leave the harmonious conditions of the garden. 'But the truth is that the step into opposition, the awakening of consciousness, follows from the very nature of man: and the same history

---

[10]*Sich verdoppelt.* This is not apparent in the English translations I am using.
[11]Genesis 3. Hegel, 1892, §24Z, 53ff; Hegel, 1895, Vol. 3, 51ff. See also Kant, 1963 in which many of these themes are first introduced into the philosophical discussion of this period.

repeats itself in every son Adam' (Hegel, 1892, §24Z, 55). In other words, we are all 'fallen', torn away from the natural state – that is our condition as self-conscious beings. However, for Hegel, that is not the end of the matter.

The story seems to imply that the first instinctive and natural state of life is the ideal. It appears to suggest the romantic view that our loss of 'innocence and harmony with nature', our exclusion from the garden, is a misfortune, and hence also that the human condition of self-consciousness is a misfortune. But Hegel questions that interpretation. The human condition is one of division from nature and of self-division – a state of contradiction, a restless state, which creates its own drive to overcome it. In the theoretical sphere this drive manifests itself as the need to know and to understand. In the practical sphere, it takes the form of the need for creative work. Thus as a result of our breach from nature we are condemned to labour. But 'if it [labour] is the result of disunion it is also the victory over it' (Hegel, 1892, §24Z, 55). For through working on the world we also come to objectify ourselves, to transform ourselves, to humanise our world and make ourselves at home in it.

The story of the Fall suggests that there is a development from the natural to the human condition, but here Hegel's interpretation of the story runs into difficulties. Hegel's thought is pre-Darwinian. He makes an absolute distinction between humans and other animals. For him there is no evolution from the natural to the human ('spiritual') realm. Nature does not evolve, it merely repeats itself. Change, in the sense of development, occurs only in the human realm. Marx's account of the difference between humans and animals in *Economic and Philosophical Manuscripts* described above and his idea that work is a distinctively human activity seem to imply a similarly sharp distinction.[12]

There are evident problems with this. As Marx (1975e, 329) acknowledges, animals such as 'the bee, the beaver and the ant, etc.' produce, in that they build nests and dwellings (though they do not produce 'universally', 'freely', or 'in accordance with the laws of beauty'). Conversely, some humans satisfy their basic needs directly, without the mediation of 'work' in Hegel's sense. Thus hunter-gatherers satisfy their material needs immediately from nature for the most part (although they work to create their tools, dwellings, clothes, utensils, etc.).[13]

---

[12]The *Economic and Philosophical Manuscripts* were also written before Darwin, but Marx was quick to welcome Darwin's work when it appeared.
[13]Of course hunting and gathering involve 'work' in other senses, e.g., the expenditure of effort.

Marx appears to be more aware of these problems in later work. Nevertheless, important aspects of the idea that work is a distinctive human activity and an essential means of human development are retained. The *German Ideology* (1845), written only one year after *Economic and Philosophical Manuscripts*, states that 'men can be distinguished from animals by consciousness, by religion or anything else you like. They themselves begin to distinguish themselves from animals as soon as they begin to *produce* their means of subsistence' (Marx and Engels, 1978b, 150).[14] Although this was written well before Darwin published his ideas, it suggests that humans evolve from animals, that being human is a matter of degree, and that labour is the main means by which human beings develop and become fully human.[15]

By the time of writing *Capital* (1867) Marx no longer regards work as such as distinctively human. He acknowledges that animals also produce. However, he distinguishes between purely natural and specifically human forms work. He argues that the labour of animals is driven by immediate need and is purely 'instinctive'. He distinguishes this from 'labour in a form that stamps it as exclusively human' as follows.

> A spider conducts operations that resemble those of a weaver, and a bee puts to shame many an architect in the construction of her cells. But what distinguishes the worst architect from the best of bees is this, that the architect raises his structure in imagination before he erects it in reality. At the end of every labour-process, we get a result that already existed in the imagination of the labourer at its commencement. He not only effects a change of form in the material on which he works, but he also realises a purpose of his own that gives the law to his modus operandi, and to which he must subordinate his will. (Marx, 1961a, 178)

Moreover, in working on the world, man not only changes the world, he also transforms his own nature.[16] 'By ... acting on the external world and

---

[14]In this book, with reference to works written jointly by Marx and Engels, I often refer only to Marx as author. This is purely for reasons of style, it is not intended to have any implications about Engels' contribution.

[15]For a fuller and post-Darwinian Marxist account, see Engels, 1958a.

[16]Marx is referring here specifically to 'labour in a form that stamps it as exclusively human'. Engels, following Darwin, applies this thought to human evolution as well: 'labour created man himself' (Engels, 1958a, 80). Given the welcome that Marx gave to Darwin's ideas, however, there is no reason to believe that at this time he would have accepted Hegel's rejection of evolution and disagreed with Engels on this.

changing it, he at the same time changes his own nature. He develops his slumbering powers and compels them to act in obedience to his sway.' (Marx, 1961a, 178)

## The realm of freedom

Hence for Marx, as for Hegel, work is not only a means to satisfy material needs, it is also a fundamental part of the human process of self-development and self-realisation. This process occurs not only in economic labour but in all forms of practical activity through which we deliberately make changes in the world, even in play. Its highest expression is in the free creative activity of art.

> Even a child's first impulse involves this practical alteration of external things; a boy throws stones into the river and now marvels at the circles drawn in the water as an effect in which he gains an intuition of something that is his own doing. This need runs through the most diversiform phenomena up to that mode of self-production in external things which is present in the work of art. (Hegel, 1975, 31)

According to Hegel these different forms of activity involve different degrees of freedom. At one pole there is consumption directly under the impulse of desire. This is the form taken by the activity of animals, which desire and immediately consume the objects around them. They are not free. They are determined by their desires and dominated by the object. Human beings can also act in this way, in which case they are not acting freely.

> The person ... caught up in the individual, restricted and nugatory interests of his desire, is neither free in himself, since he is not determined by the essential universality and rationality of his will, nor free in respect of the external world, for desire remains essentially determined by external things and related to them. (Hegel, 1975, 36)

In working on the object rather than immediately consuming it, gratification of desire is postponed, the object is preserved. People thus detach themselves from their desires and achieve a relative freedom with respect to them. At the same time they allow a degree of freedom to the object.

However, in deferring his desires, the producer achieves only a limited autonomy with respect to them, he does not transcend them altogether. The product likewise is granted only a limited freedom, it is destined ultimately to be consumed. Economic work continues to be dominated by material desires; it is still in what Marx calls 'the realm of necessity' (Marx, 1971b, 820).

Artistic activity by contrast is truly free activity, free creation.[17] It is free, first of all, in the negative sense that it is not determined by natural desire. Artistic creation is not an instrumental activity to satisfy physical needs. Moreover, the product, the work of art, is not made to be consumed. With art, determination by material desire is altogether transcended. 'From the practical interest of desire, the interest of art is distinguished by the fact that it lets its object persist freely and on its own account, while desire converts it to its own use by destroying it.' (Hegel, 1975, 38)

## Free artistic activity

For Marx, too, art is the highest form of creative activity, free creative activity, the highest form of work. Animals are not capable of such activity, they are not free. In so far as they produce, they 'produce only when immediate physical need compels them to do so, while man produces even when he is free from physical need and truly produces only in freedom from such need ... hence man also produces in accordance with the laws of beauty' (Marx, 1975e, 329).

These passages are from the *Economic and Philosophical Manuscripts*, but the same thought recurs later in Marx's work. In *Grundrisse* he describes composing music as 'really free labour', which can constitute 'attractive work, the individual's self-realization' (Marx, 1973a, 611). In 'Critique of the Gotha Programme' he envisages a time when work will become an end in itself, 'life's prime want' (Marx, 1978c, 531).

These ideas are also at the basis of Marx's almost universally misunderstood distinction between the 'realms' of 'necessity' and 'freedom' in *Capital*, volume 3.

> The realm of freedom ... begins only where labour which is determined by necessity and mundane considerations ceases.... Just as

---

[17]It should be noted that this view of art abstracts it from the social conditions in which it is produced. In concrete conditions, art is often a commodity, produced to earn a living. Only when it is freed from these constraints can it be the 'truly free' activity that Marx envisages. This point is not a new one. Plato, in *Republic* Book I, argues that 'money making' perverts the proper aims of practical activities (Sayers, 1999a, 13–15).

the savage must wrestle with Nature to satisfy his wants ... so must civilized man, and he must do so in all social formations and under all possible modes of production.... Freedom in this field can only consist in socialized man, the associated producers, rationally regulating their interchange with Nature, bringing it under their common control, instead of being ruled by it as by the blind forces of Nature.... But it nonetheless still remains a realm of necessity. Beyond it begins that development of human energy which is an end in itself, the true realm of freedom. (Marx, 1971b, 820)

Despite numerous accounts to the contrary, it is quite clear that Marx is not saying that work in the realm of necessity is unfree.[18] He spells out, quite explicitly, what freedom in 'the realm of necessity' involves ('Freedom in this field can only consist ...'). For Marx as for Hegel, it is only purely immediate consumption, dominated by immediate desire, that is unfree. Economic work has a degree of freedom in comparison with this. Human beings are for-themselves, they can stand back from desire and the activity to gratify it and subject this to rational control. There is freedom in this realm, which consists in the exercise of rational control over production and consumption.

Nevertheless, such economic activity is ultimately in the service of natural needs, it is instrumental activity to meet these needs. To that extent it is not completely free. A fuller and higher form of freedom is realised when we produce, not to meet material needs, but purely as an end in itself. This is the truly free creation of art. It is not determined by material needs or by the object. In its turn it leaves the object free to exist as it is and does not consume it.[19]

## Alienation and its overcoming

As I have shown, Marx, like Hegel, conceives of economic work as on a continuum with free artistic creation, with the implication that such work, although it is always a means to meeting material needs, is also potentially a self-realising activity and an end in itself.

Marx's account of alienation is a critical and radical version of the Hegelian ideas that I have been describing. Under conditions of

---

[18]For example, Arendt, 1958, 105–15; Gorz, 1982, 95–6.
[19]For a fuller account and discussion of these ideas see Chapter 5 below.

alienation, 'labour, life activity, productive life itself' is perverted so that it is,

> *external* to the worker, i.e. does not belong to his essential being; that he therefore does not confirm himself in his work, but denies himself, feels miserable and not happy, does not develop free mental and physical energy, but mortifies his flesh and ruins his mind.... His labour is therefore not voluntary but forced. (Marx, 1975e, 326)

It is often said that such a critical notion of alienation is absent from Hegel and distinctive to Marx. Marx himself seems to make this claim. For example, he says, 'the only labour Hegel knows and recognises is abstract mental labour' (Marx, 1975e, 386). This is a puzzling remark. At face value it is quite evidently false, as Marx is certainly aware. Hegel is notable in giving labour, in the sense of material productive activity, a central place within his philosophical system. In the *Phenomenology*, the specific subject of Marx's discussion, it plays a key role in the 'master-servant' section.

Perhaps, as Arthur suggests, 'the "abstract mental labour" to which Marx refers is the "*labour of spirit*"'.

> The *Phenomenology* is a spiritual odyssey, or, perhaps, a *Bildungsroman* of spirit, in which spirit discovers that the objective shapes given to it in consciousness and self-consciousness are nothing but its own self-determination. Spirit comes to know itself through *producing* itself, in the first instance as something which stands over against it ... spirit can come to itself only through setting up opposition and then negating it. (Arthur, 1983, 71)

For Hegel, it should be noted, (finite) 'spirit' is not something abstractly mental but rather human being; and material labour is a 'spiritual' activity in that it leads to human development. Nevertheless, Arthur is right to stress the way in which, for Hegel, this is ultimately a process which takes place primarily within consciousness and self-consciousness. Marx, by contrast, insists upon the primacy of the material and economic factors in human development.

Marx's target appears to be Hegel's idealism; but he has not got this clearly in his sights. It is true that, for Hegel, economic labour is not the highest stage of spirit's development. This continues further through art, religion and philosophy. These higher activities do not supersede labour, they supplement it. However, Marx is no position to criticise these ideas, since he holds similar views himself. For Marx too believes that art and philosophy (if not religion) constitute a higher 'realm of freedom' and a higher sphere of human development. This is a direct descendent of the Hegelian view, as I have been arguing.

## Objectification and alienation

Marx also accuses Hegel of presenting an uncritical and idealised picture of actual economic conditions. 'Hegel adopts the standpoint of modern political economy. He sees *labour* as the *essence*, the self-confirming essence, of man; he sees only the positive and not the negative side of labour. Labour is *man's coming to be for himself* within *alienation* or as *alienated man*.' (Marx, 1975e, 386)

Lukács' account of this has been particularly influential. I shall deal with it before going on to discuss the more general issues raised by Marx's criticisms. In Marx, objectification is a feature of all work (indeed of all human activity which has an effect in the world); whereas alienation, Lukács maintains, is a specific feature of work under capitalism. Hegel, by contrast, makes no such distinction, he treats alienation as a universal, ontological, characteristic of self-conscious spirit. Thus the Marxist concept of alienation is capable of serving as a critical concept in a way that Hegel's is not (Lukács, 1975, 549; cf. Mészáros, 1970).

As we have seen, Hegel does indeed regard alienation from nature as a characteristic feature of spirit. And yet, for Hegel, it is equally a part of the essence of self-conscious spirit to strive to overcome its alienation, its separation, from nature. This sets for it a historical task which is also a characteristic feature of human spirit. It strives to heal its breach with nature and be at home in the world. In other words, and paradoxical as this may sound, for Hegel spirit is essentially – ontologically – historical in character. Alienation can and will be overcome when spirit has completed its development and come to be at home in the world. This is a historical process; and, *pace* Lukács, this way of thinking provides a framework with which Hegel can criticise the society of his day, as we shall see in due course. Lukács is therefore wrong to attribute a non-historical view of alienation to Hegel in contrast to Marx. For such a view one must turn rather to an 'existentialist' such as Heidegger (1962, 220; cf. Kierkegaard, 1962).

Conversely, as regards Marx, the very idea that he has a single and clear cut 'theory of alienation' (Mészáros, 1970, 233) is questionable. In particular, Marx does not always apply the concept of alienation only to capitalism, as Lukács maintains. In the *Economic and Philosophical Manuscripts*, it is true, the term is central to Marx's critique of capitalism, as Lukács suggests; but later his account of capitalism is developed in more specific economic terms. Throughout, however, Marx also uses the term 'alienation' to describe aspects of work which are not specific to capitalism, such as that it is stultifying, externally imposed, that it is merely a means to the end of satisfying material needs, that it takes place within an oppressive division of labour, etc.. These are features of work in all class divided societies.[20]

In the *German Ideology* Marx is already beginning to develop the terms of his later account of capitalism. The language of 'alienation' plays a much less prominent role in his thought. He is even ironical about its Hegelian philosophical associations (Marx and Engels, 1978b, 161). What in 1844 he calls 'alienated labour', is now referred to simply as 'labour' which 'has lost all semblance of self-activity and only sustains ... life by stunting it' (Marx and Engels, 1978b, 191). He envisages the 'abolition' of such 'labour' and of 'the division of labour' (Marx and Engels, 1978b, 192). Arguably, 'labour' and the 'division of labour' in this sense are present not only in capitalism but in all class societies. In the *Grundrisse*, he is explicit that the features attributed to alienated labour in the *Economic and Philosophical Manuscripts* are characteristic of such societies: 'in its historic forms as slave-labour, serf-labour, and wage-labour, labour always appears as repulsive, always as *external forced labour*', however labour can become 'real freedom', 'attractive work, the individual's self-realization' (Marx, 1973a, 611) – life's 'prime want' as he says in 'Critique of the Gotha Programme' (Marx, 1978c, 531).

As with Hegel, that is to say, there are aspects of alienation which are not specific to capitalism but apply to all historical societies. Moreover, the overcoming of alienation is a fundamental human drive: a historical task, achievable historically. Thus for Marx as well as for Hegel alienation is both an ontological and a historical characteristic.

## Hegel as social critic

Let us now return to the view that Hegel's philosophy is inherently uncritical and that it gives an idealised picture of the society of his time. Undoubtedly, there are aspects of Hegel's philosophy about which this charge is fully justified. For Hegel, the overcoming of alienation is not an unattainable or even a distant ideal; it can be, and is being,

---

[20]See Chapter 6 below for further discussion.

achieved in the present. Work is an essential part of the process of spiritual self-development: it is a process objectification – of alienation and its overcoming – leading to self-realisation. The central theme of the Hegelian system is the story of human self-development, culminating in the spiritual achievements – the art, religion and philosophy – of his own age. Thus, in Hegel's system, labour is often presented in positive and uncritical terms, as playing an essential role in a story of spiritual development and progress.

However, there are other strands of Hegel's philosophy which are in contradiction with this. When Hegel focuses on the actual conditions of labour in the society of his day, he is too perceptive and honest to blind himself to the very unideal conditions which prevailed. As Lukács himself observes, 'he does not close his eyes to the destructive effects of the capitalist division of labour and of the introduction of machinery into human labour' (Lukács, 1975, 329). In these contexts, Hegel does employ the concept of alienation in a critical fashion. Indeed, he uses it to pose many of the issues that Marx addresses. Equally, however, Hegel's approach to these issues is significantly different. A discussion of Hegel's observations will help to clarify these differences.

To repeat, Hegel's philosophy revolves around a story of progress. This implies that alienation can be overcome only through a process of historical development. Hegel has no shred of romantic attachment to a 'simple' or 'natural' form of life. This may initially seem idyllic, in that our needs would be few and easily satisfied directly from nature but, Hegel argues, 'such a life will soon bore us'.

> A restricted mode of life of this kind presupposes an insufficient development of spirit.... A full and entire human life requires higher urgings, and this closest association with nature and its immediate products cannot satisfy it any longer. Man may not pass his life in such an idyllic poverty of spirit; he must work. What he has an urge for, he must struggle to obtain by his own activity. (Hegel, 1975, 259)[21]

All this suggests that Hegel would be favourably disposed towards the industrialisation which was occurring in his time. However, he regards this as just as unsatisfactory for human development, though in the opposite way. Hegel believes that modern industrial production has developed excessively. In simpler societies, the individual works to satisfy

---

[21]See Sayers, 1998, chapters 3–4, for a survey of empirical evidence in support of this contention.

his own needs and those of his household and of others directly connected with him. With the advent of large scale industry, the individual is caught up in a network of economic relations which he cannot understand or control. The economic system becomes so complex and extensive that the individual can no longer grasp how the product (or part of a product) which he creates relates to the needs of its eventual consumers, whoever they may be.

> The long and complicated connection between needs and work, interests and their satisfaction, is completely developed in all its ramifications, and every individual, losing his independence, is tied down in an endless series of dependencies on others. His own requirements are either not at all or only to a very small extent, his own work. (Hegel, 1975, 260)

Furthermore, the industrial division of labour makes work increasingly mechanical and stultifying for the worker, so that 'every one of his activities proceeds not in an individual living way but more and more purely mechanically according to universal norms' (Hegel, 1975, 260).

Such criticisms of the way in which the worker in industrial society is alienated from his product and from his activity are now more familiar from the descriptions that Marx gives in his early writings. The account of 'estranged labour' in the *Economic and Philosophical Manuscripts* echoes Hegel's account particularly closely. It is clear from this that Marx believes the non-worker – in the shape of the capitalist – is just as alienated as the worker in capitalist society. Frustratingly, however, Marx's manuscript breaks off just at the point where, having described the alienation of the worker, he is about to consider the way in which the capitalist is also alienated (and he does not deal with this topic elsewhere).

Hegel's account does not break off, and it is suggestive of the way in which Marx's ideas might have developed. Just like the workers in modern society, Hegel argues, the 'wealthy' too are caught up in a complex and impenetrable web of economic relationships. Moreover, they are freed from the need to work. But, for this very reason, they are also alienated from the world around them, since they cannot see this as their own creation nor recognise themselves in it.

> [Through] wealth ... individuals ... are freed from satisfying their needs and can devote themselves to higher interests.... In this

superfluity, the constant reflection of endless dependence is removed, and man is all the more withdrawn from all the accidents of business as he is no longer stuck in the sordidness of gain. But for this reason the individual is not at home even in his immediate environment, because it does not appear as his work. What he surrounds himself with here has not been brought about by himself; it has been ... produced by others ... and acquired by him only through a long chain of efforts and needs foreign to himself. (Hegel, 1975, 260)

*Not at home* [handwritten margin note]

## Alienation in the modern world

It is quite evident from these passages that it is wrong to suggest that Hegel is uncritical of the society of his day. On the contrary, he sees well enough that people are alienated from the world that capitalism and large scale industry were creating. The ideal, unalienated condition for him is a middle way between the extremes of simple idyllic circumstances and excessive modern development. As regards work at least, he looks back to an earlier 'golden age' when production was still on a domestic and local scale; and when producers could relate to their products and feel at home in a world which they could still comprehend as their own creation.

> In such a mode of life man has the feeling, in everything he uses and everything he surrounds himself with, that he has produced it from his own resources, and therefore in external things has to do with what is his own and not with alienated objects lying outside his own sphere wherein he is master. In that event of course the activity of collecting and forming his material must not appear as painful drudgery but as easy, satisfying work which puts no hindrance and no failure in his way. (Hegel, 1975, 261)

His primary example is the 'heroic' society portrayed by Homer.

> Agamemnon's sceptre is a family staff, hewn by his ancestor himself, and inherited by his descendants [*Iliad*, ii]. Odysseus carpentered himself his huge marriage bed [*Odyssey*, xxiii] ... everything is domestic, in everything man has present before his eyes the power of his arm, the skill of his hand, the cleverness of his own spirit, or a result of his courage and bravery. In this way alone have the means of satisfaction not been degraded to a purely external matter; we see their living origin itself and the living consciousness of the value which

man puts on them because in them he has things not dead or killed by custom, but his own closest productions. (Hegel, 1975, 261)

In other respects, of course, Hegel rejects the ancient Greek model. Such earlier societies lack what for him is the essential feature of the modern world, the sphere of 'civil society' as a realm of individual autonomy and subjectivity. As a modern example of unalienated conditions, Hegel cites Holland in the seventeenth century, as depicted in the 'genre' paintings of everyday life by artists such as Rembrandt and Van Dyck.[22] These disclose a people who, as a result of their industry and history, are at home in their world.

> The Dutch themselves have made the greatest part of the land on which they dwell and live; it has continually to be defended against the storms of the sea, and it has to be maintained. By resolution, endurance, and courage, townsmen and countrymen alike threw off the Spanish dominion ... and by fighting won for themselves freedom in political life and in religious life too.... This citizenship, this love of enterprise, in small things as in great ... this joy and exuberance in their own sense that for all this they have their own activity to thank, all this is what constitutes the general content of their pictures. (Hegel, 1975, 169)[23]

This is Hegel's vision of unalienated society, and it provides the standard by which he criticises modern industrial conditions. For Hegel that ideal is now irretrievably past and gone, large scale industry is an inescapable part of modern life. Ultimately Hegel has no wish to renounce modernity which has seen the development of individuality and freedom, despite the alienation and other problems it brings with it. These problems are insoluble, he believes, the best that can be hoped is that the state will ameliorate some of their harsher effects.

---

[22]As Hegel stresses, these paintings were an innovation of the time. Van Dyck is a curious choice on Hegel's part, he is best known for his court paintings. Vermeer and de Hooch would serve his case better.

[23]See also Hegel's (1975, 262–3, cf. 191, 1110) glowing appreciation of Goethe's 'masterpiece' *Hermann und Dorothea* and the contrast he draws with J.H. Voss, *Luise*. 'Goethe has been able to find and present out of our modern world today ... situations and complications which in their own sphere bring alive again what is undyingly attractive in the primitive human circumstances of the Odyssey and the pictures of patriarchal life in the Old Testament' (Hegel, 1975, 1110), and yet in which at the same time the 'great interests of the age, the battles of the French Revolution, the defence of [the] country' (Hegel, 1975, 262) play an essential part.

## The overcoming of alienation

Marx's account of alienation grows out of these ideas, but it develops them in a very different way. For Marx maintains that large scale industry and the division of labour associated with it, so far from being a barrier to the overcoming of alienation, is the necessary basis for it. That is Marx's view from first to last; and it is one of the fundamental points on which he diverges from Hegel.

Crucially, therefore, Marx's critique of modern society is aimed at capitalism and not at industry *per se*. Indeed, for Marx, one of the great achievements of capitalism is that it has led to the development of modern industry to the point where it can provide the basis for a new, communist society – a society in which alienation can finally be overcome and in which human beings can at last be at home in world.

Such views are often questioned. Modern industry has unleashed gigantic forces of production. It has led to economic relations which are literally global in scale. It has imposed its stamp on nature in such an inexorable fashion that the natural environment is now in danger of being overwhelmed and extinguished by it. Industry and the economy seem to be hostile forces quite beyond human control.

Nevertheless they are not mere alien phenomena, Marx insists, they are human powers and human creations. 'Industry ... is the open book of the essential powers of man' (Marx, 1975e, 354). Its forces can potentially be experienced, in unalienated fashion, as the expression of human power and creativity in and through which we recognise and affirm ourselves. The great challenge in modern society is to bring them under human control and make them serve our needs (which may of course involve limiting and curbing them). There is no reason to believe that this is impossible. If we can subdue nature as we have, then surely we can master our own creations and come to be at home with them. That is Marx's vision of the overcoming of alienation, and it lies in the future and not in some golden age which is irretrievably past.[24]

---

[24]I am grateful to members of the Hegel Reading Group in Canterbury, whose discussions first stimulated many of the ideas in this paper. This Chapter was originally given as a talk to the Philosophy Society, Brighton University, and I am indebted to the participants in the ensuing discussion for their comments and criticisms. I would also like to acknowledge the help I have been given in revising and improving this paper by the full and detailed comments of the editorial reviewers for *Historical Materialism*.

# 3
# The Concept of Labour

In recent years the character of work in advanced industrial society has been changing rapidly. Production is being automated and computerised. The factory operated by massed workers is being superseded. Industrial labour is ceasing to be the dominant form of work. Work in offices that used to require intellectual skills is now done by computers. With the enormous growth of jobs in the service sector and the increasing use of information technology, new kinds of work are being created.

These changes are often summed up by saying that these societies are moving from the industrial to the postindustrial stage. In some important respects this is questionable. Arguably, the economy is still industrial, but it now operates on a global scale. If industry is ceasing to be the predominant form of work in Western Europe and North America, that is mainly because it is being relocated to other parts of the world in a new global division of labour.

Nevertheless, it is beyond dispute that work is changing. With the widespread use of computers and information technology new kinds of work have developed. Hardt and Negri's (2000, 2005) attempt to theorise these changes has been particularly influential. The older industrial forms of labour which produced material goods, they argue, are no longer dominant. They are being superseded by new 'immaterial' forms of work. Hardt and Negri situated their thought within the Marxist tradition. However, they maintain, Marx's ideas need to be rethought in the light of the new conditions of postindustrial society (Hardt and Negri, 2005, 140). Marx takes material production as the paradigm of work, his concept of labour is based on an industrial model. In order to describe the new postindustrial forms of work, Marx's account must be supplemented with the concepts of 'immaterial' labour and 'biopolitical' production.

My aim in this chapter is to criticise these ideas. First I will explain Marx's account of labour and show that Hardt and Negri's criticisms are based on a fundamental misreading of his thought. Then I will argue that Hardt and Negri's own account is confused and unhelpful. Properly understood and suitably developed Marx's concept of labour continues to provide a more satisfactory basis for understanding the nature of work in the modern world.

## Marx's concept of labour

According to Marx, labour is an intentional activity designed to produce a change in the material world. In his early writings, he conceives of work as a process of 'objectification' through which labour is 'embodied and made material in an object' (Marx, 1975e, 324). Later he describes labour as activity through which human beings give form to materials and thus realise themselves in the world.

> In the labour-process ... man's activity, with the help of the instruments of labour, effects an alteration, designed from the commencement, in the material worked upon. The process disappears in the product, the latter is a use-value, Nature's material adapted by a change of form to the wants of man. Labour has incorporated itself with its subject: the former is materialized, the latter transformed. (Marx, 1961a, 180)

This account is often taken to assume a 'productivist' model that regards work which creates a material product as the paradigm for all work. It is much criticised on this basis. Hardt and Negri along with many others point out that many kinds of work do not seem to fit this picture, some with which Marx was familiar, others that have newly developed.

There are two versions of the view that Marx has a 'productivist' model of the labour process. Some, like Hardt and Negri (2000, 255–6, 292; 2005, 140–2), accuse him of presupposing an industrial idea of labour. Others, by contrast, maintain that Marx's ideas are based on the paradigm of craft or even artistic work. In either case, the productivist account is treated either as self-evident (Adams, 1991) or as a 'plausible' reading of Marx's language and imagery (Habermas, 1987, 65–6; Benton, 1989, 66). These interpretations are superficial and unsatisfactory. Marx's theory of labour is not self-evident, nor is it based upon mere metaphors or images. It is a central element of a systematic philosophical theory of the relation of human beings to nature in which the concept of labour plays a fundamental role.

This theory is never stated explicitly by Marx. Although he discusses the general character of labour in a number of places, he does not fully spell out his philosophical presuppositions (Marx, 1975e, 1973a, 1961a; Marx and Engels, 1978b). These are derived from Hegel. Hegelian assumptions underlie his thinking about labour, not only in his early writings where they are clearly evident, but throughout his work. For a valid understanding of Marx's concept of labour, as I shall demonstrate, it is essential to see it in this Hegelian context. However, the critics I am discussing do not take this background into account. When Marx's thought is restored to its proper context and interpreted in this light it becomes evident that the charge that he is in the grip of a 'productivist' paradigm is misconceived and unjustified. On the contrary, it is rather these critics who see all labour in these terms and project them onto Marx.

In particular, the theory that labour is a process of 'objectification' and a form-giving activity has a Hegelian origin and plays a central role in his philosophy. According to Hegel labour is a distinctively human ('spiritual') activity. Through it human beings satisfy their needs in a way that is fundamentally different to that of other animals. Non-human animals are purely natural creatures. They are driven by their immediate appetites. They satisfy their needs immediately, by devouring what is directly present in their environment. The object is simply negated and annihilated in the process. Appetites arise again, and the process repeats itself. Natural life is sustained, but no development occurs.

Human labour by contrast creates a mediated relation to our natural appetites and to surrounding nature. Work is not driven by immediate instinct. In doing it we do not simply devour and negate the object. On the contrary, gratification must be deferred while we labour to create a product for consumption only later. Through work, moreover, we fashion and shape the object, and give it a human form. We thus 'duplicate' ourselves in the world.

Through this process we establish a relation to the natural world and to our own natural desires which is mediated through work. We objectify ourselves in our product, and come to recognise our powers, embodied in the world. We develop as reflective, self-conscious beings. Moreover, Hegel (1977, 118) maintains, relations with others are a necessary condition for these developments. Labour is not a purely instrumental activity to meet only individual needs, it is always and necessarily a social activity. It involves and sustains relations with others.

As we have seen in the previous chapter, these ideas are taken over and developed by Marx. They apply not only to industrial or craft work, but to work of all kinds, as Hegel makes clear in the following passage.

> In empirical contexts, this giving of form may assume the most varied shapes. The field which I cultivate is thereby given form. As far as the inorganic realm is concerned, I do not always give it form directly. If, for example, I build a windmill, I have not given form to the air, but I have constructed a form in order to utilize the air.... Even the fact that I conserve game may be regarded as a way of imparting form, for it is a mode of conduct calculated to preserve the object in question. The training of animals is, of course, a more direct way of giving them form, and I play a greater role in this process. (Hegel, 1991, §56A, 86)

Hegel here treats all these different sorts of work as form-giving activities in the sense that they are all ways of imparting form to matter. 'Productivist' types of work that create a material product, such as craft and manufacture, figure as particular kinds of labour, but it is quite clear that Hegel is not trying to assimilate all work to this model. On the contrary, he is emphasising the great variety of forms that it may take. Its result need not be the creation of a material product, it may also be intended to conserve an object, to change the character of animals or people, to transform social relations, etc..

The wider purpose of Hegel's theory is to give a systematic account of the different forms of labour; and this is part of a still larger theme. One of Hegel's most fruitful and suggestive ideas is that subject and object change and develop in relation to each other. He thus questions the enlightenment idea that a fixed and given subject faces a separate and distinct external world. As the activity of the subject develops, so the object to which the subject relates develops and changes too.

This is the organising principle of Hegel's account of labour.[1] He conceives of different kinds of labour as different forms of relation of subject to object (nature). In characteristic fashion, moreover, the

---

[1]This is also the organising theme in Hegel's accounts of the development of 'spirit' (*Geist*) (Hegel, 1977, 1975, 1895). The first seeds of this theory of labour appear very early in Hegel's work (Hegel, 1979). It is well worked out by time of the Jena lectures (Hegel, 1983). It is presented again in his later work (Hegel, 1991, §§196–207, 231–9). The latter work was well known to Marx. The earlier accounts were not published in Marx's time and would not have been available to him.

different forms of labour are arranged on an ascending scale according to the degree of mediation that they establish between subject and object. Marx draws extensively on these ideas. They provide an indispensable key to understanding Marx's account of labour, as I will now show.

### Direct appropriation

The simplest form of work, involving the most immediate relation to nature, is direct appropriation from nature, as in hunting, fishing, or the gathering of plants, etc.. In work of this kind, nature is taken as it is immediately given. This is the limiting case, still close to unmediated, natural appropriation in that it does not involve transformation of the object in itself. However, such work is a distinctively human rather than a purely natural and unmediated form of activity in that, in its human form, it is intentional, socially organised and usually involves the use of tools or weapons.[2]

Benton argues that such labour cannot be fitted into Marx's account (1961a, 180, quoted above).

> The conversion of the 'subject [i.e., object] of labour' into a use-value cannot be adequately described as 'Nature's material adapted by a *change of form* to the wants of man'. This conversion is rather a matter of selecting, extracting and relocating elements of the natural environment so as to put them at the disposal of other practices (of production or consumption). These primary labour-processes, then, *appropriate* but do not transform. (Benton, 1989, 69)[3]

This is not correct. Such labour does transform the object. Appropriation is a kind of transformation, it is wrong to oppose these as though they were exclusive of each other. According to Marx (1961a, 178), direct appropriation transforms the object in that it separates it from nature. The object is thus made useable: it is caught and killed, plucked, extracted,

---

[2]'All those things which labour merely separates from immediate connexion with their environment, are subjects [i.e. objects] of labour spontaneously provided by Nature. Such are fish which we catch and take from their element, water, timber which we fell in the virgin forest, and ores which we extract from their veins' (Marx, 1961a, 178). Such work is mentioned briefly by Hegel (1997, §103, 179–80).
[3]Cf. Grundmann, 1991b; Benton, 1992, 59ff.

moved, etc.. Labour is thereby embodied and objectified in it through a change of form.

It might be objected that a mere change of place affects only the object's 'external' relations and does not alter the thing itself. This objection assumes that an object's external relations are not part of its being. This view is questioned by Hegelian and Marxist philosophy which are often described as philosophies of 'internal relations' for this reason (Sayers, 1990b; Ollman, 1971). In the context of economic life the fact that game or fish have been caught makes a great deal of difference: 'a bird in the hand is worth two in the bush'.

## Agriculture

As productive activity develops our relation to nature alters and subject and object are changed. This is a crucial theme in Hegel that is taken over and developed by Marx. It is overlooked by Benton, Habermas, Hardt and Negri and many other writers. With the development of agriculture we no longer relate to nature as a mere given, we cease to be entirely dependent on the contingencies of what is immediately present. We actively arrange the natural environment to meet our needs. Thus we begin the process of freeing ourselves from passive dependence on natural contingency.[4]

Furthermore, in agriculture, our relation to nature is mediated through previous work. Agriculture employs raw materials that are themselves the results of previous labour (seeds, cultivated land, livestock, etc.), and which are then used to create useful products (crops, animals), as well as the materials for future production. In the process, it satisfies not only present needs, it necessitates planning for the future and determining future needs. In these ways, agriculture involves a more mediated and developed relation of subject and object than direct appropriation.

Benton argues that agriculture is another case that does not fit the productivist model that he attributes to Marx. The products of farming are not created by forming the object but grow on their own. 'Human labour does not *bring about* the transformation of seed to plant to crop, but secures optimal conditions for an organic transformation to occur by itself. Contrast this with the carpenter who works with tools to change the form of a piece of wood' (Benton, 1992, 60). Agriculture, he

---

[4]Of course, agriculture remains dependent on the natural contingencies of the seasons, climate, weather, etc., until we begin to free ourselves from these factors too through further technological advances.

maintains, is primarily 'a labour of sustaining, regulating and reproducing, rather than transforming' (Benton, 1989, 67–8).

Both Hegel and Marx are of course aware that farming depends on natural processes, but they do not regard this as conflicting with the view that agricultural work is a formative activity. In thinking that it must do, again Benton is taking the notion of form-giving activity to refer specifically to work which creates a material product. This is a misreading of this concept, as I have stressed. For both Hegel and Marx agriculture is 'formative' in that we realise our purposes in nature by means of it. It involves the control of natural conditions and processes for human ends.

## Craft and industry

Craft work involves a further development of our relation to the object of labour and to nature. By comparison with agriculture, craft is less reliant on natural processes and less dependent on natural contingencies. It involves the creation of a material product by the direct activity of the worker. It is thus a directly formative activity. Nevertheless, as I have been arguing, it is not the only kind of formative activity. What differentiates it is that the worker uses his or her own skills to make the object from raw materials that are themselves the products of previous labour.

Craft work is the basis upon which industry develops. Under the impact of capitalism, first the division of labour and then the character of the labour process itself is transformed. There are two distinct phases to this process. The first involves what Marx (1976, 1019–23, 1025–34) terms the 'formal subsumption' of labour under capital. The traditional methods of work are not altered, but the social organisation of work, the division of labour, is transformed.

With the introduction of machinery, the labour process itself is altered. This is what Marx (1976, 1023–5, 1034–8) calls the 'real subsumption' of labour under capital. In craft production, the worker controls the tool. In industrial production, the tool is operated by the machine. The craft element is progressively eliminated from the labour process (Marx, 1973a, 705), the industrial factory is created. Subject and object are again changed.

Moreover, with the transition from handicraft to manufacture and industry, labour becomes an intrinsically cooperative and social process. The product ceases to be something that the worker creates individually, it becomes the collective result of collective activity (Marx, 1973a, 709). The scale of production also increases enormously. Production is no longer designed to meet particular and local needs, it becomes what Hegel (1991, §204, 236) calls a 'universal' process aimed at satisfying 'universal' needs by means of market exchange using the 'universal' medium of money. Thus both activity and product become more abstract and universal, and the relation of subject to object in work is further mediated and distanced.

The increasingly universal character of work is also a central theme in Marx's account. Craft labour is rooted in particularity. It involves specialised processes and skills tied to particular materials and products. Its products are designed to satisfy individual and local needs. Industry does away with these limitations. 'What characterizes the division of labour in the automatic workshop is that labour has there completely lost its specialized character.... The automatic workshop wipes out specialists and craft-idiocy.' (Marx, 1978a, 138)

With the introduction of machinery, work is reduced to routine and mechanical operations dictated by the machine, or to the feeding, minding and maintaining of machines. However, the industrialisation and mechanisation of work prepares the way for still fuller forms of automation. The more mechanical work becomes, the more it can be taken over by machines altogether. In the end, the human being can 'step aside' (Marx, 1973a, 704, 705; echoing Hegel, 1991, §198, 233).

In this way, through the development of industry, the relation of worker to product becomes increasingly mediated and distanced. The labour process ceases to involve the direct transformation of the object by the worker. The craft element is almost entirely removed from the work activity itself. In the production process, machines act on their own, nature acts upon itself. Human purposes are realised through the use of science and technology and the application of knowledge. The craft model of production becomes less and less appropriate. However, that is not to say that the notion of labour as a form-giving activity is rendered inapplicable. On the contrary, industrial production is still formative in that it is intentional activity that gives form to materials and creates use values that embody human labour.

## Universal work

Industry creates a highly mediated relation of the worker to nature and to the social world. Work become increasingly distant from the direct production process as such, and the product is no longer related in a direct way to the satisfaction of particular needs. However, even automated industry is not the final stage of the process of development that I have been tracing. For modern industrial society has spawned entirely new kinds of work that seem to have no relation at all to the creation of material products or the satisfaction of material needs. These include commercial, administrative and other kinds of service work. Such work has become increasingly significant in modern society.

Hegel and Marx witnessed the beginning of these developments. Hegel treats commerce as a type of work essentially connected with and subordinated to manufacturing industry. However, he regards public administration and education as distinct spheres which involve the universal work of a separate class of public servants. Such work is universal in that it is abstracted from the creation of particular objects to meet particular material needs. Furthermore, it is the outcome of the exercise of universal, intellectual and rational powers. Marx also sees such work as employing intellectual abilities and creating a more universal and abstract relation between the worker and the object.

Commerce, administration and service work do not have direct material products, yet both Hegel and Marx include these sorts of work under the same heading of formative activities as other kinds of work. As economic activity grows from a local to an industrial scale, mechanisms of administration, distribution and exchange are needed to organise production, and to maintain the connections between producers and consumers. Commercial, administrative and service work are formative activities in that they create and sustain these economic and social relations.

## Postindustrial work

How do these ideas stand up today with the great changes in work since Hegel and Marx's time? As we have seen, Hardt and Negri argue that Marx's concept of labour is a product of the industrial society that was emerging at the time. It must now be rethought.

What sort of rethinking is needed? Hardt and Negri are not clear about this. At times they suggest that their project is to develop and extend Marx's theory to comprehend work and politics in post-industrial society. They portray mechanisation and automation as the paths along which industry has been developing since its inception, in the way that I have been arguing. Postindustrial forms of work using computers merely continue and extend this process (Hardt and Negri, 2000, 292). More commonly, however, they suggest that postindustrial forms of work are completely novel and necessitate a radically new theoretical approach. Marx's account of labour, they imply, presupposes an industrial and productivist model which is ceasing to apply. Industry is being superseded by the 'immaterial' production of the information economy. New 'immaterial' forms of labour are becoming predominant (Hardt and Negri, 2005, 107–15).

Hardt and Negri (2000, 281–5; 2005, 107–9, 140–3) have taken the concept of 'immaterial labour' from Lazzarato (1996) and extended it to become central to their account of postindustrial society. Immaterial labour, like all labour, they acknowledge, involves material activity: what makes it 'immaterial' is its product. Lazzarato (1996, 133) defines it as 'the labor that produces the informational and cultural content of the commodity'. According to Hardt and Negri (2005, 108), it creates 'immaterial products, such as knowledge, information, communication, a relationship, or an emotional response'. It makes not just objects but 'subjectivities' (Hardt and Negri, 2000, 32). It is 'biopolitical production, the production of social life itself' (Hardt and Negri, 2000, xiii).

These ideas have considerable initial appeal and plausibility. However, they will not bear detailed examination. Precisely what kinds of work are these concepts referring to? Hardt and Negri's account is hazy and shifting. In *Empire*, they distinguish three types of immaterial labour.

> The first is involved in an industrial production that has been informationalized and has incorporated communication technologies in a way that transforms the production process itself.... Second is the immaterial labour of analytical and symbolic tasks.... A third type ... involves the production and manipulation of affect. (Hardt and Negri, 2000, 293)

More recently, the first of kind of work on this list has been dropped (Hardt and Negri, 2005, 108). Quite rightly so. Although industry uses computer control this does not make it an 'immaterial' process. The fact that many aspects of car production, for example, are now computerised, does not mean that car making has ceased to be a material process, or that car workers are no longer engaged in material production. Although machines now do the work and shop floor workers no longer 'get their hands dirty', nevertheless, by controlling these machines, they still have material effects and produce material goods. Their work is still material and formative in character.

### Symbolic labour

Hardt and Negri no longer include computerised industrial work under the heading of immaterial labour. That leaves two 'principle forms' of such work: 'symbolic' or intellectual labour and 'affective' labour, dealing with feelings or attitudes.[5] Both are types of immaterial labour, they maintain, in the sense they do not have material products nor are they designed to meet material needs. For this reason also such work seems to fall outside Marx's model of work as formative activity.

Symbolic work is primarily intellectual or artistic. It 'produces ideas, symbols, codes, texts, linguistic figures, images, and other such products' (Hardt and Negri, 2005, 108). It includes computer programming, graphic design, various sorts of media work, work in advertising and public relations, etc.. Work of this kind, it is true, does not directly create a material product. In this respect it resembles commercial, administrative and other kinds of service work. However, it is wrong to think that a new category of immaterial labour is needed to comprehend it. The error here is to imagine that 'symbolic' work of this sort has no material result and that only work which directly creates a tangible product, like industry or craft, is material activity. It is not the case that symbolic work creates only symbols or ideas: products that are purely subjective and intangible. All labour operates by intentionally transforming matter in some way, as Marx maintains. Symbolic labour is no exception: it involves making marks on paper, making sounds, creating electronic impulses in a computer system, or whatever. Only in this way is such activity objectified and realised as labour. In this way, all labour is material.

Economically speaking, symbolic work is not primarily concerned with creating a material product as such, but rather with the realisation of value through distribution, exchange, marketing, etc.. However, it is important to see that these activities are essential to the processes of material production in an industrial economy. They are needed in order to establish, maintain and facilitate the economic and social relations required for production. A modern economy cannot function without managers, accountants, computer programmers, designers, etc.. Their work does not directly create a material product, nevertheless it has material effects which produce and reproduce social and economic relations and alter consciousness.

In this way, there is also an immaterial aspect to such labour, as Hardt and Negri maintain. However, the same is true for other kinds of work as well. All labour has an immaterial as well as a material aspect. For all labour takes place in a context of social relations. In altering the

---

[5]The distinction between these forms is not clear cut, as Hardt and Negri (2005, 108) acknowledge, 'most actual jobs involving immaterial labor combine these two forms'.

material world, labour at the same time sustains and alters these social relations. In the process, it affects – creates, alters – subjectivities. *All* labour, it must be stressed, does this. It is not peculiar to a special sort of 'immaterial' labour or 'biopolitical' activity alone. 'Social relations are just as much produced by men as linen, flax, etc.... In acquiring new productive forces men change their mode of production; and in changing their mode of production, in changing the way of earning their living, they change all their social relations.' (Marx, 1978a, 103)

In a quite different way, Marx's account is also criticised by Habermas (1972, chapter 2; 1996). He conceives of work as a purely instrumental activity to meet individual needs, and he treats the sphere of communicative action and social interaction as a separate and autonomous realm. The result is a dualistic distinction between work on the one side and the sphere of social relations (communicative action and social interaction) on the other.

Hardt and Negri (2000, 404–5) criticise Habermas for thus 'compartmentalising' work and communicative action into separate spheres. In the postindustrial period with the development of immaterial labour, they argue, work has become 'biopolitical' and *essentially* communicative and social in character. By separating social relations from the sphere of work, Habermas detaches them from their real, material basis and idealises them.

This criticism of Habermas is valid as far as it goes but it should be taken further, for it applies to his account of labour and social relations quite generally. By restricting their argument to 'immaterial' labour only, Hardt and Negri end up reproducing a dualism between material and immaterial activity of the sort that they criticise in Habermas. All human labour is social and necessarily involves a communicative element; and at the same time all human social relations are rooted in material labour. This is Marx's theory, and neither Hardt and Negri nor Habermas presents a valid critique of it.

### Affective labour

There are similar problems with the account that Hardt and Negri give of their second form of immaterial labour, 'affective' labour. This is 'labor that produces or manipulates affects such as a feeling of ease, well-being, satisfaction, excitement, or passion. One can recognise affective labor, for example in the work of legal assistants, flight attendants, and fast food workers (service with a smile)' (Hardt and Negri, 2005, 108). Such affective labour also includes caring and helping work. According to Hardt and

Negri this is a further form of 'immaterial' labour that cannot be accounted for by Marx since it has no material product.

To support their case they appeal to Hannah Arendt's philosophy. She maintains that there is a fundamental distinction between what she calls 'labour' and 'work' which Marx fails to make. What she terms 'labour' is activity to satisfy immediate consumption needs. It is concerned primarily with the maintenance of natural life, it creates no lasting products. Arendt's main examples of such labour are cleaning, cooking and other forms of housework, but her account applies to other kinds of service work as well. Hardt and Negri's 'affective' labour is 'labour' in this sense. What Arendt calls 'work', by contrast, makes an enduring object for 'use' rather than for immediate consumption. It thereby creates a 'world'. Arendt (1958, chapters III–IV) criticises Marx for treating all productive activity in terms applicable only to 'work' in this specific sense, and hence for ignoring the fact that much productive activity is devoted to 'labour' which has no enduring product.

Again we must avoid thinking that only work which results in a material product counts as work or form-giving activity for Marx. This is at the basis of both Arendt's and Hardt and Negri's criticisms of him. It is wrong to imagine that Arendt's 'labour', or Hardt and Negri's 'affective' labour have no products. Such work operates, as does all labour, by intentionally forming matter and altering the material environment in some way, including through speech and other forms of communicative action. It does not simply disappear, it is objectified in the world, it creates use values.

Affective labour is necessary in order to establish and maintain economic and social relations. Housework is needed to create and maintain a home, education to produce socialised individuals. Receptionists, social workers, cleaners, shop workers, etc., are needed to maintain social and economic relations in a modern economy. None of these activities directly creates a material product, yet they are formative activities and modes of objectification nonetheless. As with the other kinds of so-called 'immaterial' production discussed earlier, they have material results which serve to produce and reproduce social relations and subjectivity.

Hardt and Negri are aware of some of the problems with the concept of immaterial labour to which I have been pointing. The 'labor involved in all immaterial production', they admit,

> remains material.... What is immaterial is *its product*. We recognize that *immaterial labor* is a very ambiguous term in this regard. It might be better to understand [it] ... as 'biopolitical labor', that is, labor

that creates not only material goods but also relationships and ultimately social life itself. (Hardt and Negri, 2005, 109)

The concept of 'biopolitical' labour does not resolves these problems, they go deeper than Hardt and Negri appreciate. As I have argued, just as all immaterial labour necessarily involves material activity, so all material labour has an immaterial aspect, in that it alters not only the material immediately worked upon but also social relations and subjectivity. There is no clear distinction between material and immaterial labour in this respect. Resort to the concept of 'biopolitical' activity is no help. The same point applies. *All* productive activity is 'biopolitical' to some degree in that all labour transforms relationships and social life. In this way all labour is ultimately a form of self-creation (Marx, 1973a, 712). In short the notion of 'biopolitical' activity is no more satisfactory than that of 'immaterial' labour as a way to distinguish postindustrial forms of work.

## Political implications

Hardt and Negri are right to argue that work has changed radically since the industrial revolution. Despite the initial plausibility of their account, however, their categories of immaterial labour and biopolitical activity are little help in understanding these changes. Properly understood and suitably developed, Marx's theory of work as objectification and form-giving activity provides a more satisfactory and illuminating conceptual framework for understanding the nature of work, including its new postindustrial forms.

According to this theory, different kinds of labour involve different degrees of mediation in our relation to nature ranging from the most immediate relationship of direct appropriation to the most abstract and universal kinds of work. This is primarily a logical sequence rather than a historical one (though historical changes are associated with it). In Hegel's case, there is also an ethical and political dimension to his account. With the development of our relation to nature through labour comes the emergence of self-consciousness from immediate natural conditions towards a developed, reflective and mediated state and with that a growth of freedom.

It is not immediately clear whether Marx adopts a similar perspective. His theory of labour is developed in an economic context. In purely economic terms, Marx does not differentiate between different kinds of labour, still less make a hierarchy of them. Like other classical economists, in the labour theory of value he equates different forms of labour together as 'abstract' labour. This may appear to suggest that he does not rank different kinds of work morally or politically, but that is not the case: there is clearly an evaluative dimension to Marx's theory. The writers I have been discussing all criticise it in this respect, and they are not wrong to do so. However, they fail to take account of the Hegelian dimension to Marx's thought and so misunderstand its implications.

The view that Marx's account relies on a 'romantically transfigured prototype of handicraft activity' (Habermas, 1987, 65–6; cf. Benton discussed above) is a complete misconception. Marx could not be clearer in his rejection of the craft ideal. He is scornful of the 'idiocy' and small mindedness engendered by handicraft work (Marx, 1978a, 138). His critical attitude is grounded on the account of the labour process that I have been describing which sees craft work as a limited and purely individual activity aimed at the satisfaction of particular and local needs.

For Marx, the coming of industry means a liberation from these constraints. This is the positive aspect of its development. However, the change from craft to industrial production takes place under the contradictory conditions of capitalism in which the pressure towards universality inherent in industry comes into conflict with the system of private ownership and the free market in which it develops. The result is the 'devastation caused by a social anarchy which turns every economic progress into a social calamity' (Marx, 1961a, 487). In the longer term, however, the coming of industry means the elimination of brute physical effort and the reduction of repetitious and mechanical toil. Work becomes more productive, rational, and universal, hence 'more worthy of ... human nature' (Marx, 1971b, 820).[6]

These points about Marx are widely understood. Marxism is thus often seen as a philosophy rooted in industrial conditions that idealises industrial labour and the industrial working class. This is Hardt and Negri's position. However, the reading that I have been proposing suggests a different view. Marx is a historical thinker. At the time he was writing, industry was becoming the predominant form of production and the industrial proletariat was emerging as the most advanced political force. But things have moved on. Hardt and Negri are right to insist that Marx's ideas must be rethought and developed to take account of this.

---

[6]This is the logic of Marx's account. It should be Hegel's outlook too, but Hegel does not fully accept the implications of his own theory as argued in Chapter 2 above.

Marxism should not be seen as eternally linked to an industrial perspective. Indeed, its underlying philosophy suggests that industry is not the highest development of our productive and creative powers. It points to higher forms of labour, beyond industry, in more universal kinds of work. Hegel assigns this mainly to a universal class of civil servants. This is not Marx's idea. Marx envisages the eventual emergence of forms of work in which the universal tendencies of modern industry are realised, and in which,

> the detail-worker of to-day, crippled by one and the same trivial operation, and thus reduced to the mere fragment of a man, [will be replaced] by the fully developed individual, fit for a variety of labours ... to whom the different social functions he performs, are but so many modes of giving free scope to his own natural and acquired powers. (Marx, 1961a, 488)

It is easy to dismiss this as a utopian dream, but that would be a mistake. Aspects of it are already coming true, though within the contradictory conditions of capitalism. In contemporary society, as Hardt and Negri (2000, 285) observe, 'jobs for the most part are highly mobile and involve flexible skills.... They are characterized in general by the central role played by knowledge, information, affect and communication.'

As I have argued, Marx's concept of labour, properly understood, continues to provide a more helpful basis than the concepts of immaterial labour and biopolitical production for understanding these developments. In more favourable conditions, such universal work might extend our rational and creative powers. It could become something we do not only because we are forced by economic necessity but as a free activity. This is Marx's ideal (Marx, 1971b, 820).[7]

---

[7]An earlier draft of this Chapter was first read at a Marx and Philosophy Society Seminar on 28 May 2005. I am particularly grateful to David McNally for his comments.

# 4
# The Individual and Society

This chapter deals with Marx's account of the individual and society and its roots in Hegel's philosophy. In outline Marx's views on this theme are well known, and so too is their connection with the theme of alienation which I shall describe. The Hegelian roots of these ideas are less well documented. Moreover, a knowledge of the Hegelian context helps to clarify the philosophical assumptions involved in Marx's views, assumptions which Marx himself often does not make explicit. The contrast with Hegel's outlook is also useful in bringing out what is distinctive in Marx's approach.

Recent philosophical discussion of the topic of individual and society has been dominated by the debate between liberalism and communitarianism. I will situate Hegel and Marx's accounts in this context. My aim is to show that Hegel and Marx have a different and, I shall argue, more fruitful approach which raises large and important issues about the character of modern society.

## Starting from society

Much liberal social thought starts from the assumption that the individual is an atomic entity, 'unencumbered' (Sandel, 1982) by any necessary social relations. Individuals are taken to exist and to have an identity which is logically prior to and independent of any social relations. Work is treated as an individual activity to meet individual needs which involves relations with others only contingently, and society is regarded as a mere collection of such individuals interacting together.

Both Marx and Hegel reject this approach. According to Hegel,

There are always only two possible viewpoints in the ethical realm: either one starts from substantiality, or one proceeds atomistically

48

and moves upward from the basis of individuality. The latter view-point excludes spirit, because it leads only to an aggregation, whereas spirit is not something individual, but the unity of the individual and the universal. (Hegel, 1991, §156A, 197)

Marx is equally insistent that social and economic theory must start from the social totality. 'Whenever we speak of production ... what is meant is always ... production by social individuals' (Marx, 1973a, 85). He explicitly contrasts his starting point with the atomistic approach adopted by Adam Smith in *The Wealth of Nations*. According to Marx, Smith begins with the assumption of an isolated individual, a Robinson Crusoe like figure, working alone to satisfy his own needs. Only subsequently does this figure encounter others, exchange products and enter into social and economic relations (Marx, 1973a, 83–5).[1]

Marx's objections to this approach are partly empirical. The supposition of an initial pre-social, purely individual condition – the idea of a 'state of nature' which runs through eighteenth century liberal social thought – has no historical basis.

> The more deeply we go back into history, the more does the individual, and hence also the producing individual, appear as dependent, as belonging to a greater whole: in a still quite natural way in the family and in the family expanded into the clan [*Stamm*]; then later in the various forms of communal society arising out of the antitheses and fusions of clans. (Marx, 1973a, 84)

However, Marx also rejects the individualistic starting point on philosophical, ontological grounds. Production should not be thought of simply as an instrumental activity to meet individual needs, it is always and necessarily a social activity. In working to create a material product, at the same time we produce and reproduce our social relations (Marx, 1978a, 103). Human beings are *essentially* social creatures.

## Communitarian accounts

Ideas such as these are now familiar and widely held. The rejection of the idea of the atomic individual has been a fundamental aspect of the

---

[1]This account of Smith (1900) is widely shared, but it is also questioned, see e.g. Denis, 1999.

contemporary communitarian critique of liberalism.[2] This critique is also applied to liberal society. According to the liberal account, a society based on the free market, in which autonomous individuals can pursue their own interests, best accords with human needs and human nature. In criticism of this, communitarian philosophers argue that liberalism threatens communities by fragmenting them into a mass of competing individuals.

Two contrasting accounts of the nature of that threat are evident among these thinkers. Some argue that in liberal society the bonds of traditional community have actually been shattered and destroyed. According to MacIntyre (1985), for example, the picture of the individual and society given in liberal social theory is true: not as an account of universal human nature, but as an account of the way people have become in modern society. Under the impact of the market, society has been dissolved into a mass of separate individuals each pursuing their own independent interests.

However, other communitarian writers have pointed out that this sort of account is not compatible with the social ontology of communitarianism. If we are necessarily social beings, then liberal society cannot be understood as the mere negation and loss of community. If the idea of the 'unencumbered' self is a myth of liberal philosophy, it cannot at the same time give a true picture of the individual in modern society. This point is made by Walzer. Modern society cannot involve the total dissolution of community, he argues, 'the deep structure even of liberal society is ... communitarian, we are in fact persons and ... we are in fact bound together' (Walzer, 1990, 10; cf. Taylor, 1991).

Walzer is right to criticise MacIntyre in this way and to insist on our social nature. However, his position takes a more questionable turn when he goes on to argue that the liberal notions of individuality and society are only superficial and mistaken appearances and that all that is required to overcome them is a change in consciousness. For on the other side MacIntyre is right to point out that there is a basis of objective truth in the liberal account of modern fragmentation that Walzer denies (Sayers, 1999b).

In short there is a connection between the liberal account of the individual and society and the objective conditions of liberal society

---

[2]See MacIntyre, 1985; Sandel, 1982; Taylor, 1985. It should be noted that none of these philosophers is happy with the 'communitarian' label; nevertheless it is standardly applied to them and is useful to indicate the anti-atomistic approach that they share.

that have produced it. Though both strands of communitarianism that I have described have some awareness of this, neither gives a satisfactory account of it.

## Marx

For this one must turn to Marx. He gives a historical account of liberal society and of the sort of individuality it involves. In pre-modern societies, he argues, people are much more closely embedded in the community than in modern conditions. Social roles are largely fixed and determined for individuals by their place in the social order. In such societies, people 'enter into connection with one another only as individuals imprisoned within a certain definition, as feudal lord and vassal, landlord and serf, etc.' (Marx, 1973a, 163). It is only with the development of modern society and the free market that individuals get separated from fixed and predetermined roles and become independent agents, free to pursue their own particular interests. 'In this society of free competition, the individual appears detached from the natural bonds etc. which in earlier historical periods make him the accessory of a definite and limited human conglomerate' (Marx, 1973a, 83).

Of course, the market and money are not inventions of capitalism, they existed long before it developed. In earlier periods, however, the main form of economic activity was production for use and direct extraction of surplus value. It is only with the development of capitalism that production of commodities for exchange on the market comes to predominate.

> Prices are old; exchange also; but the increasing ... dominance of the latter over all relations of production, only develop[s] fully ... in bourgeois society, the society of free competition. What Adam Smith, in the true eighteenth-century manner, puts in the prehistoric period, the period preceding history, is rather a product of history. (Marx, 1973a, 156)

And only at the end of this process, according to Marx, does the situation finally come to be reflected in the realm of ideas.

> Only in the eighteenth century, in 'civil society' [*bürgerliche Gesellschaft*], do the various forms of social connectedness confront the individual as a mere means towards his private purposes, as external necessity. But the epoch which produces this standpoint, that of the

isolated individual, is also precisely that of the hitherto most developed social ... relations. (Marx, 1973a, 84)

In short, the liberal idea that the isolated individual is a universal, presocial given must indeed be rejected on philosophical grounds. However, a purely ontological critique of liberalism does not give the whole picture. For the atomistic way of thinking reflects real historical conditions. The error of liberalism is to mistake this form of individuality for human nature as such and to treat it as universal and existing independent of and prior to any social relations.

> This eighteenth-century individual – the product on one side of the dissolution of the feudal forms of society, on the other side of the new forces of production developed since the sixteenth century – appears as an ideal, whose existence they project into the past. Not as a historic result but as history's point of departure. As the Natural Individual appropriate to their notion of human nature, not arising historically, but posited by nature. (Marx, 1973a, 84)

## Hegel

In arguing in this way, Marx is basing himself on an important Hegelian insight, although he develops and extends it greatly. For Hegel was one of the first philosophers to identify and describe the social changes to which Marx is referring and to take cognisance of the economic theorists who were beginning to analyse them. As Marx suggests (1973a, 84, quoted above), Hegel analyses them under the heading of 'civil society' (*bürgerliche Gesellschaft*).[3] He uses this term to denote the sphere of social and economic life governed by the principles of 'subjectivity' and 'individual freedom' in which the individual acts as an independent agent, responsible for his own beliefs and pursuing his own interests, particularly in the economic sphere of the competitive market.

Civil society, thus understood, is one of the three spheres or 'moments' into which Hegel analyses modern society.[4] According to Hegel, a sep-

---

[3]Hegel, 1991, §§182–256, 220–74. This term has a prior history in political thought that can be traced back to Aristotle, but Hegel's use is distinctive and innovative (Riedel, 1984). The same term is taken over by Marx to describe capitalist society as a whole. When Marx is using it in this way, it is usually translated as 'bourgeois society'.

[4]The other two 'moments' of the modern social whole are the family and the state (Hegel, 1991, §157, 198).

arate social sphere of this sort, in which people are free to form their own ideas and pursue their own interests, is a distinctively modern development. Of course he is not suggesting that independent thought or self interest as such are new phenomena. However, in earlier periods, Hegel argues, independent thought and the pursuit of self interest were both regarded as threats to social stability. Attempts were made to curb free thought, particularly on religious matters, and to control independent economic activity.[5] The implications of this are the same as those of Marx's ideas just described: the creation of an arena of social life in which people are at liberty to follow their own beliefs and the growth of an economic sphere in which they are free to pursue their own interests is a distinctive development of liberal society: 'the realm of civil society belongs to the modern world' (Hegel, 1991, §182A, 220).

According to Hegel, the sphere of civil society is governed by two principles. These appear to be independent and unrelated, but they are not: both must be grasped in order to understand civil society. The error of the communitarian approaches that I have identified, I shall argue, is that each sees only one of these principles and emphasises it exclusively.

Hegel's (1991, §182, 220) first principle is that of 'the particular individual', with the subjective freedom and autonomy just described. The liberal account suggests that this is the sole component of a free market society, which is conceived as nothing more than a collection or 'aggregation' of individuals all freely pursuing their own interests in their own ways.[6] MacIntyre in effect endorses this account when he maintains that modern society has involved the complete destruction of all communal ties and relations.

However, this is only one side of the story for Hegel. Such 'particular individuals' do not exist on their own. Although individuals in modern society appear to be acting quite independently, they are in fact

---

[5]It is in this light that Hegel interprets Plato's hostility, in *The Republic*, to any sphere of individual autonomy and his arguments against the Sophists (Hegel, 1991, §185, 222–3; Sayers, 1999a, 12–15). He maintains that the principle of individuality is introduced into Western philosophy by Socrates and with Christianity. However, it reaches its full development only in modern times in Europe after going through a series of earlier stages (Hegel, 1956).

[6]At least within broad limits imposed by the state in order to prevent the outbreak of a Hobbesian 'war of all against all'.

essentially related to other such individuals and bound up in 'a system of all-round interdependence' (Hegel, 1991, §§182–3, 220–1). People are related to each other in such a way that they can achieve their ends only by simultaneously satisfying those of others. In this way, 'the subsistence and welfare of the individual ... are interwoven with, and grounded on, the subsistence [and] welfare ... of all, and have actuality ... only in this context' (Hegel, 1991, §183, 221). Thus in acting as an individual in civil society we each further a 'universal' (i.e., social) end. This 'universality', according to Hegel, is the second principle at work civil society.

Walzer stresses this aspect of social connection in his account of modern society; but, like MacIntyre, he does so in a one-sided – though opposite – way. Hegel, by contrast, insists that both aspects are simultaneously at work in civil society. What this means and how it is possible becomes clearer when one sees that what Hegel is describing in abstract philosophical terms is in fact the operation of the division of labour in a system of market exchange. In such a system, individual agents seem to operate separately: one person farms, another build houses, still others work in factories and offices, and so on. Though people act independently, they can do so only within an overall division of labour in which each is providing for the needs of the others. The division of labour is simply another term for the social organisation of labour. This social arrangement is established and maintained through the operation of the market.

Hegel's (1991, §189R, 227) account of the way the market operates is sketchy and vague. It is drawn mainly from the work of economists such as Smith, Say and Ricardo, but it lacks the empirical and economic detail that these writers bring to their studies. In a free market situation, individuals seem to be free and independent agents, their social interconnection appears to be external and accidental to them. The social totality seems to have dissolved and to be 'lost in its extremes' (Hegel, 1991, §184, 221). Particular and universal, individual activity and social relations, appear to have fallen apart and become detached from each other. However, the outcome of numerous individuals all pursuing their own economic interests is not the mere chaos of a Hobbesian state of 'war' (Hobbes, 1985, chapter 13). Rather it is a situation governed by apparently objective regularities, the economic laws of the market. These regularities constitute the subject matter of economics. 'This proliferation of arbitrariness generates universal determinations from within itself, and this apparently scattered and thoughtless activity is subject to a necessity which arises of its own accord. To discover the necessity at work here is the object of political economy' (Hegel, 1991, §189A, 227).[7]

Hegel has an optimistic view of the outcome of this economic system. The result of all these particular self interested individuals competing in the market place is that the common good will be served. Particular and universal are reconciled.

> Subjective selfishness turns into a contribution towards the satisfaction of the needs of everyone else. By a dialectical movement, the particular is mediated by the universal so that each individual, in earning, producing and enjoying on his own account, thereby earns and produces for the enjoyment of others. (Hegel, 1991, §199, 233)

This echoes the ideas of Adam Smith who talks of an 'invisible hand' benignly governing the market, and Mandeville who suggests that the 'private vice' of self interest leads to 'public benefits' (Smith, 1900; Mandeville, 1970).[8] In related contexts, Hegel talks of the way in which the 'cunning of reason' mysteriously ensures that a rational result comes from the pursuit of individual ends (Hegel, 1988b, 35; 1892, §359, 350; 1969, 746). He holds that civil society creates a framework in which liberty and individuality are both realised. In this way, although he rejects the individualistic ontology of liberalism, he shares much with liberalism in his political and economic views (Rawls, 2000).

## Alienation

Marx's analysis of the workings of capitalism and the market develops out of Hegel's analysis of civil society, but the critique of liberalism that results is much deeper and more thoroughgoing than Hegel's. Marx questions the idea that the market always acts to harmonise the interests of competing individuals; its operation leads also to conflict,

---

[7]The implication of this is that economics and the laws it describes are products of the modern world – an implication which Marx makes explicit: 'the categories of bourgeois economy ... are forms of thought expressing with social validity the conditions and relations of a definite, historically determined mode of production, viz., the production of commodities' (Marx, 1961a, 76).

[8]Uncritical advocates of laissez-faire capitalism ('vulgar' economists, as Marx calls them) still hold such views (Hayek, 1960).

stagnation and crisis.[9] So far from being the benign mechanism of reconciliation that Hegel describes, it imposes on individuals and even on whole communities as an apparently independent and inexorable force. Indeed, we are so used to perceiving the economy in this way that we accept it as normal and it passes almost unnoticed. 'You can't buck the market', people say, for it appears to be a separate and autonomous power governed by its own objective laws which operate despite the will of individuals or even of society. The Rev. Dr Colin Morris gave a graphic account of such attitudes in a recent radio broadcast.

> The Sunday newspapers were full of reactions to the Budget. They said things like: before [the Budget] the Stock Market had been 'sceptical' or 'nervous', but now it's 'pleased' or 'happy' – as though it's a sort of living being. It's the kind of language people once used about that other invisible force called God. In Old Testament times, the people feared Jehovah's reaction to what they'd done. These days, it's the Market's verdict that is awaited with anxiety. (Morris, 2004)

Marx uses the same analogy in his account of our attitudes to the market. Just as in religion, where things which are our own creations 'appear as independent beings endowed with life, and entering into relation both with one another and the human race' (Marx, 1961a, 72), so too in economics we find ourselves at the mercy of forces which we ourselves have created. We have lost control of our own social relations, our own creations and powers, which now appear to rule over us.

Thus in liberal society, on the one hand there are a mass of apparently autonomous individuals each independently pursuing their own interests, though in reality they are interdependent and their activities are connected together. On the other hand, the form of their connection and interdependence resides in an apparently separate economic system which appears to operate according to its own objective laws

---

[9]'The real point is not that each individual's pursuit of his private interest promotes the ... general interest. One could just as well deduce ... that each individual reciprocally blocks the assertion of the others' interests.' (Marx, 1973a, 156)

and which confronts these individuals as a power independent of them.

In fact, these two aspects go together, they are correlative aspects of the same situation. Marx describes it under the heading of 'alienation'.

> The social character of activity ... here appear[s] as something alien and objective, confronting the individuals, not as their relation to one another, but as their subordination to relations which subsist independently of them and which arise out of collisions between mutually indifferent individuals. The general exchange of activities and products, which has become a vital condition for each individual – their mutual interconnection here appears as something alien to them, autonomous, as a thing. (Marx, 1973a, 157)

The Marxist notion of alienation is most frequently encountered in relation to labour. Work is alienated when we relate to our own product or creative activity as to something which is independent and opposed to us (Marx, 1975e, 322–34). In the present case, alienation is from economic and social relations. At root, however, these two forms of alienation are the same. For in producing objects we are also producing and reproducing our economic and social relations, as we have seen. Economic relations are also products of human labour. So far from providing conditions for the realisation of individuality and social reconciliation as suggested by Hegel and other liberal philosophers, in conditions of alienation these relations form an independent order which is hostile and opposed to us.

## Marx's critique of liberalism

Both Marx and Hegel agree that when individuals pursue their own interests in a market society, differences and inequalities will emerge: specialisation and division of labour are inevitable features of modern economic life. Hegel argues that these need not constitute a barrier to the realisation of individuality and liberty. On the contrary, 'the individual attains actuality only by entering into existence [*Dasein*] in general, and hence into determinate particularity; he must accordingly limit himself *exclusively* to one of the particular spheres of need [i.e., economic activity].' (Hegel, 1991, §207, 238)

Again Hegel takes a benign view of the impact of the economic system. No doubt it is true that to achieve anything determinate *in a particular activity* one must limit oneself, as Hegel is fond of reminding us (Hegel, 1991, §13A, 47; cf. 1892, §92A, 173). It does not follow from this that one must confine oneself exclusively to one specific occupation for the whole of one's life. However, this is what Hegel is recommending and what the modern division of labour in effect dictates. So far from facilitating the realisation of individuality and freedom, it limits and restricts it.

> As soon as the distribution of labour comes into being, each man has a particular, exclusive sphere of activity, which is forced upon him and from which he cannot escape. He is a hunter, a fisherman, a herdsman, or a critical critic, and must remain so if he does not want to lose his means of livelihood. (Marx and Engels, 1978b, 160)

This, too, is a manifestation of social alienation. The economic relations that we ourselves have created come to act as coercive constraints on us.[10] 'This fixation of social activity, this consolidation of what we ourselves produce into an objective power above us, growing out of our control, thwarting our expectations, bringing to naught our calculations, is one of the chief factors in historical development up till now.' (Marx and Engels, 1978b, 160)

This line of thought provides the basis both for Marx's analysis of liberal society and for his critique of liberalism, a form of critique absent from both communitarianism and Hegel's social thought. Communitarian accounts, as we have seen (p. 49f above), fail to understand the way in which, in liberal society, atomised individuality coexists with objectified social relations and so they stress one or other of these aspects one-sidedly. Hegel, I have been arguing, has a deeper understanding of this connection, and Marx draws heavily on his analysis in this respect. However, Hegel believes that liberal society creates the conditions for the realisation of individuality and liberty. Though he has some awareness of the alien and negative aspects of liberal society, as we shall see, he tends to discount these as mere anomalies. To repeat, in many respects he is a liberal in his political and economic views.

Marx's critique goes further. He argues that the social relations of the market and the atomised individuality associated with it are forms of alienation which limit individuality and freedom. Genuine community

---

[10]For Marx the full development of individuality involves the all-round development of our powers and abilities, unconstrained by such limitations, see Chapter 8 below.

and full individual development will become possible only when we regain control of our economic and social relations and organise society in such a way as to allow for our all-round activity as universal beings. This is impossible, Marx argues, in liberal – i.e., capitalist – society. Economic alienation is an ineliminable feature of this kind of society because it is rooted in the economic system of the market itself. His argument goes as follows.

Each individual in a market economy appears to be operating separately and to be producing independently. In reality, however, their activities are socially connected and coordinated, as Hegel describes. They are part of the overall social organisation and division of labour. But what is the basis of their social connection? It is located in the economic system of exchange through which their products and needs are related. Their social connection becomes explicit and asserts itself only when the products of their separate activities are exchanged in the market. The connection between the activities of individuals, therefore, resides in the economic relations between the goods they produce.

The precise way in which this social connection is established through economic exchange is spelled out by Marx in his account of the 'fetishism of commodities' in *Capital*.

> As a general rule, articles of utility become commodities, only because they are products of the labour of private individuals or groups of individuals who carry on their work independently of each other.... Since the producers do not come into social contact with each other until they exchange their products, the specific social character of each producer's labour does not show itself except in the act of exchange. In other words, the labour of the individual asserts itself as a part of the labour of society, only by means of the relations which the act of exchange establishes directly between the products, and indirectly, through them, between the producers. (Marx, 1961a, 72–3)

In this way, both the autonomous individuals in market society and the apparently alien economic system which confronts them go necessarily together. The alienation involved is not only a subjective appearance, it is an objective feature of the situation. Its causes lie in the fact that both our apparent separation and our social connections are made through the economic mechanisms of the market. The relations between producers are established via the relation of their products in the market. Social relations are thus not established directly between people, but indirectly via a relation between things, or rather between the economic value bestowed on things within the economic system. To the producers, therefore, 'the relations connecting the labour of one individual with that of the rest appear, not as direct social relations between individuals at work, but as what they really are, material relations between persons and social relations between things' (Marx, 1961a, 73). Social relations between people are transformed into economic relations between things – economic relations which operate in an alien way, independently of us.

What this means is that in order to overcome this alienation, regain control over our social lives and relate to each other in a directly social and unalienated way, more than a mere change of consciousness is needed. The overcoming of alienation can be accomplished, Marx's argument implies, only with the abolition of the predominance of market exchange and the whole system of economic life which goes with it.

## The free individual

Thus there is a dimension of social criticism in Marx's theory which is entirely absent from the communitarian critique of liberalism. Moreover, Marx's account of social alienation and its overcoming is located within a larger historical picture. Again Marx's ideas have Hegelian origins. But even though Marx's account of historical development follows a Hegelian pattern, he uses it to reach a very different assessment of modern individuality and social relations and their place in historical development.

In the earliest forms of society, according to the Hegelian scheme, individuals are in immediate unity with the community. They are united primarily by natural bonds of family and kinship. Society takes the form of a tribe or clan. Its members accept its customs and traditions as unquestioned laws. The individual is submerged in the community, separateness and particularity have not yet developed, the universal (i.e., the social) predominates.[11]

However, individuality starts to develop within such communities. The resulting tensions and conflicts lead eventually to their breakup. A new historical stage commences in which freedom and autonomous individuality begin to develop. This stage evolves through a series of different historical shapes. With the Protestant Reformation and the French Revolution, according to Hegel, the third stage is reached. The conditions are finally created for the modern liberal state. This contains a developed

---

[11]This initial stage reaches its highest development in the ancient Greek *polis* on Hegel's account.

sphere of civil society which allows individuals to pursue their own interests, yet within the overall legal and political framework of the state. Liberal society thus combines the individualism of civil society within the larger whole of the state. The community is no longer a merely immediate unity, it is now a unity which contains individuality and difference within it: it has a concrete and developed form. For Hegel this is the final stage of historical development, the 'end of history'. The fully developed, free individual is at home in such a society, alienation is overcome (Hegel, 1988a, 92–8).

This is not to suggest that Hegel is blind to the problems of liberal society. As we have seen (in Chapter 2 above), he is by no means an uncritical advocate of free market capitalism and industrial society (nor are the economists on whom he relies, such as Adam Smith). He is particularly concerned by the huge gulf of inequality that, as he could see, was a consequence of the development of capitalism and which, he feared, would spawn an excluded and disaffected underclass or 'rabble'.[12] But he can see no effective remedies. He half-heartedly suggests a number of possibilities, including charity, the founding of colonies to which the poor could be exported, even simply 'to leave the poor to their fate' (Hegel, 1991, §245R, 267). He holds out little hope for any of these policies.

Poverty and social exclusion remain as unfortunate 'anomalies' in Hegel's account of liberal society, but they are not usually allowed to disrupt his optimistic picture of it.[13] For Hegel's historical horizons are limited by liberal society, he cannot see beyond it. When he does despair

---

[12]Hegel, 1991, §244, 266. Cf. Marx and Engels' (1978c, 474) view that capitalist society was dividing into the 'two great hostile camps' of the bourgeoisie and proletariat. If the situation appears different now (at least from the perspective of the economically developed part of the world), arguably that is not because capitalism has ceased to be like this, but because these effects are now being worked out on a global rather than national scale.

[13]According to Knowles, Hegel gives a penetrating analysis of the problem of poverty in capitalist society, he should not be criticised for failing to come up with a solution for it. 'The mistake of Marx and ... of his followers was to suppose that deep and plausible social criticism somehow delivers up distinctive and effective policy prescriptions. This is not a mistake to which Hegel was prone' (Knowles, 2002, 293). This is to misunderstand the purpose of both these writers. Neither Hegel nor Marx is trying to give 'policy prescriptions' about what ought to be done. Rather they are seeking to analyse and understand what is actually the case. If there are inherent and ineliminable conflicts in modern society then the liberal order cannot be stable and harmonious, as Hegel maintains. It is inherently contradictory, it is destined to change and be superseded, regardless of what policies are pursued. That is Marx's argument (Sayers, 1998, 106–10).

of a resolution of its problems, instead of looking beyond it, he looks back to an earlier and simpler form of life, where economic activity is still at a local and immediately comprehensible level. His ideal here is the 'heroic' society of Homeric legend (as we have in Chapter 2 above). 'In such a mode of life man has the feeling, in everything he uses and everything he surrounds himself with, that he has produced it from his own resources, and therefore in external things has to do with what is his own and not with alienated objects lying outside his own sphere wherein he is master.' (Hegel, 1975, 261)

Though romantic visions of this sort have had and still have great influence, they were unrealistic in Hegel's day, as Hegel himself was aware, and they are even more so today. It is impossible for us to return to such simple conditions. Moreover, such romanticism conflicts with Hegel's historical framework which assumes a progressive development. In this, development occurs through a process of alienation and its overcoming. Society moves from an initial stage of simple and immediate unity, through a period of particularity and separation in which individuals are alienated from each other and from the community. The third and final stage is one of synthesis and reconciliation. The individual is reintegrated with the community and with others: alienation is overcome.

It is important to see that alienation, on this account, is not a purely negative phenomenon. On the contrary, it is a necessary stage in the process of development. Equally, however, alienation is not a condition to remain in; for in it individuals are divided from each other and from their social connections. There is a drive to overcome it and find reconciliation; and this, Hegel believes, is achieved in modern liberal society.

The Marxist notion of alienation is often interpreted as a purely critical and negative concept, but seen in the light of its Hegelian roots it is clear that this is incorrect. Marx's account of history makes use of the same basic Hegelian framework. He too sees history as a development in which alienation forms a necessary stage in the process of its eventual overcoming (Sayers, 1998, 88–9, 136–41). Moreover, like Hegel, Marx divides history into three basic stages: an initial condition of immediate unity, followed by a stage of division and alienation, and finally a synthesis of the early stages, a higher form of unity in which concrete individuality can develop within community (Gould, 1978).[14]

---

[14]See Chapter 6 below for elaboration of this line of thought.

However, Marx's specific application of this framework is quite different to Hegel's.

> Relations of personal dependence (entirely spontaneous at the outset) are the first social forms, in which human productive capacity develops only to a slight extent and at isolated points. Personal independence founded on *objective* [*sachlicher*] dependence is the second great form, in which a system of general social metabolism, of universal relations, of all-round needs and universal capacities is formed for the first time. (Marx, 1973a, 158)

This 'second' form is liberal society, in which independent individuals are bound together by the alien economic relations of exchange and the market. Marx (1973a, 83) dates its beginning between the sixteenth and eighteenth centuries in Europe when these relations come to predominate.

As we have seen, Marx rejects the view, shared by Hegel and liberalism, that this creates the conditions in which true individuality and freedom can be realised and alienation overcome. This is not to deny that modern liberal society involves a real development of individuality and freedom, particularly in comparison with the relative absence of individual autonomy in earlier forms of society. However, even in the freest of liberal societies, individuality and liberty are limited by the alienation which is a pervasive feature of modern life. On the one hand, individuals seems detached and isolated from each other, while on the other hand the enormous economic powers and social relations which we ourselves have created have escaped our control and rule over us as independent and hostile forces. Marx describes the situation with a graphic and powerful metaphor.

> Modern bourgeois society, with its relations of production, of exchange and of property, a society that has conjured up such gigantic means of production and of exchange, is like the sorcerer who is no longer able to control the powers of the nether world whom he has called up by his spells. (Marx and Engels, 1978c, 478)

The implications of this account are radical and far reaching. The alienation from our productive powers which Marx is here describing, he insists, is an essential and objective feature of capitalist society, it is rooted in the economic forms of market exchange which are constitutive of it. The 'sorcerer' is 'modern bourgeois society', and the powers it has summoned up are those of capitalism and the market as such.

But this is not the end of the historical story for Marx. There can and will be another stage for which capitalism has created the necessary material conditions. 'Free individuality, based on the universal development of individuals and on their subordination of their communal, social productivity as their social wealth, is the third stage' (Marx, 1973a, 158). Only with this further stage, Marx maintains, will we be able to overcome our present alienation and reappropriate the economic and social powers that now rule over us. This will involve a complete transformation of society: the supersession of the predominance of monetary exchange, and of 'civil' or bourgeois society as such. Only then will the full and free development of individuality in a true community become a genuine possibility.[15]

---

[15]Earlier versions of this Chapter were presented at the Philosophy Departments of Lancaster University, University of New Hampshire, and at Bertell Ollman's Political Theory Colloquium, New York University. I am grateful to participants in these discussions, and to David McLellan and Andy Denis for helpful comments and criticisms.

# 5
# Freedom and the 'Realm of Necessity'

It is sometimes argued that there are two conflicting strands in Marx's thought on work and freedom. In his early writings Marx maintains that, although work in contemporary society is an alienated activity, it need not be so. Alienation can and will be overcome in a future society. Potentially, work can be a fulfilling and liberating activity (Marx, 1975d, 1975e). This is what I have been arguing in this book so far. In his later work, however, some say that he changes his outlook and that this is evident in the following well known passage from *Capital*.

> The realm of freedom actually begins only where labour which is determined by necessity and mundane considerations ceases; thus in the very nature of things it lies beyond the sphere of actual material production. Just as the savage must wrestle with Nature to satisfy his wants, to maintain and reproduce life, so must civilized man, and he must do so in all social formations and under all possible modes of production. With his development this realm of physical necessity expands as a result of his wants; but, at the same time, the forces of production which satisfy these wants also increase. Freedom in this field can only consist in socialized man, the associated producers, rationally regulating their interchange with Nature, bringing it under their common control, instead of being ruled by it as by the blind forces of Nature; and achieving this with the least expenditure of energy and under conditions most favourable to, and worthy of, their human nature. But it nonetheless still remains a realm of necessity. Beyond it begins that development of human energy which is an end in itself, the true realm of freedom, which, however, can blossom forth only with the realm of necessity as its

basis. The shortening of the working day is its basic prerequisite. (Marx, 1971b, 820)

Here, it is often said, Marx adopts a more 'sombre' and 'realistic' (Berki, 1979, 53), a 'gloomy' and 'pessimistic' (Cohen, 1988b, 207), perspective on the place of work in human life. He appears to say that economically necessary labour is inescapably alienating and unfree. Cohen (1988b, 207), for example, glosses this passage as follows: 'being a means of life, [labour] cannot be wanted, and will be replaced by desired activity as the working day contracts'. 'True freedom' is attainable only outside work. The aim of a future society, therefore, is not to humanise work but rather to reduce it to the unavoidable minimum and to expand the 'realm of freedom'.[1]

My aim in this Chapter is to question this reading of what Marx is saying in this passage and to clarify his views on work and freedom. It is a mistake, I shall argue, to interpret Marx as opposing the realms of necessity and freedom. Moreover, properly understood, this passage provides no grounds for thinking that Marx's views on work and freedom changed significantly in his later writings.

## Work and freedom in Hegel and Marx

By the 'realm of necessity', Marx means the sphere of economically necessary labour, labour to meet material needs.[2] He contrasts it with the 'realm of freedom', the sphere of activities not so determined. This encompasses time for 'idleness or for the performance of activities which are not directly productive (as e.g. war, affairs of state) or for the development of human abilities and social potentialities (art, science, etc.) which have no directly practical purpose' (Marx, 1988, 190). However, it is a mistake – though a common one – to infer that the realm of necessity must therefore be a realm of unfreedom. This inference is predicated on the assumption that economic labour is necessarily unfree. There is no evidence that Marx makes this assumption,

---

[1]For similar accounts, see also Arendt, 1958, 105–15; Berki, 1979, 53–4; Cohen, 1988b, 207–8; Marcuse, 1969; McMurtry, 1978, 51–2; Plamenatz, 1975, 143ff. Klagge (1986) gives an account closer to the one presented here.

[2]Marx makes related distinctions between 'necessary' and 'surplus' labour and labour time. These apply only in capitalist society (Marx, 1988, 190–3; Marx, 1973a, 708–9).

either here or elsewhere. Quite the contrary. In this very passage, Marx explicitly talks of freedom *in the realm of necessity* ('freedom in this field ...') and spells out the conditions for it. Elsewhere he asserts that labour can be 'self-realization, objectification of the subject ... real freedom' (Marx, 1973a, 611).

The idea that economically necessary work can be free and fulfilling is fundamental to Marx's outlook, both here and throughout his work. However, it is unfamiliar to many contemporary philosophers. Indeed, it is denied, implicitly at least, by most traditional philosophies. Plato and Aristotle regard a fully human life as a life of reason, requiring exemption from labour which they look upon as a lower activity catering only to lower needs. For Kant, too, we are rational beings and our material nature is a lower and merely animal aspect of our being. Such attitudes are also evident in an important strand of Christian thought which treats work as a 'curse', a punishment for our 'fallen' nature. Work is seen as painful toil by the hedonism which underlies utilitarianism and classical economics.[3] On this view we are essentially consumers rather than producers who work only as a means to satisfy our needs (see Chapter 2 above; Anthony, 1978; Sayers, 1998, chapters 2–4).

Views such as these are pervasive in both philosophy and everyday life, and Marx is often interpreted in the light of them. As we have seen, however, according to Marx work has a quite different place in human life. We are essentially active and creative beings who can develop and fulfil ourselves only through productive activity. In his early writings Marx describes work as the 'vital activity' of human beings, their 'species activity', the 'essential activity' by which human beings are distinguished from other animals (Marx, 1975e, 328–9; Marx and Engels, 1978b, 150). He maintains these views throughout his life. In the *Grundrisse* he describes labour as potentially a 'free' activity; in the 'Critique of the Gotha Programme' he envisages that it may become 'life's prime want' (Marx, 1978c, 531). However, he does not spell out the philosophical basis for these views.

As I have argued, this derives from Hegel. For Hegel, as for Marx, work plays an essential role in human life. It is the basis on which human beings are distinct from other animals. Non-human animals, on Hegel's view, have a purely immediate relation to nature, both to their own nature and to the surrounding natural environment. They

---

[3]Cf. Marx's (1973a, 611) criticisms of Adam Smith's views on work as a 'sacrifice' of freedom and happiness, and a 'curse'.

are driven by their own immediate instincts and desires, and they consume the objects they desire immediately and directly. Humans, by contrast, are self-conscious beings, they have 'being-for-self'. They can stand back from their immediate instincts and from what is immediately present to them, both through conscious reflection and in a practical way. Work is a form of such practical being-for-self. In work, gratification is deferred, the object is not consumed immediately; nor is it simply annihilated, rather it is formed and altered for later consumption or use. Thus a mediated and distinctively human relation to nature is established.

Through work we separate ourselves from nature and establish a self apart. At the same time we begin the process of overcoming this division from nature. By objectifying ourselves in our products, we come to recognise our powers and capacities as real and objective, and thus we develop a consciousness of self. Moreover, by humanising the world we come to feel increasingly at home in it. For Marx, too, it is through the productive activity of work that we overcome our alienation from nature and develop and recognise our distinctive powers.

> It is ... in his fashioning of the objective [world] that man really proves himself to be a *species-being*. Such production is his active species-life. Through it nature appear as *his* work and his reality. The object of labour is the *objectification of the species-life of man*: for man reproduces himself not only intellectually, in his consciousness, but actively and actually, and he can therefore contemplate himself in a world he himself has created. (Marx, 1975e, 329)

Thus both for Hegel and for Marx work is not only a means to satisfy material needs, it is also an activity of self-development and self-realisation. Moreover, this process of objectification and self-realisation is present in other forms of practical activity as well. Its fullest development is in artistic creation. This is the highest form of productive activity for both of these philosophers.

A distinctive account of freedom is associated with these views. According to this, freedom is not an all-or-nothing affair, it is present by degrees. Different kinds of practical activity involve different degrees of freedom for the agent and, correlatively, allow different degrees of freedom to the object. Purely natural, animal consumption under the impulsion of immediate desire is not free. It is directly determined by the appetites which drive it. Direct consumption of this sort is also determined by its object. The creature driven by hunger is governed by the food in its environment. Moreover, in such consumption no freedom is granted to the object: it is simply devoured and destroyed.

By working on the object and deferring gratification, human beings detach themselves from their appetites and desires and acquire a degree of freedom with respect to them. At the same time, work allows a measure of freedom to the object. The object is not immediately consumed; it is transformed and hence preserved for later consumption or use. Nevertheless, the object is destined ultimately for consumption and destruction, for the purpose of economic work is the satisfaction of needs. Such work is thus still in the 'realm of necessity'.

Artistic creation, by contrast, is truly free activity. It is not in the service of material needs and its product is not for consumption: determination by natural desire is entirely transcended. Such activity is not a means to the end of satisfying material needs, it has no economic function. Its aims are aesthetic not economic, it is an end-in-itself. This is what Marx is referring to when he talks of activity in the 'realm of freedom'.

These ideas are held by Marx throughout his life. What he says in *Capital* in his maturity is entirely consonant with what he says in his youth, in the *1844 Manuscripts*, 'animals ... produce only when immediate physical need compels them to do so, while man produces even when he is free from physical need and truly produces only in freedom from such need ... man also produces in accordance with the laws of beauty' (Marx, 1975e, 329).

In short, freedom is a matter of degree according to this conception. It ranges all the way from the unfreedom of instinctive and purely natural ('animal') activity, through different kinds of labour and other activity more or less immediately determined by need, up to the truly free activity of artistic creation.

## Freedom and necessity

Thus, contrary to the views of the commentators cited above, there can be freedom in the sphere of necessary work. Marx is explicit on this score. He specifies two conditions for such freedom in the passage from *Capital* that I am discussing.[4] First, alienation from the process of

---

[4]There is a similar account of the conditions for free labour in Marx, 1973a, 611.

production must be overcome. 'The associated producers' must 'rationally [regulate] their interchange with Nature, bringing it under their common control, instead of being ruled by it as by the blind forces of Nature'. Note here that freedom involves not simply an absence of constraint, but the positive aspect of rational self-determination. Second, necessary economic labour must be carried out 'with the least expenditure of energy and under conditions most favourable to, and worthy of, their human nature'. What Marx means is that through the use of human intelligence, especially with the introduction of machinery, the brute physical exertion involved in work can be minimised and the intelligent and 'scientific' aspects of work enhanced (cf. Marx, 1973a, 611).

Marx also insists that the time devoted to necessary labour must be reduced so that 'disposable time' for free activity, the 'realm of freedom', can be increased. Is there not a contradiction here? If activity in the realm of necessity can be free, as I have been arguing is Marx's view, why should it be reduced? Does this passage from *Capital* not imply after all that, for Marx, work in the realm of necessity is a regrettable necessity, as writers like Berki and Cohen assert?

Marx does not explicitly answer these questions. What he does say, however, suggests a response along the following lines. To maintain that economic work can be a liberating and fulfilling activity is not to say that it is the only such activity or that it should be our sole activity. Yet in industrial society, particularly when Marx was writing in the middle of the nineteenth century, working hours had been extended to extreme lengths, as Marx describes in the celebrated chapter of *Capital* on 'The Working Day' (Marx, 1961a, chapter 10). Since then they have gradually decreased, but they still dominate the lives of most working people, leaving little time for anything else (Zeisel, 1958). Marx wants work time to be reduced to what he calls 'a normal length' (Marx, 1972, 257, quoted below), not because he thinks that in ideal conditions necessary work should be eliminated altogether, but so that people can have time and energy for other kinds of activities as well, and fulfil themselves in a variety of ways. In these conditions, and with the removal of class subordination, economic labour can become a free activity. 'It is self-evident that if labour-time is reduced to a normal length and, furthermore, labour is no longer performed for someone else, but for myself, and, at the same time, the social contradictions between master and men, etc., being abolished, it acquires a quite different, a free character.' (Marx, 1972, 257)

Historically, up to now, the surplus labour of the majority has been the basis on which a small elite has been exempt from labour and able to enjoy free time.

> The free time of the non-working parts of society is based on the surplus labour or overwork, the surplus labour time, of the working part. The free development of the former is based on the fact that the workers have to employ the whole of their time, hence the room for their own development, purely in the production of parti-cular used values; the development of the human capacities on one side is based on the restriction of development on the other side. The whole of civilization and social development so far has been founded on this antagonism. (Marx, 1988, 191; cf. Marx, 1973a, 705–6, 708)

Work time and free time have stood in antagonistic opposition to each other. To be free has meant not working, and to work has meant being unfree. Neither condition has been satisfactory. Alienated and oppres-sive work has existed alongside an alienated and disconnected sort of freedom. Philosophical theories for the most part have reflected this situation. Activities which provide for material needs have been looked down upon and disparaged as 'lower' forms of activity, in contrast to intellectual and rational pursuits which are regarded as 'higher' and more worthy. Plato is the extreme here. At times he suggests that our bodily and natural appetites are a burden and that we would be better off without them. Other philosophers, such as Aristotle, Kant and even Hegel, sometimes appear to accept this line of thought as well. At other times, however, all these writers (including Plato) recognise that we are physical as well as rational beings and that our bodily needs are essen-tial to us (Sayers, 1999a, 142–4). Our happiness lies not in opposing the rational to the bodily aspects of our being, but in finding ways of overcoming this antagonism and harmonising these aspects.

Marx, I am suggesting, follows this latter line of thought. In a society of the future, Marx envisages that the antagonism which has hitherto prevailed between these aspects can be transcended.[5] The purpose of limiting the working day is not to minimise or eliminate work in the 'realm of necessity' as such, but rather to overcome the antagonistic

---

[5]This antagonism is ultimately related to the division between mental and manual labour (Sayers, 1998, chapter 2).

relation which has existed historically between work and freedom. The aim is to create the conditions in which alienation can be overcome – conditions in which necessary work can become a free activity, and in which free creative activity can itself become a universal human need (Marx, 1973a, 708). This is Marx's idea, not only in his early writings but also in *Capital* and throughout.

## Overcoming the distinction?

A number of questions are thrown up by the account that I have been developing. Will the aim of society continue to be to minimise necessary labour in order to maximise free time? Will the distinction between the realms of necessity and freedom persist even when the antagonism between them is overcome?

It is not easy to interpret what Marx says on these issues, there are different and possibly divergent strands to his thought. On the one hand, in the passage from *Capital* that I am discussing, Marx insists that the realm of necessity will continue to exist 'in all social formations and under all possible modes of production'. This follows simply from the fact that we are creatures of physical need, a fact which no social changes can alter. 'So far ... as labour is a creator of use-value, is useful labour, it is a necessary condition, independent of all forms of society, for the existence of the human race; it is an eternal nature-imposed necessity, without which there can be no material exchanges between man and Nature, and therefore no life.' (Marx, 1961a, 42–3)

Marx also maintains that the aim of society will continue to be to minimise the time devoted to satisfying material needs (necessary labour time). In the *Grundrisse* Marx spells this out as follows. In a future society,

> The *surplus labour of the mass* has ceased to be the condition for the development of general wealth, just as the *non-labour of the few*, for the development of the general powers of the human head. With that, production based on exchange value breaks down, and the direct, material production process is stripped of the form of penury and antithesis. The free development of individualities, and hence not the reduction of necessary labour time so as to posit surplus labour, but rather the general reduction of the necessary labour of society to a minimum, which then corresponds to the artistic, scientific etc. development of the individuals in the time set

free, and with the means created, for all of them. (Marx, 1973a, 705–6)

All this seems to imply that the distinction between the realms of necessity and freedom must continue to exist in any future society.

However, other themes in Marx's thought point in a different direction, towards the reduction and ultimate overcoming of the very distinction between these realms. Fundamental to Marx's outlook is the view that human needs develop and change historically. As Marx puts it in the passage from *Capital* under discussion, the realm of necessity 'expands', needs become more developed and differentiated. This is a theme that Hegel also emphasises. He gives an illuminating example of the process.

> Hercules was attired in a lion skin, and this is a simple way of satisfying [the need for clothing]. Reflection fragments this simple need and divides it into many parts: according to its particular nature, each individual part of the body – head, neck, feet – is given particular clothing, and one concrete need is divided into many needs and these in turn into many others. (Hegel, 1997, 167–8)

Moreover, clothing also comes to have a social and even an aesthetic function. The work to meet our need for clothing, which is in the realm of necessity, thus acquires an aesthetic aspect, a creative and free dimension. A similar process occurs with food, housing and other basic necessities, all of which expand and come to have an aesthetic dimension.

Conversely, as needs develop, free creative activity itself becomes a need. The expansion of needs increasingly takes in the requirement for self-expression and self-realisation.[6] Marx foresees the emergence of the person 'rich in needs' who is 'simultaneously the man *in need* of a totality of vital human expression ... the man in whom his own realization exists as inner necessity, as need' (Marx, 1975e, 356).[7]

---

[6]The growth of such needs is apparent in the expansion of leisure activities (Sayers, 1998, chapter 4), and in education, which now normally involves a significant component of art, music, dance, creative writing, etc., at least at lower levels, in a way that even a century ago it did not.

[7]Agnes Heller (1976) attempts to theorise these developments with her concept of 'radical needs'.

With human development, that is to say, basic necessities are aestheti-cised and free expression becomes a necessity. Work to satisfy basic needs becomes free activity and free activity becomes a need. In this way, Marx seems to envisage that not only the antagonism but ultimately even the distinction between the realms of necessity and freedom will eventually be overcome.

Thus, on the one hand, Marx says that the distinction between the realms of necessity and freedom must persist even in a classless society. On the other hand, he implies that the distinction between these realms can eventually be overcome. He does not resolve this contradiction. However, even if his view is that the distinction persists, this goes no way towards vindicating the accounts of writers like Berki and Cohen. For as I have argued, in distinguishing a realm of 'freedom' from a realm of 'necessity', Marx is not making a distinction between spheres of freedom and unfreedom. Nor is he implying that necessary work can never be free. On the contrary, a proper understanding of Marx's accounts of labour and freedom shows clearly that he believes that necessary labour can indeed be a free and self-realising activity. This is what I have been arguing.

## Arendt on labour and work

Arendt is one the writers who criticises Marx for holding contradictory views on work and freedom. The passage from *Capital* that I have been discussing is, she maintains, only one example of 'a fundamental con-tradiction which runs like a red thread through the whole of Marx's thought', for 'Marx's attitude toward labor, and that is toward the very center of his thought, has never ceased to be equivocal' (Arendt, 1958, 104). Since her criticisms are based on what she herself acknowledges to be idiosyncratic concepts of 'labour' and 'work' (Arendt, 1958, 79–80), I shall deal with them here separately.

According to Arendt, there is a fundamental distinction between 'labour' and 'work' which Marx fails to make. Labour, she maintains, is what we do to satisfy our basic physical needs. It is a natural activity to satisfy bodily needs; it is an animal-like activity in the sphere of necessity, a form of activity which we share with other animals and which is necessary for the maintenance of life. Such labour is carried out by what she terms *'animal laborans'*. It involves the repetitive and cyclical process of maintaining natural life by continually satisfying needs which constantly re-arise. It is thus 'primarily concerned with the means of its own reproduction' (Arendt, 1958, 88). Either it creates no product at all, or its products are consumed almost as soon as they are created. Work, by contrast, creates durable objects, enduring products for 'use' and not merely for consumption. Work thereby creates a 'world'. It is the distinctively human activity of what she calls '*homo faber*'.

According to Arendt, Marx fails to make this distinction. He talks of 'labour' in terms which are applicable only to 'work'. He looks upon 'all labor as work and [speaks] of the *animal laborans* in terms much more fitting for *homo faber*' (Arendt, 1958, 87, cf. 102). He maintains that the labour of '*animal laborans*' can lead to fulfilment and freedom, whereas Arendt maintains that they can be attained only through the work of '*homo faber*'.

> The *animal laborans* [can] be redeemed from its predicament of imprisonment in the ever-recurring cycle of the life process, of being forever subject to the necessity of labor and consumption, only through the mobilization of another human capacity, the capacity for making, fabricating, and producing of *homo faber*, who ... not only eases the pain and trouble of laboring but also erects a world of durability. (Arendt, 1958, 236)

These arguments are unsatisfactory in several ways. The way in which Arendt conceives of 'labour' muddles the distinction between animal and human activity. She describes human 'labour' as a sort of animal activity and looks upon it as something almost sub-human. Likewise, as the term '*animal laborans*' itself suggests, she tends to treat those who perform it as in effect a sub-human species. In a corresponding way, she elevates 'work' (and what she calls 'action') above the material realm. She thus makes 'work' transcendent and gives it an exaggerated significance. More generally, Arendt's attempt to detach 'labour' from 'work' is confused and untenable, the two are necessarily and inextricably combined in human productive activity. The 'labour' which meets consumption needs also creates a product, it is thus at the same time a form of 'work' in Arendt's sense.

As Hegel and Marx maintain, and as we have seen above, labour is a distinctively human activity which creates a distinct product. It is this product which we then consume. As Hegel observes, 'man, as consumer, is chiefly concerned with human products.... There are few immediate materials which do not need to be processed ... perhaps water is unique in that it can be drunk as it is found' (Hegel,

1991, 232).[8] Animals, by contrast, consume what is around them directly without transforming it into a product through work.

In short, human labour does not simply vanish in consumption, it creates a product. Indeed, according to Marx, consumption itself is a form of production. 'In taking in food, for example, which is a form of consumption, the human being produces his own body' (Marx, 1973a, 90).[9] Moreover, human labour takes place in a context of social relations, and it produces and reproduces those relations, and with them the social world (Marx, 1978a, 103). Arendt does not appear to have understood this either.

Arendt's account of labour, it is often claimed, applies particularly to domestic labour, to the tasks of cooking, cleaning, mending, etc., usually performed by women. Such labour indeed seems to be end-lessly repetitive and cyclical; it appears to vanish as soon as it is done and to create nothing enduring, just as Arendt describes. This is not the case, however. Such labour not only sustains life, it also produces and reproduces a home, a family, a social world.

Conversely, 'work' in Arendt's sense, the creation of enduring objects of use and a human world, cannot be separated from the activity of production to meet consumer needs. The human and social world always and necessarily arises out of and exists on the basis of produc-tive activity to meet material needs. This is Marx's materialist theory, at any rate, and Arendt gives no good reasons to question it.

Seyla Benhabib argues that Arendt's distinction should be under-stood as an attempt to construct 'ideal types' (Benhabib, 1996, 131). Arendt's categories should be treated as mere 'conceptual' abstractions which are useful for theoretical understanding even if they do not exist as distinct forms in reality. Elsewhere, I have argued at length that Marx questions the validity of abstractions of this sort. Integral to his approach is the attempt to comprehend social reality in concrete terms as a totality (Sayers, 1990b), but to pursue that line of argument here would take me too far from the theme of freedom.

However, there are other problems with the abstractions created by Arendt's account. As we have seen, Arendt degrades 'labour' and those who do it to an almost sub-human level. In a corresponding way, she

---

[8]This is no longer so. The water we drink is now invariably the product of elabo-rate processing, we even get our 'natural spring water' out of plastic bottles.
[9]'The product ... of individual consumption, is the consumer himself.' (Marx, 1961a, 183)

elevates 'work' (and what she terms 'action') above the material realm. She thus gives it an exaggerated and false human significance. Such views were prevalent among the ruling class in the ancient world who relied on slave labour to provide them with the necessities of life, as Arendt (1958, 80–5) well describes. They looked down upon the slave who did such labour, the *animal laborans*, with disdain and contempt. Although Arendt explicitly dissociates herself from such views, she criticises modern society in terms which echo them. She describes modern society as a mass 'consumer' society in which the needs and interests of the modern *'animal laborans'* have become dominant. She treats with disdain and contempt the labour which meets consumer needs and those who do it. Such elitist attitudes may have been tenable in the ancient world, where they corresponded to the prevailing social conditions. They are inappropriate and unacceptable in the modern world where such conditions have long passed. It is one of the great achievements of the Hegelian and Marxist theories that I have described that they have criticised and replaced views such as these with an account of the place of labour in human life more fitting for modern conditions.[10]

[10]An earlier version of this Chapter was presented at ISSEI VIII International Conference, Aberystwyth, July 2002. I am grateful to the participants in the ensuing discussion, and particularly to Daniel Brudney and Andrew Chitty, for their comments and criticisms.

# 6
## Alienation as a Critical Concept

Marx talks of alienation in connection with a number of areas of life – religion, politics, social and economic relations – but particularly labour. I shall focus on the area of labour in this Chapter.[1] In this area, at least, he clearly uses the concept of alienation in a critical manner. But what sort of criticism does it involve?

Very often it is taken to be a moral and humanist criticism based upon a notion of universal human nature. This is supposed to provide the standard by which Marx criticises alienating social conditions. Honneth gives a typical account of this approach.

> According to Marx, human beings' central feature is their capacity for objectifying and realizing themselves in the product of their labor; it is only by this act of objectification that individual subjects are in a position to achieve certainty of their own powers and thereby attain self-consciousness. Thus the possibility of freely and willingly experiencing their own labor as a process of self-realization forms the deciding precondition for a good life. However, this condition is destroyed by the establishment of the capitalist mode of production, since wage labor robs the active subjects of any control over their activity. Capitalism therefore represents a social form of life that sets human beings in opposition to their own essence, thus robbing them of any prospects of a good life. (Honneth, 2007, 14)

Although there has been an immense amount of argument about the place of the concept of alienation in Marx's work, this sort of account

---

[1]Similar arguments apply to these other areas as well, I believe, but I will not try to establish that here. I hope to return to it on another occasion.

is seldom disputed. It is at the basis of the 'humanist' Marxism which celebrates the concept of alienation (and Marx's early writings in which it is prominent) for adding an ethical dimension to his thought – a dimension which, it is argued, is missing from his later work (Fromm, 1963). A similar account of alienation is also given by structuralist 'anti-humanists' who argue that Marx abandoned the idea of universal human nature and the concept of alienation in his later work (Althusser, 1969). Others question both these positions and argue that Marx retained the concept of alienation throughout – but many of these also regard alienation as a humanist moral concept.

In this chapter I will argue that there are serious problems with this sort of account. The concept of alienation is more complex and less readily assimilated to the familiar pattern of universalist moral thought than it suggests.

One more preliminary: as I have made clear, I share the view that the concept of alienation remains a part of Marx's thought throughout his work, though I shall not attempt to establish this point here. However, the most extensive explicit account of it is in the *Economic and Philosophical Manuscripts of 1844*. I shall focus mainly but not exclusively on this work in this chapter.

## Hegel on work

As Honneth says, Marx's concept of alienated labour is based on a distinctive theory about the place of work in human life. This derives from Hegel as we have seen. Labour is a fundamental concept in Hegel's philosophy. It is also a fundamental concept in classical economics, one of the other main sources of Marx's ideas in this area. In economics, work is generally treated as a purely instrumental activity, a mere means to the end of meeting our needs. For Hegel, by contrast, work is also a 'spiritual' activity, an activity that distinguishes humans from other animals. Other animals are purely natural beings. They have a direct and immediate relation to nature. Work involves a break with this natural and immediate relation to nature. Although it entails a breach with natural immediacy and leads to a condition of alienation, it is also the means by which this breach is overcome. For through it we give human form to the world and change ourselves. We begin to make ourselves at home in the world and overcome our alienation.

The process of development involved here follows a characteristic pattern. Starting from an initial condition of immediacy and simple

unity, it moves through a stage of division and alienation. It culminates eventually in a higher form of unity, a mediated and concrete
unity which includes difference within it. According to Hegel all
human ('spiritual') phenomena follow a path of development of this
sort. Individual human development proceeds from an initial state
of infant simplicity and innocence, through stages of division and
alienation, to adult maturity and self-acceptance.

A similar pattern is present also in the course of social and
historical development. The earliest societies are simple unified
communities. For example, clan groups and the early stages of
ancient Greek society take this form. With historical development, division and alienation occur and individuality and difference are increasingly manifest. In Europe, the eventual culmination,
according to Hegel (1956), is a modern liberal form of society.
This, he believes, is a higher form of social unity in which individuality and difference are contained within a unified social
order.

As we have seen (in Chapter 2 above), Hegel uses the Biblical story
of the Fall of Man to explain this account. As he interprets the story,
the Garden of Eden embodies the idea that human beings initially
led a simple life, in harmony with each other and with nature.
Social development disrupts this innocent state. With the Fall comes
division: alienation from others and from nature. According to
the Bible, Adam and Eve eat the forbidden fruit and they are expelled
from the Garden as a punishment. The usual interpretation is that
the original condition of simplicity is the ideal to which we should
aspire, and the story is taken to imply an idyllic and romanticised
vision of life before the Fall and a yearning to return to it. Hegel's
interpretation is very different. He does not idealise the past or
advocate a return to it. On the contrary, historical development
is leading towards a higher and different form of unity in the
future.

> The disunion that appears throughout humanity is not a con-
> dition to rest in. But it is a mistake to regard the natural and
> immediate harmony as the right state.... Childlike innocence
> no doubt has in it something fascinating and attractive; but
> only because it reminds us of what the spirit must win for itself.
> The harmoniousness of childhood is a gift from the hand of
> nature: the second harmony must spring from the labour and
> culture of the spirit. (Hegel, 1892, §24Z, 55)

## Marx on alienation

Marx takes over these Hegelian ideas and develops them in a radical and critical way. Like Hegel, he sees labour as a distinctively human form of activity. It is an 'essential' human activity, it is our 'species' activity. Moreover, he regards labour – all labour – as a process in which we objectify ourselves in our products. However, Marx makes a crucial distinction between 'objectification' (*Vergegenständlichung*) and 'alienation'. Work does not always lead to self-realisation. In conditions of alienation, this does not occur. 'The object that labour produces ... stands opposed to it as *something alien*, as a *power independent* of the producer.' (Marx, 1975e, 324)

In the *1844 Manuscripts*, Marx distinguishes four aspects of alienated labour, of which such alienation from the *object* of labour is the first. Workers are also alienated in relation to the *activity* of labour. This is the second aspect. Work is experienced as externally imposed, as forced and not free. This is how classical economics usually conceives of work, and it is how work is often experienced in fact. According to Marx, however, this is characteristic of *alienated* labour, it is a feature only of specific social and historical conditions. For implicit in the concept of alienation is the idea that labour need not have this character. Work can be a self-realising activity, alienation can be overcome.

Marx takes over the Hegelian account of human nature and of the role of work in human life that I have been explaining. This is embodied by Marx in the notion of 'species being'. This is our distinctively human being. Work is our 'species activity', the activity which distinguishes humans from other animals. These are driven by appetite and instinct. Their activities are directly the means to satisfy their material needs. In conditions of alienation, work is reduced to its 'animal' character, it becomes a mere means to satisfy our purely material needs. Thus we become alienated from our 'species being'. This is the third aspect of alienation that Marx distinguishes.

For the classical economists, work is an essentially individual activity to satisfy individual needs. It may or may not take place within the context of relations with others, these are purely contingent and external. Marx rejects this account. Like Hegel he sees human beings as essentially social. Work, as a human activity, always and necessarily occurs within a context of social relations. In the *1844 Manuscripts* and subsequently Marx makes this point by maintaining that in work we create not only a material product, at the same time we also produce and reproduce our social relationships.

> Through estranged labour man not only produces his relationship to the object and to the act of production as to alien and hostile powers; he also produces the relationship in which other men stand to his production and product, and the relationship in which he stands to these other men. (Marx, 1975e, 331)

In other words, social relations are just as much the creation of human labour as are its more tangible material products, and labour is objectified in them just as it is in our material products.[2] As the products of our labour we should be able to recognise them as a confirmation of our powers and abilities. In conditions of alienation, however, they become independent of us and opposed to us. This is the fourth aspect of alienation, the alienation of 'man from man' In the *1844 Manuscripts* Marx's account of it is brief and sketchy. However, what Marx is referring to is the way in which economic forces have dissolved communal bonds with the result that individuals are atomised, and economic forces take on a life of their own and obey their own objective laws.[3] This is how both individuals and the economy are usually regarded in economics. However, Marx argues, individuals are not separate atoms; and economic laws, unlike natural laws, are specific to particular forms of society. Classical economics thus presents what are the alienated forms of specific societies as though there were objective and universal. In this way, Marx's critique of political economy in this area parallels his critique of the economists' picture of labour described earlier, in that alienated labour is treated as if it were the universal form of it.

---

[2]Colletti, 1975, 50–1. This is true not only of alienated labour but of all labour. 'M. Proudhon the economists understands very well that men make cloth, linen, or silk materials in definite relations of production. But what he has not understood is that these definite social relations are just as much produced by men as linen, flax, etc.' (Marx, 1978a, 103).

[3]Cf. Leopold, 2007, 65–6. These ideas are much more fully developed later, in Marx, 1973a, 156–65, and in the analysis of 'the fetishism of commodities' in Marx, 1961a, chapter 1.4, discussed below.

## Marxism as critique

Marx describes his project as the 'critique of political economy'.[4] The main categories of political economy are criticised for portraying the capitalist system as in accord with universal human nature. The concept of alienated labour plays a central role in this, as we have seen. His account of alienation is usually taken to imply a humanist moral critique of present kinds of work and social relations. Alienation is portrayed as a purely negative condition that thwarts the realisation of a universal human nature. Work and its products should be avenues of self-realisation but they are turned into their opposites.

One should be cautious about attributing such ideas to Marx. Of course Marx condemns capitalism, but the view that the main purpose of the concept of alienation is moral criticism is mistaken, even in relation to his early work. Like Hegel and others in the post-Kantian philosophical tradition, Marx insists that his primary aim is theoretical understanding rather than moral condemnation.[5] This is not to suggest that the moral account is entirely mistaken. Marx does indeed hold the view that work can be a self-realising activity, and that in conditions of alienation this potentiality is thwarted. However, human nature is not an unchanging universal, it is an historical phenomenon which develops dialectically. Work and alienation play an essential role in this process. Hence alienation is not a purely negative phenomenon, its impact is more complex and contradictory.

In Hegel, as we have seen, work entails a break with purely natural conditions. It involves a separation of humans, as self-conscious beings, from an initial situation of natural immediacy. Equally, however, it is through work that we overcome this division from nature. We give human form to the world around us and come to recognise our powers and capacities as real and objective. We transform our environment and our relationship to it, and in the process we transform ourselves. As we have seen, Marx follows Hegel in comprehending work in these

---

[4]This is the title of Marx, 1971a. It is also subtitle of *Capital* in its original version, though this is changed in the English translation of 1867 supervised by Engels. However, it is also the title that Engels (1964) gave to his article of 1844 cited by Marx (1975e, 281; 1978b, 5) as an important influence on the early development of his thought.

[5]Cf. Hegel, 1991, Preface; Nietzsche, 1994, Preface; Heidegger, 1962, 211; etc..

terms, and he derives his views directly from Hegel, as he explicitly acknowledges.

> The importance of Hegel's *Phenomenology* ... lies in the fact that Hegel conceives the self-creation of man as a process, objectification as loss of object, as alienation and as supersession of this alienation ... he therefore grasps the nature of *labour* and conceives objective man – true, because real man – as the result of his *own labour*. (Marx, 1975e, 385–6 quoted above p. 15)

The full significance of what Marx says here has not been sufficiently noticed. The process of human development that Marx describes follows the characteristic Hegelian and dialectical pattern described earlier, though of course the specific stages of development are quite different to Hegel's. Starting from an initial condition of immediacy and simple unity, this moves through a stage of division and alienation, to culminate eventually in a higher form of unity, a mediated and concrete unity which includes difference within it.[6]

As Marx makes clear in the passage just quoted, his account of the role of alienated labour in human development conforms to this Hegelian pattern. It must be comprehended in these terms. An important implication of this is that alienation is *not a purely negative or critical concept*. Alienation does not involve the pure negation of human possibilities in the way that the moral interpretation implies.[7] On the contrary, a stage of division and alienation is an essential part of the process of human development. It represents the beginning of the process of emancipation through which human beings are gradually freed from a condition of natural immediacy and develop self-consciousness and freedom. Alienated labour and alienated social relations play an essential role in this process.[8]

This is not to suggest, of course, that alienation is a satisfactory state or a condition to 'rest in' as Hegel puts it. On the contrary, it is a con-

---

[6]Cohen, 1978, chapter 1, gives an excellent account of this process, though he does not connect it with the concept of alienation. See also Cohen, 2000, chapters 3–6.

[7]'Alienation has not only a *negative* but also a *positive* significance' (Marx, 1975e, 388, 391). This a central theme of the sections on 'Private Property and Communism' and 'Critique of Hegel's Dialectic and General Philosophy' in Marx, 1975e, see Chapter 7 below for further discussion.

[8]Cf. Arthur, 1986, 12, 67, 72, 148; and Leopold, 2007, 86.

dition of disunity, it involves distress and suffering. However, these negative aspects themselves drive us to try to overcome them and seek unity. According to Hegel, this cannot be found by a return to earlier conditions. Rather, we are driven on, to look for a 'higher' unity. This is not given immediately, it must be created; and this can be achieved only through the activity of labour. Marx gives specific detail to this picture. Thus, alienated labour creates the material conditions for a higher, communal form of society. This is what Marx (1971b, 819) calls 'the civilizing mission' of capitalism. However, it does not contribute to human development in only an external and instrumental way, it is also the way in which the producers transform themselves. Through alienated labour and the relations it creates, people's activities are expanded, their needs and expectations are widened, their relations and horizons are extended. Alienated labour thus also creates the subjective factors – the agents – who will abolish capitalism and bring about a new society.

Seen in this light, alienated labour plays a positive role in the process of human development, it is not a purely negative phenomenon. It should not be judged as simply and solely negative by the universal and unhistorical standards invoked by the moral approach. Rather it must be assessed in a relative and historical way. Relative to earlier forms of society – strange as this may at first sound – alienation constitutes an achievement and a positive development. However, as conditions for its overcoming are created, it becomes something negative and a hindrance to further development. In this situation, it can be criticised, not by universal moral standards but in this relative way.

This sort of account is criticised for implying a quasi-theological narrative of fall and redemption (cf. Lear in Honneth, 2008). In some respects it does conform to that pattern. Hegel is quite explicit about this, as we have seen, he appeals to the Biblical story of the Fall to explain his position. In and of itself, the fact that this account has this form is not a valid objection to it. There is nothing wrong with portraying human development in this way, provided that reality actually conforms to this pattern and it is illuminating to see it like this. However, Hegel is also criticised for presenting his account of history as a 'theodicy' which is designed not just to describe the pattern of historical development but to reconcile us to the evil and suffering that it has involved. Again he is explicit about this.

> Our approach is a theodicy, a justification of the ways of God. Leibniz attempted a theodicy in metaphysical terms ... so that once

the evil in the world was comprehended in this way, the thinking mind was supposed to be reconciled to it. Nowhere ... is there a greater challenge to such intellectual reconciliation than in world history. This reconciliation can be achieved only through the recognition of that positive aspect, in which the negative disappears as something subordinate and overcome. (Hegel, 1988a, 18)

Marx's idea of progress is criticised for portraying historical development in similar terms.[9] However, Marx cannot be accused of trying to justify the destructive impact of historical development, particularly not in its capitalist form. His outrage at the suffering and misery caused by capitalism is evident in almost everything that he wrote. Nevertheless, he does argue that this suffering does not refute the idea of progress. Indeed he portrays it as an inescapable part of the process. While historical development proceeds through conflict and strife like a blind process of nature this is the way it occurs. In this sense, Marx does seek to 'reconcile' us to it, but his description is far from what is usually understood by a 'theodicy'. 'Has the bourgeoisie ... ever effected a progress without dragging individuals and peoples through blood and dirt, through misery and degradation?' (Marx, 1978e, 662) Only in the future – when 'a great social revolution shall have mastered the results of the bourgeois epoch, the markets of the world and the modern powers of production, and subjected them to ... common control' – only then can historical development be made to take a more benign form (Marx, 1978e, 664).

## Alienation as an historical condition

This is Marx's Hegelian, historical and dialectical account of alienation and its role in human development. At least, these are its abstract and formal outlines. However, as a historical condition alienation is a feature of concrete and specific societies. It comes about at a certain point in the history of particular societies and it will be overcome given certain historical developments. When does it start? How will it end?

For Hegel, modern liberal (i.e. capitalist) society means an end to the alienation of individual and community which characterises earlier

---

[9] I am grateful to Meade McCloughan for making me aware of this.

forms. Marx, of course, rejects this view. He regards alienation as an inescapable feature of capitalist society. It is also clear that he believes that alienation can be overcome with the advent of communism.[10] But is alienation confined to capitalism, or does it also exist in precapitalist conditions? Marx is surprisingly inexplicit about this, particularly as regards alienated labour specifically (Elster, 1985, 77n). What he does say on the topic seems contradictory. In the *1844 Manuscripts* for the most part he appears to assume that alienated labour is specific to capitalism. This is Lukács' view. He points out that when Marx (1975e, 330–1, 324) talks of the product of alienated labour being 'owned by another' he is clearly describing the situation of 'the so-called free worker who has to work with the means of production belonging to another and for whom, therefore, these means of production as well as his own product exist as an independent, alien power' (Lukács, 1975, 549).

Marx is even more explicit that alienation is specific to capitalism in his celebrated account of 'The fetishism of commodities and the secrets thereof' in *Capital* (Marx, 1961a, chapter 1.4). There he describes the way in which social relations under capitalism take on the alien and 'fantastic form of a relation between things' (Marx, 1961a, 72). He contrasts this with the 'simple', 'clear' and 'intelligible' way in which social relations appear, both in precapitalist forms of society and in a future 'community of free individuals, carrying on their work with the means of production in common' (Marx, 1961a, 77–9).

A similar account is presented in a passage in the *Grundrisse* which is a preliminary draft for this section of *Capital*. In this, moreover, Marx presents the development as a dialectical process which moves from an initial condition of simple unity, through a stage of alienation, towards a higher form of unity. The process of social and economic development, as he describes it, begins with precapitalist conditions in which there are 'fixed personal (historic) relations of dependence in production' (Marx, 1973a, 156). These are 'the first social forms, in which human productive capacity develops only to a slight extent and at isolated points' (Marx, 1973a, 158). With the coming of capitalism

---

[10]This is the explicit theme of Marx, 1975e. It is fundamental to his account of genuine as contrasted with 'crude' communism (Marx, 1975e, 345–51), see Chapter 7 below. It remains Marx's view throughout his work.

they are dissolved and replaced by the alienated relations of the market in which,

> The social character of activity, as well as the social form of the product, and the share of individuals in production ... appear as something alien and objective, confronting the individuals, not as their relation to one another, but as their subordination to relations which subsist independently of them and which arise out of collisions between mutually indifferent individuals. The general exchange of activities and products ... appears as something alien to them, autonomous, as a thing. (Marx, 1973a, 157)

These alienated relations will eventually be overcome. 'Free individuality, based on the universal development of individuals and on their subordination of their communal, social productivity as their social wealth, is the third stage' (Marx, 1973a, 158). Marx is explicit that 'the second stage creates the conditions for the third' (Marx, 1973a, 158) – that is, a passage through capitalism and alienation is necessary in order to create the conditions for their overcoming and for communism.[11]

In other places, however, Marx appears to maintain that alienation is a more pervasive phenomenon, not confined to capitalism. Thus at one point in the *1844 Manuscripts* he describes feudal land-ownership as a form of 'alienation' (Marx, 1975e, 318). Elsewhere, too, he seems to suggest that features of work usually associated with alienation are present in other kinds of society as well. In *The German Ideology*, for example, he suggests that the division of labour as such is a form of alienation (Marx and Engels, 1978b, 160). This has existed throughout known history. Similarly, in the *Grundrisse* he suggests that work is regarded as purely instrumental and unfree, not just in capitalism but in all class divided societies (Marx, 1973a, 611).

Is alienation, then, specific to capitalism or is it present in all societies with class divisions? The question is wrongly posed, I believe. Rather than trying to answer it, the concept of alienation that it

---

[11]There is an extended account of this passage in these terms in Gould, 1978, chapter 1.

presupposes should be questioned. The historical account that I have been describing sees alienation as a necessary stage in a larger process of development. This is a general theoretical schema for thinking about the course of human change. It is quite possible to apply it in different ways, even to the same historical phenomena. There is no single right way. We should not be looking for a single unique condition of alienation. Rather, we should ask whether specific historical changes can usefully be seen as following a pattern of alienation and its overcoming – and, if so, how? There are various ways in which this can be done, various time scales on which these stages can be seen to occur. Different conceptions of alienation will correspond to these.

For example, the entire course of human social development can be thought of as starting with a stage of natural simplicity and unity. Engels explicitly posits such a stage which he calls 'primitive communism' (Marx and Engels, 1978c, 473n; Engels, 1958c, chapter IX). With class divisions, humanity enters into a long development taking it through numerous forms of division and alienation. Eventually, according to Engels, it will transcend these in a future classless society. On this view, alienation has been a feature of class divided societies throughout history.

It is unclear whether Marx accepted the hypothesis of an initial prehistoric stage of 'primitive communism'. Some passages, as I have suggested, seem to imply a similar picture.[12] More frequently, however, he treats alienated labour as a specific feature of capitalism, with the implication that labour in precapitalist societies is not alienated. This is not to suggest that people in precapitalist conditions do not experience their work as toil and as unfree. Of course, in such societies work is often felt to be harsh and unpleasant; and it is often experienced as a forced imposition, either by the imperatives of natural needs or by coercion from others or both. On the reading that I am arguing for, however, alienated labour means something more precise and definite than mere dissatisfaction with work. It is not a universal and abstract moral notion, it has a specific historical reference.

---

[12]The account of history in terms of changes in the division of labour in Marx and Engels, 1978b can be read as suggesting such a picture. See also Cohen, 1978, 24, 299 for some further evidence. Cohen's evidence is not convincing in my view, but I will not pursue the question here.

It is illuminating to interpret Marx's account of the four aspects of alienated labour in the *1844 Manuscripts* in this light, as descriptions that apply specifically to labour in capitalist conditions.[13]

1) The crucial factor that creates alienated labour with the coming of capitalism is the predominance of commodity production and wage labour. In precapitalist conditions commodity exchange plays only a limited role. Production is to satisfy needs that seldom extend beyond the household and the local community. There is a direct and immediately visible connection between work and the needs it satisfies. With the coming of capitalism this changes. The direct connection between work and needs is broken. Money and the market now intervene between producer and consumer. The product is no longer created to satisfy local and immediately apparent needs, it is made for exchange on the wider market.

Moreover, in the capitalist system the direct producers no longer control the exchange process. They are dispossessed of everything except their ability to labour. They are now wage labourers who own neither their tools, nor the materials they work on, nor the products of their labour. These now take the form of capital which becomes a power independent of the workers and opposed to them. This is the concrete meaning of the first aspect of alienation described by Marx, alienation from the object of labour (Marx, 1975e, 325). It is not a vague, subjective lack of connection with the product, but a specific and objective economic condition.

It is important to see that the impact of alienated labour thus understood is not purely negative. By severing its connection with the object, labour is at the same time freed from the subservience, even bondage, to the object that exists in precapitalist forms of labour – in serf labour, where it is quite explicit and in craft labour within a restrictive guild context. Alienated labour thus creates the conditions in which more universal forms of work and life can develop (cf. Chapter 3 above). In this way, the loss of connection with the object in alienated

---

[13]Marx is referring specifically to the alienation of the worker. In the *Economic and Philosophical Manuscripts of 1844* he promises to go on to discuss the alienation of the non-worker (capitalist) but the manuscript breaks off as he about to do so. One can only speculate about what he might have said, see pp. 28–9 above.

labour also liberates it and creates the conditions through which the object can later be reappropriated in a fuller fashion.[14]

2) As to the second aspect, alienation from the activity of labour, again what Marx is referring to is not a general sort of discontent but a specific condition brought about by the advent of wage labour. Work in all conditions is an instrumental activity in that it is aimed at producing goods that satisfy human needs (use values). In precapitalist societies work is an autonomous activity which for the most part directly meets the needs of the household and locality. With the coming of capitalism, work itself becomes a commodity, undertaken for wages. People no longer work for themselves but for another, and their activities are owned and controlled by that other, by capital. 'The external character of labour for the worker is demonstrated by the fact that it belongs not to him but to another, and that in it he belongs not to himself but to another.... The activity of the worker is not his own spontaneous activity. It belongs to another, it is a loss of his self.' (Marx, 1975e, 326–7)

Again such alienation is not a purely negative phenomenon. Though work is no longer done to meet the particular needs of the household or community, it now caters for more general needs. These are mediated through the market, they appear in an alien form. In working for another, for wages, work is freed from an immediate connection with the satisfaction of particular needs, it acquires a more universal character. In this way, the worker is no longer connected only with particular individuals and the locality but is brought into a wider network of social relations. In becoming a wider social activity, moreover, work becomes part of a more extensive division of labour. And even though this division of labour appears to be an alien and external imposition, it is in fact the estranged form taken by the social character that the labour has acquired.

> The social power, i.e. the multiplied productive force, which arises through the cooperation of different individuals as it is determined by the division of labour, appears to these individuals ... not as their

---

[14]As Engels (1958e, 563–4) puts it, 'Only the proletariat created by modern large-scale industry, liberated from all inherited fetters, including those which chained it to the land ... is in a position to accomplish the great social transformation which will put an end to all class exploitation and all class rule.' See Sayers, 1998, chapter 5.

own united power, but as an alien force existing outside them, of the origin and goal of which they are ignorant, which they thus cannot control. (Marx and Engels, 1978b, 161)

These alienated forms of activity will ultimately be reappropriated and brought back under conscious human control. Alienated labour and the relations it creates play a crucial role in preparing the way for this.

> *All-round* dependence, this natural form of the *world-historical* co-operation of individuals, will be transformed ... into the control and conscious mastery of these power, which, born of the action of men on one another, have till now overawed and governed men as powers completely alien to them. (Marx and Engels, 1978b, 164)

3) In precapitalist conditions, work is a direct response to natural need. In this respect it is like a natural activity, such as eating or breathing. It is not a *means* external to life, it is inseparable from life itself. With wage labour, the direct connection between work and needs, production and consumption, is broken. The result is that productive and socially useful work – our 'essential' and distinctive 'species' activity – is made into a means to earn a wage. Work becomes a purely instrumental activity, related only externally to the needs it satisfies: any kind of work will do as long as it pays. Our species activity is reduced to a mere means to satisfy physical needs and we are alienated from it. This is the third aspect of alienation. However, this alienation of productive activity also constitutes a step on the way towards our emancipation from purely natural conditions. For in this way productive activity ceases to be quasi-natural and quasi-instinctive, it is on the way to becoming a conscious and, ultimately, a freely chosen activity.

4) The fourth aspect is the alienation of 'man from man'. In the *1844 Manuscripts* Marx's account is sketchy, as I have said, but in later works he analyses this aspect of alienation in detail: for example, in the *Grundrisse*, and in *Capital* under the heading of the 'fetishism of commodities' (Marx, 1973a, 156–65; 1961a, Chapter 1.4). In these places, moreover, he explicitly presents such alienation as specific to capitalism and commodity production.

In precapitalist conditions, people are bound together in a quasi-natural community. The market destroys this. In working for wages, individuals appear to be working purely for themselves, independently of others. The community seems to be fragmented into a mass of atomic individuals. At the same time, the goods produced appear to take on an economic life of their own in the market. On the one hand, society appears to be composed of a mass of separate individuals each pursuing their own interests; and on the other hand, the economy appears to obey laws which are objective and independent of human will. Both appearances are deceptive. Unlike natural laws, these economic laws are historical phenomena specific to capitalist society, and so too are these individuals who are alienated from each other. 'The categories of bourgeois economy ... are forms of thought expressing with social validity the conditions and relations of a definite, historically determined mode of production, viz., the production of commodities' (Marx, 1961a, 76). What appear to be impersonal economic laws of the market operating between commodities, between *things*, are in fact alienated social relations between their producers, between *people*. They are the social form of human creative activity, but in an alien and external form.[15]

Such alienated economic forces do not exist in precapitalist societies, in which the market does not dominate, and where 'the social relations between individuals in the performance of their labour, appear ... as their own mutual personal relations' (Marx, 1961a, 71–2). They are specific to capitalism. And such alienation will be overcome in a future society, in which productive activity will be brought back under conscious social control. The global economic system of capitalism creates the necessary conditions for this by developing economic and social relations in a universal fashion.

In these ways, the conditions for the overcoming of alienation are created by alienated labour itself. Alienated labour thus creates not only the objective, material conditions for its overcoming (it does create these and they are essential), it also creates the subjective and human conditions. For alienated labour is not simply a means to an economic end, as it is portrayed to be by economic theory. It is not a purely negative activity which leads also to a desired result. It is a more complex and contradictory phenomenon. It contains a positive as well as a negative aspect within itself. It itself produces the conditions for its own supersession. 'Labour is man's coming to be for himself within alienation or as an alienated man.' (Marx, 1975e, 386)

The idea that alienated labour is a necessary stage in historical development is sometimes thought to be inherently conservative. So far from explaining the critical force of the concept of alienation, it is said, it

---

[15]See Chapter 4 above for a fuller account of these ideas.

has the effect of rationalising capitalism and justifying it as 'progressive'. Marx's own arguments are targeted mainly at the political economists who try to justify capitalism by claiming that it accords with universal human nature. The moral critique of capitalism condemns it in similarly universal terms as conflicting with universal human nature. These are equally unsatisfactory, I have argued. The historical approach judges capitalism relatively. It does indeed maintain that capitalism forms a necessary stage in historical development. However, it is *only* a stage, its necessity is limited and relative. It is progressive, but only relative to previous conditions, not inherently. With time it ceases to be progressive and becomes a hindrance to development. It can then be criticised in these terms, relative to the conditions of the future whose advent it is impeding. Likewise, it is necessary, but only for a specific time, for capitalism is only a stage which in time will be superseded (Engels, 1958d, section 1; Sayers, 1998, chapter 8).

This is Marx's historical theory at least, but it would be wrong to be too dogmatic about it or assert it as an inviolable law. Marx himself did not do so. Towards the end of his life, he considered it possible that there might be a revolution in Russia which would build communism on the basis of existing Russian rural communes without going through a capitalist stage. Marx and Engels discuss this in the Preface to the *Communist Manifesto* written for the Russian edition of 1882.

> In Russia we find, face-to-face with the rapidly flowering capitalist swindle and bourgeois property, just beginning to develop, more than half the land owned in common by the peasants. Now the question is: can the Russian *obshchina* [peasant commune], though greatly undermined, yet a form of primeval common ownership of land, pass directly to the higher form of Communist common ownership? (Marx and Engels, 1978c, 471–2)[16]

Marx and Engels do not rule out this possibility. Such a transition might occur, they go on to say, given the right international circumstances (viz., if a 'proletarian revolution' in the West occurs at the same time to support it). Historical processes are complex and unpredictable, Marx acknowledges, they cannot be foretold with any certainty.

---

[16]There has been some speculation that this expresses Engels views and that Marx's were different, but there is no convincing evidence for this. For a good account of the arguments see Chattopadhyay, 2006, 54–5.

More recently, these issues have been raised by the Russian and the Chinese revolutions. Both attempted to leap over the capitalist stage and create communist societies on the basis of predominantly precapitalist conditions. Lenin and Mao each argued that exceptional international conditions had made this possible (Lenin, 1969b; Mao Tsetung, 1967). With the collapse of the Soviet system and the evolution of China into a rampantly capitalist society, doubt must be cast on the very idea that the forms of 'actually existing communism' that were created in these societies were forms of communism at all. It is possible therefore that these developments, so far from being exceptions to the theory that capitalism is a necessary stage, are rather confirmations of it (McCarney, 1991).

## The overcoming of alienation

How can alienation be overcome? This too must be understood in terms of the historical and dialectical account that I have been giving. According to this, as we have seen, alienated labour is not the purely negative phenomenon implied by the moral account of it. It is not the mere thwarting of an unchanging human nature. It has an essential role in the process of human self-development, it constitutes a necessary stage in the process. Moreover, the overcoming of alienation is not accomplished simply by negating or abolishing the conditions that give rise to it. It cannot be achieved by a return to earlier, precapitalist conditions. Even though these are not alienating, they would no longer satisfy us. On the moral account, by contrast, there is no reason why alienation should not be overcome in this way. Kamenka (1966, 124–8), for example, takes Marx's concept of alienation to criticise capitalism in a way that implies this. He is then puzzled by its inconsistency with Marx's insistence that communism requires an industrial base. According to the historical account, however, overcoming alienation presupposes the achievements of alienated labour and builds upon them. It involves an advance beyond alienation to a higher stage.

In short, the overcoming of alienation is not a bare negation of it. It takes the form of a dialectical supersession in which the conditions of alienation are not only transcended and negated, but also preserved and built upon for the result.[17] Hegel uses the word *'aufheben'* to

---

[17]'The negative which emerges as a result of dialectic, is, because a result, at the same time the positive: it contains what it results from, absorbed into itself, and made part of its own nature.' (Hegel, 1892, §81Z, 152)

describe this sort of development. This term has been variously translated into English as to 'supersede', 'transcend', or 'sublate', but none of these adequately captures the German meaning. According to Hegel (1969, 107), 'to sublate (*aufheben*) has a twofold meaning in the language: on the one hand it means to preserve, to maintain, and equally it means to put an end to…. Thus what is sublated is at the same time preserved.'

Again these are the formal and abstract philosophical outlines of the process. What is its concrete character? How can the alienation that is a specific feature of capitalist society actually be superseded? Marx says little about this, either in the *1844 Manuscripts* or subsequently. He was famously reluctant to speculate about the future. However, what he does say, in the *1844 Manuscripts* and elsewhere, sometimes seems to imply that alienation results from the fact that the product of labour is owned by capital and not the producer, and that it is used to dominate and exploit the worker. In other words, Marx seems to be suggesting that the capitalist system of private property is the main cause of alienation. That fits in well with a common understanding of Marx's ideas, and it suggests that what is needed to overcome alienation is the abolition of capitalist property, private property in the means of production.

Undoubtedly this is an essential aspect of Marx's account, but it is not the full story. It is not sufficient, either as an account of Marx's views or of the realities of the situation. In a passage towards end of the manuscript on 'Estranged labour', Marx (1975e, 331–2) insists that private property is not the cause of alienated labour but rather its consequence. This has puzzled a number of commentators (Arthur, 1986, 156n). It is particularly problematic if, as is often the case, alienation is taken to be a purely subjective attitude towards work. On the other hand, if 'alienated labour' is interpreted as I have been suggesting, to refer to wage labour and to the objective economic system of which it is a part, then Marx's words make good sense and cohere with the rest of his philosophy. What Marx is saying is that it is the economic system of wage labour and capitalism that gives rise to the property system, not vice versa. This is the basic thesis of what later becomes known as 'historical materialism'.[18]

What this also implies is that more needs to be changed than the property system in order to overcome alienation. It is important to see that this is Marx's position, both in the *1844 Manuscripts* and in

---

[18]For a different account see Arthur, 1986, 20–2.

subsequent works. One of his most extended accounts of the overcoming of alienation is contained in the section of the *1844 Manuscripts* entitled 'Private Property and Communism'. Marx there criticises what he calls 'crude' communism. This involves the abolition of private property and its conversion into communal or state property. This is contrasted with what he regards as genuine communism which requires a much deeper and fuller transformation in order to create the conditions for the 'true appropriation of the human essence' (Marx, 1975e, 348).

In his later writings, this account is superseded by the theory that postcapitalist society will be divided into two stages. The first stage has many of the features attributed to inadequate conceptions of communism in 1844.[19] In particular, it involves the abolition of capitalist private property by transforming it into communal property. In the *1844 Manuscripts*, Marx criticises this as resting on a restricted and unsatisfactory idea of 'appropriation'. In his later work, however, he regards this as a necessary first stage (Marx, 1978c, 531). Only after a period (of unspecified duration) will the conditions be created for the transition to the second stage of 'full communism' and 'true appropriation'. As Marx makes clear this will involve not only the legal and political changes achieved in the first stage, but the much wider and deeper human and social transformation required for alienation to be decisively overcome.

The idea that such a transformation is needed in order to overcome alienation is a constant feature of Marx's thought, but he indicates only in general terms what it will involve or how the overcoming of alienation can actually be brought about.[20] In the *1844 Manuscripts*, however, there are indications of some of the human changes to which it will lead. The account is vague, but suggestive and even visionary nevertheless. Two sets of themes emerge. 'True appropriation' will entail a transformation of our relations i) to objects and ii) to our fellow human beings. These themes can be related to the four aspects of alienated labour that Marx describes, though Marx does not explicitly do so.

---

[19]Particularly the type of communism described briefly in Marx, 1975e, 347–8, as communism that 'has not yet comprehended the positive essence of private property' and which thus 'is still held captive and contaminated by private property'.

[20]I return to these topics and deal with them at length in Chapters 7–9 below.

1) All our ways of relating to objects – 'seeing, hearing, smelling, tasting, feeling, thinking, contemplating, sensing, wanting, acting, loving' – are, for Marx (1975e, 351), ways we have of 'appropriating' them. Alienated labour and the system of private property limit and constrict these relations, narrowing them down to issues of ownership and utility. 'Private property has made us so stupid and one-sided that an object is only ours when we have it, when it exists for us as capital or when we directly possess, eat, drink, wear, inhabit it, etc., in short, when we *use* it' (Marx, 1975e, 351).[21] For example, 'the dealer in minerals sees only the commercial value, and not the beauty and peculiar nature of the minerals, he has no mineralogical sense' (Marx, 1975e, 353).[22] Such limitation is a form of alienation. The 'true appropriation' involved in its overcoming goes beyond a mere change in ownership. It will lead to 'the complete emancipation of all human senses and attributes' (Marx, 1975e, 352). It will liberate the senses and allow them to function in a fully human way.

2) Overcoming alienation from the activity of work will transform it into a self-realising activity. A change from private property to common ownership will not bring this about by itself. Much work is intrinsically unsatisfying, it is *inherently* limiting and stultifying. A mere change in the form of ownership may well increase the motivation to work, but it will not fundamentally alter the intrinsic nature of the activity itself. Deeper changes are needed that will transform the present form of work and the division of labour. The changes that Marx envisages can be achieved only on the basis of the advanced industrial economy created by the alienated labour of capitalism. These thoughts are central to Marx's discussions of future forms of work in *German Ideology* and *Capital*. However, there is little mention of them in the *1844 Manuscripts*. I will not pursue this topic further here except to note that this is a major limitation of his account in this work, I will return to it in Chapter 9.

3) In work, as we have seen, we produce not only goods but also social relations, and indeed we produce and transform human nature itself. 'The whole of what is called world history is nothing more than the

---

[21]One can imagine that one has truly appropriated an object (a book, for example) simply by owning it.
[22]I doubt that this is always the case.

creation of man through human labour' (Marx, 1975e, 357). This process involves passing through a stage of alienation, as I have stressed. Its outcome is not only wealth in the form of property and goods, wealth in the narrow economic sense, but also ultimately the fully developed social individual, the truly wealthy individual 'rich in needs'. This is the realisation of our 'species being'. 'The *rich* man and the wealth of human need take the place of the wealth and poverty of political economy. The rich man is simultaneously the man *in need* of a totality of vital human expression; he is the man in whom his own realisation exists as inner necessity, as need' (Marx, 1975e, 356). These developments are predicated on the fullest growth of human productive and creative powers.

4) The elimination of the alienation of 'man from man' means ending economic fetishism, bringing social and economic relations back under conscious social control. Again this entails a radical transformation that eliminates not only private property in the means of production, but commodity production and the market altogether. And this is to be achieved, not by a return to precapitalist conditions where production is centred around the immediate locality and dictated by the imperatives of natural needs, but in a fully communal and social fashion.

> Let us suppose that we had produced as human beings. In that event ... in the individual expression of my own life I would have brought about the immediate expression of your life, and so in my individual activity I would have directly *confirmed* and *realized* my authentic nature, my *human, communal* nature. Our productions would be as many mirrors from which our natures would shine forth. (Marx, 1975d, 278–9)

The idea that the overcoming of alienation means regaining control over our own productive activity and social and economic lives is not an explicit theme in the *1844 Manuscripts*,[23] but it is implicit

---

[23]This idea is made explicitly in Engels, 1964. Engels' article was already published when Marx was writing the *1844 Manuscripts* and is referred to in by Marx (1975e, 281) in that work.

in the notion of alienated labour and its overcoming as the 'true appropriation' of human powers (Marx, 1975e, 348) which I discuss at length in Chapter 7 below. It is spelled out in a number of Marx's later works.[24] These themes, I have been arguing, have a historically specific critical content which cannot be comprehended when alienation is interpreted as an abstract and universal moral concept. They become visible only when Marx's account of alienated labour is interpreted against the background of the Hegelian ideas in which it was developed.[25]

---

[24]'The life-process of society, which is based on the process of material production, does not strip off its mystical veil until it is treated as production by freely associated men, and is consciously regulated by them in accordance with a settled plan.' (Marx, 1961a, 80. Cf. Marx, 1971b, 819; 1973a, 159, 611–12; etc.)

[25]I am grateful to Christopher Arthur, Andrew Chitty and Meade McCloughan for their detailed and helpful comments on an earlier draft of this Chapter.

# 7
# Private Property and Communism

> The distinguishing feature of communism is not the abolition
> of property generally, but the abolition of bourgeois property.
> But modern bourgeois private property is the final and most
> complete expression of the system of producing and appropri-
> ating products that is based on class antagonisms, on the
> exploitation of the many by the few. In this sense, the theory
> of the Communists may be summed up in the single sentence:
> Abolition of private property. (Marx and Engels, 1978c, 484)

Marx defines communism as the abolition of 'bourgeois property', that
is, private property in the means of production. This familiar formula
runs through Marx's later work. His ideas about what it might mean in
practice are developed and filled out in various ways as his political
experience accumulates and as his thought matures. These developments are traced by Lenin in *State and Revolution* (1969b), which gives
the classic account of the evolution of Marx's ideas about communism
from 1847, when he wrote *Poverty of Philosophy* (Marx, 1978a), onwards.

Since Lenin's time, earlier works by Marx have come to light which
reveal earlier phases of his thought.[1] In these, as in the later works, communism is regarded as the overcoming of private property. In them,
however, Marx conceives of property in ways that seem to bear little relation to the familiar juridical idea that he uses later. He treats property

---

[1]These go back to before the time when Marx first identifies himself as a communist in 1843–4 (Löwy, 2003, 49–61). Lenin was unaware of *The German
Ideology* as well as what are now usually classified as Marx's 'early works' with
the exception of *The Holy Family*, written with Engels and published in 1845.

as an ethical phenomenon. He describes private property as 'human self-estrangement', and maintains that communism will lead to the 'true appropriation of the human essence' (Marx, 1975e, 348). Indeed, in the *1844 Manuscripts,* Marx dismisses the idea that communism can be achieved simply by abolishing bourgeois private property in the narrow legal sense as 'crude' communism. Communism, he insists, means a far deeper social and human transformation. For Marx at this time, as Arthur says, communism 'is no narrowly political and juridical adjustment of existing powers and privileges. It has fundamental ontological significance' (Arthur, 1986, 35). It involves the creation of what Marx (1975e, 333) calls 'truly human and social property', and a 'true' form of appropriation (1975e, 346) through which 'man' will be 'completely restored to himself as a social [and] human being' and alienation overcome (1975e, 348).

My aim here is to explain these ideas and to show that, although there are indeed major changes in Marx's conception of communism between his early and later work, not least in the language he employs, there are also significant continuities in his thinking. Important aspects of Marx's early conceptions of private property and communism are retained in the later work. So far from expressing views that he later comes to abandon, Marx's early writings on private property and communism, I shall argue, give expression to radical and visionary themes which run right through Marx's work and help to illuminate aspects of Marx's thought that are often overlooked.

## Private property and communism in 1844

Marx discusses private property and communism in a number of his early works of which the section on 'Private Property and Communism' in the *1844 Manuscripts* is the most extensive and important.[2] In this Marx explains and defends his conception of communism by contrasting it with what he calls 'crude' communism.[3] Some aspects of 'crude' communism are similar to features of what he later comes to believe will be a necessary transitional stage between capitalism and 'full' communism. This has led a number of writers to identify this early notion of 'crude' communism with the later idea of a transitional stage (Avineri, 1968, 223;

---

[2]See also Marx, 1975e; Marx, 1975c.
[3]*der rohe Kommunismus*, literally 'raw' communism.

Tucker, 1961, 154–6), but that is clearly wrong. In 1844, Marx appears to believe that communism can be achieved immediately after the overthrow of capitalism, the idea that a transitional stage between capitalism and communism might be needed has not yet occurred to him.

By 'crude' communism Marx is referring to what he regards as various mistaken ideas of communism held by his contemporaries (Arthur, 1983, 36–8; Elster, 1985, 451). There is considerable disagreement about whom specifically Marx has in mind.[4] Nevertheless, 'crude' communism has some features in common with what Marx later regards as the transitional first stage of communism. '(For crude communism) the community is simply a community of *labour* and equality of *wages*, which are paid out by the communal capital, the *community* as universal capitalist' (Marx, 1975e, 346–7). In other words, private capital is abolished in the sense that it is taken over by the state, the 'community' becomes the 'universal capitalist' (Marx, 1975e, 347). No individual can live by mere ownership, everyone must work for wages, hence 'the category of *worker* [i.e., wage worker] is not abolished but extended to all men' (Marx, 1975e, 346).

Marx makes two basic criticisms of this crude notion of communism. First, it does not understand the 'human nature of need'. It envisages a simple ascetic community which negates wealth and 'levels down'. It abstractly negates 'the entire world of culture and civilization', and seeks to 'return to the *unnatural* simplicity of the *poor*, unrefined man who has no needs' (Marx, 1975e, 346). It does not see that the growth of production and of needs for which capitalism has been responsible means also the growth of human powers and capacities. This is a familiar theme in Marx; it runs through Marx's work from first to last. Marx rejects the romantic desire for the simple life. The growth of needs is a positive development: it means the growth of production, the growth

---

[4]According to Löwy (2003, 47, 87) Marx's targets are Weitling, Babeuf, Cabet and Villegardelle. The editors of *Marx and Engels Collected Works*, volume 3, suggest French secret societies of followers of Babeuf (Marx and Engels, 1975a, 602). The editor of the Penguin *Early Writings* suggests Fourier, Proudhon and Babeuf (Marx, 1975a, 345n). As regards Fourier and Proudhon, this is clearly mistaken (Arthur, 1986, 157–8). In *The Communist Manifesto* the ideas of early 'critical utopian socialists' (specifically excluding Babeuf) are described as follows: 'the revolutionary literature that accompanied these first movements of the proletariat … inculcated universal asceticism and social levelling in its crudest form' (Marx and Engels, 1978c, 497).

of human powers and capacities, the growth of human nature (Sayers, 1998, 65–8). But crude communism does not comprehend this, it does not understand the alienated form that industry takes under capitalism.

Marx's second criticism of crude communism is that by taking private property into common ownership, it achieves only a partial and abstract negation of it. Crude communism 'has not yet comprehended the positive essence of private property' and hence 'it is still held captive and contaminated by private property' (Marx, 1975e, 348).

The very idea that there is such a thing as a 'positive essence' of private property is itself striking. Many on the left at that time and still today regard private property as an entirely detrimental phenomenon. It is important to realise that Marx takes a quite different view. Great development has occurred within the social framework of private property. Under capitalism this development has occurred in an estranged or alienated form. Communism should not simply negate and destroy this development, rather it must build upon it and transform it. As we have seen (Chapter 6 above), communism should be the dialectical supersession (*Aufhebung*) of capitalism not the abstract negation of it. Hence capitalist private property should not be repudiated absolutely, or in an 'abstract' way. Rather, its alienated form must be overcome and its positive aspects appropriated in an unalienated fashion.

Similarly, as Marx goes on to say, in capitalist conditions, industry and its products often seem to have detrimental effects, but they should not be repudiated entirely. Rather we must see that they constitute the realisation of human powers in an alienated form. 'In everyday, material industry ... we find ourselves confronted with objectified powers of the human essence, in the form of sensuous, alien, useful objects, in the form of estrangement.' (Marx, 1975e, 354)

The economy, likewise, confronts us as an independent system which rules over our lives. In fact, however, the market is nothing but our own social activities and relations in an estranged and alien form. 'Exchange ... is the social species-activity, the community, social commerce and integration of man within private property, and for that reason it is the external, alienated species-activity.' (Marx, 1975d, 267)

True communism recognises the real character of these alienated powers, activities and relations. It does not simply repudiate or 'abstractly' negate them; rather, it seeks to overcome them dialectically and to reappropriate them in an unalienated form. This will not happen as the result of superior theoretical understanding. Even in these early writings, communism for Marx is not simply a better theory or set of ideals to be counterposed to the mistaken ideas of 'crude' communism. As in his later work, he sees communism as the projected culmination of real historical processes that are actually occurring: 'it is the complete restoration of man to himself as a *social* – i.e., human – being, a restoration which has become conscious and which takes place within the entire wealth of previous periods of development' (Marx, 1975e, 348).

## The nature of property

What does Marx mean when he talks of 'true appropriation' and of 'truly human and social property'? There is little explanation of these phrases by Marx himself.[5] However, this way of talking about property is characteristically Hegelian and, to understand it, it helps to set Marx's ideas in the context of Hegel's theory of property and of the liberal philosophical tradition from which it emerges.

We commonly think of property as the right to possess, use and dispose over things, enforceable by law. This is how property is conceived by the natural rights and utilitarian accounts of property that dominate liberal social philosophy in this area. The idea that property is a universal natural right is given its classical philosophical expression by Locke. The natural right of private property, he claims, is founded on the universal right that every individual supposedly has to the ownership of themselves and their activities, to 'the labour of his body, and the work of his hands' and hence to 'whatsoever ... he hath mixed his labour with' (Locke, 1988, 287–8).[6] By contrast, utilitarian thinkers, such as Hume (1894, chapter 5), Bentham and the classical economists (Bentham et al., 1987), reject the notion of natural rights as a philosophical fiction and argue that property is a socially created right – an institution that is useful and hence justified only when and because it is conducive to social order and prosperity.

Hegel's account of property draws on both these philosophies but goes beyond them. Crucially, Hegel does not see private property simply in legal or economic terms, he places it in a much wider context. It has a fundamental – 'spiritual' – role in human life. It is the basis on which individuality and freedom develop. 'The rational aspect property is to be found not in the satisfaction of needs but in the superseding of mere

---

[5]For helpful commentaries see Stillman, 1980a; Gould, 1978; Plamenatz, 1975.
[6]This is often referred to as the principle of 'self-ownership'.

subjectivity of personality. Not until he has property does the person exist as reason.' (Hegel, 1991, §41A, 73)

Hegel agrees that the institution of property serves to maintain order and create the conditions for prosperity as the utilitarians and classical economists argue, but for Hegel it is not a merely contingent arrangement. It plays an essential role in human life. It is a basic aspect of the way in which a person relates to things, including other persons and even their own body. As Plamenatz explains,

> It is partly in the process of coming to own things, and to be recognized as their owners, that human beings learn to behave rationally and responsibly, to lead an ordered life. It is partly in the process of learning to distinguish mine from thine that the child comes to recognize itself as a person, as a bearer of rights and duties, as a member of a community with a place of its own inside it. (Plamenatz, 1975, 121)[7]

Property is what a person has the socially recognised right to regard as their own. For Hegel, as for Locke, it is founded on the act of appropriation by which a person puts their will into some thing and makes it their own. By thus appropriating things we distinguish ourselves from mere things that have no wills. We develop our abilities and liberate ourselves from domination by nature (including our own nature) and by others. Hence we develop our freedom and individuality (Stillman, 1980b, 108; Reyburn, 1921).

For Hegel property is thus a fundamental condition for self development and a feature of all human societies. However, its social form is not unchanging, it develops historically (Stillman, 1974). In the earliest societies, property is communal, and individuals have an immediate and indissoluble unity with the collective. As private property spreads, it provides the basis on which individuals achieve autonomy

---

[7]Marx's critique of private property depends on these Hegelian insights, as Plamenatz (1975, 120) observes. '[Hegel] did not deny that private property is a useful institution because it enables men to provide for their wants more efficiently; he merely saw other virtues in it. And so Marx, who learnt so much from Hegel, in attacking the institution of property, attacked it ... not only on the utilitarian and economic front but also on what might be called the cultural or even, in the Hegelian sense of the word, the *spiritual* front.'

from the collective. It thus liberates individuals from submersion in the community and enables them to form a will and an identity apart.[8]

In earlier periods, moreover, the right to own property is not universal, only some have this right. Other human beings can themselves be made property, as with slaves or serfs. The idea that another person cannot be made into property is characteristic of the modern age. It goes together with the idea that all have the inalienable right of 'self ownership', the right to own property at least in themselves and their own labour.

For Hegel private property is the external embodiment of individual freedom; and modern civil society (i.e., bourgeois society), based on the universal right to private property within a liberal state, is for him the fullest development of individuality and liberty. Hegel's philosophy runs into problems here. The liberal right to own property that Hegel is defending is purely formal. 'What and how much I possess is ... purely contingent as far as right is concerned' (Hegel, 1991, §49, 80). My right to property exists undiminished even if I own nothing but my ability to labour. This seems unsatisfactory. The Hegelian view that property is at the basis of liberty and individuality can plausibly be taken to imply that everyone must have some actual external property in order to be able to exercise their freedom and realise themselves (Knowles, 2002, 125–7).

The social problems that were being created by the advent of industrial capitalism made this a pressing issue at the time, as Hegel was aware. Previously independent workers were being dispossessed of everything but their ability to labour and forced to work for wages in factories. They were thus deprived of even the minimum necessary property for the exercise of the most basic freedoms. In response Hegel (1991, §230, 259–60) makes some gestures towards the idea that everyone should be guaranteed a basic minimum livelihood through welfare provision for the very poor, but he is inclined to think that poverty is inevitable in capitalist society and he is not optimistic that it can be eliminated (Hegel, 1991, §§243–5, 266–7, 453–4). Despite being aware of its problems, capitalism based on private property remains, for him, the fullest realisation of freedom, and he cannot envisage a more satisfactory alternative.

---

[8]It is for this reason that Plato, in the *Republic*, is hostile to it, as Hegel (1991, §46, 77–8) observes.

## The early Marx

At first sight Marx's views on property may appear to be the very opposite of Hegel's, and that is how they are often taken. According to
Avineri, for example,

> For Marx property is not the realization of personality but its
> negation.... Consequently the problem is not the assurance of
> property to all – to Marx an inherent impossibility and immanent
> contradiction – but the abolition of all property relations as such.
> (Avineri, 1968, 109)[9]

In fact Marx's position is more complex. Seeing it in the context both
of the Hegelian philosophy he is drawing on and of the later development of his ideas that are reviewed below makes it clear that he follows
Hegel in regarding property relations as the social form within which
we appropriate things. He thus sees property as a universal human
phenomenon which exists in all forms of society.[10] Moreover, as we
have seen already, he does not see the impact of private property as
purely negative. In the *1844 Manuscripts*, as we have seen, he insists
that there is a 'positive essence' of private property that must be preserved when that particular form of property is transcended. Avineri is
wrong, therefore, to suggest that Marx advocates 'the abolition of all
property relations as such'.

However, Avineri is right to say that communism will not attempt to
assure an equal distribution of property. Marx (1975e, 332–3) rejects
Proudhon's demand to equalise wages, and he denounces the idea of
'an enforced rise in wages' as 'nothing more than better pay for slaves
[that] would not mean an increase in human significance or dignity
for either the worker or the labour' (Marx, 1975e, 332). According
to Marx (1975e, 332), 'wages and private property are identical', and
communism involves the transcendence of both.

Moreover, Marx, like Hegel, sees property in historical terms. We see
this historical approach taking shape in the *1844 Manuscripts*. The
advent of private property under capitalism leads to a development of

---

[9]Cf. Stillman, 1980a, 131, 'Marx criticizes capitalist private property as suppress-
ing individuality'. However, Stillman goes on to give a more nuanced and valuable account than these words suggest.
[10]Marx makes this explicit in the *Grundrisse* (Marx, 1973a, 87), see below p. 118.

human powers, but in an estranged and alienated form. These powers must be reappropriated, their alien form must be overcome. This is what will be achieved by the 'true appropriation' of communism. It will reclaim these powers for individuals as members of a free and conscious community. This reappropriation is not the absolute negation of all property, it is the concrete negation of a specific form of property, namely (as Marx later calls it) bourgeois private property and the creation of what he calls, in the *1844 Manuscripts,* 'truly human and social property' (Marx, 1975e, 333). Communism will establish this, and the new form of appropriation it involves, for the first time (Lobkowicz, 1967, 367).[11]

In capitalist society dominated by private property individuals appear to pursue their own separate interests. I produce for myself, not for you, and vice-versa. 'Society appears as a framework extraneous to the individuals, as a limitation on their original independence. The only bond that holds them together is natural necessity, need and private interest, the conservation of their property and their egoistic persons' (Marx, 1975c, 230). In communism, by contrast, the domination of private property and self interest are overcome. Individuals are brought together not separated in their relations. We each work for each other as well as for ourselves as part of a common society (Lebowitz, 2010, 66ff).

In some of these early writings, Marx gives visionary glimpses of what these new forms of appropriation and production will mean in human terms. He talks of the 'emancipation of all human senses and attributes' that will occur when they are freed from their instrumental dominion by private property (Marx, 1975e, 352); and as we have seen in the previous Chapter he gives a remarkable description of what unalienated creation will be like. If we produced in this way, as social and 'human beings', moreover, our individuality would also be developed and realised.

> Each of us would have ... *affirmed* himself and his neighbour in his production.... Our productions would be as many mirrors from which our natures would shine forth. This relationship would be mutual: what applies to me would also apply to you: My labour

---

[11]Perhaps this is what is referred to as 'individual property' in Marx, 1961a, 763, see p. 115 below.

would be the *free expression* and hence the *enjoyment of life*....
Moreover, in my labour the *specific character* of my individuality
would be affirmed because it would be my *individual* life. Labour
would be *authentic, active, property.* (Marx, 1975d, 277–8)

Communism, as 'true appropriation', he says, will be

the complete restoration of man to himself as a *social – i.e.*, human –
being.... It is the genuine resolution of the conflict between man
and nature, and between man and man, the true resolution of the
conflict between existence and being, between objectification and
self-affirmation, between freedom and necessity, between individual
and species. It is the solution of the riddle of history and knows
itself to be the solution. (Marx, 1975e, 348)

## Later developments

In Marx's early writings there are few details about how this new form
of appropriation will be brought about. What the overcoming of private property means in practical terms is left vague. Some of these
details are worked out gradually in subsequent writings.

A big step forward in this direction is taken in *The German Ideology*
where Marx and Engels begin to work out a detailed historical account
of the development of the division of labour and the changes in forms
of property associated with it, these for them being equivalent:
'the various stages of development in the division of labour are just
so many different forms of ownership.' (Marx and Engels, 1978b,
151)

Marx, like Hegel, rejects the idea that individuals initially exist in a
pre-social 'state of nature'. On the contrary, in the earliest conditions,
individuals live in immediate unity with their tribe or communal
group, the apparently separate individual is a later creation of historical development. Likewise, the earliest forms of property are communal. 'The first form of ownership is tribal ownership [*Stammeigentum*]'
(Marx and Engels, 1978b, 151, cf. 186). Property evolves through stages
that are sketched out by Marx and Engels, but only roughly at this
stage. Private property is a late development. 'Tribal property evolved
through various stages – feudal landed property, corporative movable
property, capital invested in manufacture – to modern capital, determined by big industry and universal competition, i.e. pure private
property, which has cast off all semblance of a communal institution'

(Marx and Engels, 1978b, 186). The idea that such private property is the result of an individual will asserted over things is a 'juridical illusion' (1978b, 188) – property is, always, a form of social
relation.[12]

This historical account of the evolution of property is deepened
and extended in subsequent works. In an important section of the
*Grundrisse*, Marx gives a detailed analysis of precapitalist economies
and the kinds of property associated with them.[13] Developing the
account given in the *German Ideology*, he argues that in these societies
in contrast to capitalism individuals associate together as members of
the community and property is communal.

> Individuals relate not as workers but as proprietors – and members
> of a community, who at the same time work. The aim of this work
> is not the *creation of value* – although they may do surplus labour
> in order to obtain *alien*, i.e. surplus products in exchange – rather,
> its aim is sustenance of the individual proprietor and of his family,
> as well as of the total community. (Marx, 1973a, 471–2)

The modern form of private property is a historical product and so
too is the 'free' worker who owns nothing but his own power to
labour. 'The positing of the individual as a *worker*, in this nakedness,
is itself a product of *history*' (Marx, 1973a, 472). In other words,
the idea that private property is derived from the 'natural' right of
'self ownership' is a myth. The 'self-owning' worker is a modern
creation. In earlier periods, 'the individual can never appear in the
dot-like isolation [*Punktualität*] in which he appears as mere free
worker' (Marx, 1973a, 485). The modern individual worker, detached
from the community and the means of production, is a creation of
history.[14]

> It is not the *unity* of living and active humanity with the natural,
> inorganic conditions of their metabolic exchange with nature, and

---

[12]The correlative idea that the state is above social relations is equally illusory.
[13]Marx, 1973a, 471–514, separately translated as *Precapitalist Economic Formations*
(Marx, 1964). Gould (1978, chapter 5) gives a good account of Marx's ideas about
property and justice in the *Grundrisse*.
[14]"Human beings become individuals only through the process of history. He
[*sic*] appears originally as a *species-being* [*Gattungswesen*], *clan being, herd animal*.'
(Marx, 1973a, 496)

hence their appropriation of nature, which requires explanation or is the result of a historic process, but rather the *separation* between these inorganic conditions of human existence and this active existence, a separation which is completely posited only in the relation of wage labour and capital. (Marx, 1973a, 489)

This process of separation is described by Marx in *Capital,* in his celebrated account of the 'primitive accumulation' of capital (Marx, 1961a, chapter 32). It begins with the spread of individual private property in the late middle ages in Europe. The initial result is a society of small scale individual or household producers in which individual energies are liberated from what had increasingly become communal constraints.

The private property of the labourer in his means of production is the foundation of petty industry, whether agricultural, manufacturing, or both; petty industry, again, is an essential condition for the development of social production and of the free individuality of the labourer himself. Of course, this petty mode of production exists also under slavery, serfdom, and other states of dependence. But it flourishes, it lets loose its whole energy, it attains its adequate classical form, only where the labourer is the private owner of his own means of labour set in action by himself: the peasant of the land which he cultivates, the artisan of the tool which he handles as a virtuoso. (Marx, 1961a, 761)

However, this mode of production and the individual form of property associated with it is suitable only for small-scale individual production, and the degree of individual development that can be achieved on the basis of such property is limited.

[It] presupposes parcelling of the soil and scattering of the other means of production. As it excludes the concentration of these means of production, so also it excludes co-operation, division of labour within each separate process of production, the control over, and the productive application of the forces of Nature by society, and the free development of the social productive powers. It is compatible only with a system of production, and a society, moving within narrow and more or less primitive bounds. (Marx, 1961a, 762)

As industry develops and the productive forces become more social in character, this individual form of private property is increasingly at odds with them. It itself becomes a hindrance to further economic development. Small property is taken over and large capital accumulates.

> At a certain stage of development, [this mode of production] brings forth the material agencies for its own dissolution. From that moment new forces and new passions spring up in the bosom of society; but the old social organization fetters them and keeps them down. It must be annihilated; it is annihilated. (Marx, 1961a, 762)

Small producers are driven off the land. They are dispossessed of their means of livelihood, forced into cities to become industrial workers, employed by capital, working for wages. Thus there comes to exist at one pole large capital and at the other a mass of dispossessed workers who own nothing but their power to labour – dispossessed, not in the sense that they are destitute (though they often were and still are where these processes are still occurring), but in the sense that they do not have the minimum of property to enable them to exercise control over their basic conditions of life.

As we have seen, these developments were beginning to be evident to Hegel in the early years of the nineteenth century. They became more apparent as the century progressed. The impoverishment and distress of the working class became a major issue of social concern. Some maintained that these were unavoidable consequences of a free market economy, but since this had also led to huge economic development it was a price worth paying. Others advocated welfare measures to ensure a minimum of property as the necessary condition for freedom and self-development; and some influential thinkers questioned the purely formal notion of property right on these grounds. Thus T.H. Green, a nineteenth century British Hegelian, says of the industrial working class,

> In the eye of the law they have rights of appropriation, but in fact they have not the chance of providing means for a free moral life, of developing and giving reality or expression to a good will, an interest in social well-being. A man who possesses nothing but his powers of labour and who has to sell these to a capitalist for bare daily maintenance, might as well, in respect of the ethical purposes which the possession of property should

serve, be denied rights of property altogether. (Green, 1999, §220, 168)

The lesson for Green is that there should be welfare provision to ensure a basic minimum for all.[15] Of course, Marx is also critical of the dispossession of the working class but his response is very different.

Since the time when Green and Marx were writing, capitalism has changed greatly, and largely in the direction that Green was advocating. Welfare measures of the sort that he was arguing for have become widespread, absolute destitution has been almost entirely eliminated, at least in the more advanced capitalist societies (although poverty and deprivation remain). A minimum wage, unemployment benefit, free education, state funded health services and old age pensions, and many other forms of welfare provision exist in most of these societies. Moreover, the standard of living of working people has increased very greatly. It may well seem that Marx's account of the way in which capitalism 'dispossesses' the working class has simply ceased to apply.

However, this misses the point of Marx's critique. When Marx talks of the 'dispossession' of working people under capitalism he is not referring only to the deterioration of their standard of living,[16] but to their alienation from – their loss of control over – their work and its products which comes with capitalism and wage labour. This is the deeper meaning of the dispossession that working people have suffered under capitalism. Even the most radical welfare measures within capitalism will achieve only a more equal distribution of resources, they do not address this fundamental dispossession. Marx is calling for something far more radical. He is arguing for the abolition of private property and wages altogether, and for a new, social form of property which will lead to the reappropriation by working people of their work and social relations.

Moreover, he maintains that the forces at work within capitalism are themselves leading towards this outcome. 'Capitalist production begets, with the inexorability of a law of Nature, its own negation' (Marx,

---

[15]Similar arguments are voiced still by supporters of social welfare. Some argue on such grounds that there should be a guaranteed basic minimum income (Van Parijs, 1992; Gorz, 1989).

[16]Marx believed that the standard of living of working people declined in the initial period of capitalism. This is sometimes disputed, see: Hobsbawm, 1964, chapters 5–7.

1961a, 763). On the one hand, it leads to the growth of large scale social productive forces that are increasingly restricted by the individual form of private property. These require a social form of ownership and control for their further development. At the same time, moreover, capitalism creates the agents who will bring such a change about, in the shape of a working class 'disciplined, united, organized by the very mechanism of the process of capitalist production itself' (Marx, 1961a, 763; cf. Marx and Engels, 1978c, 480–3).

The communist society that will eventually result,[17] Marx believed, will not redistribute private property to the producers, as suggested by those who advocate welfare measures to ameliorate the impact of capitalism. It 'does not re-establish private property for the producer, but gives him individual property [*individuelle Eigentum*] based on the acquisition of the capitalist era: i.e., on co-operation and the possession in common of the land and of the means of production' (Marx, 1961a, 763). This 'possession in common'[18] – social property – is the appropriate form for an advanced industrial society with highly social and cooperative means of production.

Let me first note that in *Capital* Marx casts this historical process in the dialectical form of a 'negation of the negation' in which large capitalists first expropriate small producers and then are themselves expropriated.[19] Thus Marx's mature account retains the Hegelian form of his earlier one, though his language is much altered and now his account is filled out with historical detail and made more concrete.

The phrase 'individual property' [*individuelle Eigentum*] in the passage just quoted is puzzling and calls for some comment. The dialectical form of the 'negation of the negation' that Marx uses implies a 'return' to individual property but in a higher form; and that, no doubt, partly accounts for Marx's use of the phrase here (Arthur, 2002, 124). But what form does property take in communist society and in what sense does it remain 'individual'? As Marx says explicitly, he is not suggesting a return to private property, but beyond that his meaning is not clear.

---

[17]Marx does not make it clear whether he is referring in this passage to the first, second or to both stages of communism, see further discussion below.

[18]That is, the social ownership of the means of production introduced after a communist revolution. See below.

[19]Marx's use of the phrase 'negation of the negation' has been enormously controversial. I simply note it here, without either endorsing or criticising it.

Engels gives the following account of this passage.

> The state of things brought about by the expropriation of the expro-
> priators is ... characterized as the re-establishment of individual
> property, but *on the basis* of the social ownership of the land and of
> the mean of production produced by labour itself.... This means
> that social ownership extends to the land and the other means of
> production, and individual ownership to the products, that is, the
> articles of consumption. (Engels, 1962, 180)

Arthur questions Engels' interpretation on the grounds that 'it intro-
duces a division between production and appropriation that is rather
foreign to the spirit of Marx's thought' (Arthur, 2002, 114). However,
such a division is a feature of the first stage of communism, in which
there is social ownership of the means of production and yet there is
still payment of individual wages and private property in consumption
goods. This may be what Engels takes Marx to be referring to here. But
it is not clear that Engels is referring to the first stage only since he also
quotes a passage earlier in *Capital* where Marx notes specifically that at
different stages of the development of communist society different
principles of distribution will apply (Engels, 1962, 180, quoting Marx,
1961a, 61).

Nevertheless, as Arthur argues, the restoration of property to the
individual worker is a recurrent theme in Marx's work. In this connection, Arthur quotes Marx's defence of the Paris Commune against its
critics.

> The Commune, they exclaim, intends to abolish property, the basis
> of all civilization! Yes, gentlemen, the Commune intended to
> abolish that class-property which makes the labour of the many the
> wealth of the few. It aimed at the expropriation of the expropria-
> tors. It wanted to make individual property a truth by transforming
> the means of production, land and capital, now chiefly the means
> of enslaving exploiting labour, into mere instruments of free and
> associated labour. (Marx, 1958, quoted by Arthur, 2002, 126)

In this way, with communism society regains control over its economic life and makes individual property a 'truth' by restoring it to
the individual as a member of the community, as a 'social individual'
– that is, not on the basis of separate individual right but rather as an
agreed share of the common property.

The story that Marx tells of the historical development of property forms in these later writings thus extends and deepens the account initially sketched in *The German Ideology*. It is an Hegelian story of the emergence and growth of individuality and freedom, first on the basis of the petty private property of the peasant and artisan at the end of the middle ages. Then human powers develop in an alienated form under capitalism, and finally they are reappropriated by social individuals under communism.

Again it is important to see that private property is by no means the purely negative phenomenon it is often thought to be in Marx's work. On the contrary, in the passage from *Capital* that I am discussing, Marx argues that 'petty' individual property forms the basis on which the individual is liberated from immediate unity with the community and it unleashes individual productive energy and creativity. As the productive forces develop and become more cooperative, however, their private ownership becomes a limitation. Capitalist property transcends this limit and makes possible an enormous development of human social productive powers. In capitalism these powers take an alienated form. The expropriation of capitalist private property will reclaim these powers by appropriating them as powers for the social individual in a conscious and unalienated way. Property will no longer be regarded as exclusively private and individual. It can be freely appropriated and used by the individual to satisfy their needs, without regard to their particular contribution or abilities.[20] This is what Marx refers to in 1844 as 'true' appropriation.[21] Thus the picture that Marx paints in *Capital* is a development of the ideas he put forward in this earlier work.

Of course, there are many reasons why one might wish to question Marx's account of the future trajectory of capitalism, but that is not the issue I am dealing with here. The point I am making is that, according to Marx, communism does not attempt to create a fairer or more humane distribution of private property, it abolishes it. However, this is not to say that communism will eliminate 'all property relations as such' (whatever

---

[20]This is what Marx later refers to as distribution 'according to need'. I shall come back to this in Chapter 9 below.

[21]Arthur criticises the historical reading of this passage that I am giving (and of Marx's dialectic in general), and attempts to develop a purely structural account. In my view this is untenable, particularly as regards this passage which is entitled 'The Historical Tendency of Capitalist Accumulation' and whose theme is explicitly historical.

that might mean), as Avineri suggests. Marx, like Hegel, sees property relations as the social form within which we appropriate things.[22] They are a necessary feature of all forms of society. 'All production is appropriation of nature on the part of an individual within and through a specific form of society. In this sense it is a tautology to say that property (appropriation) is a precondition of production' (Marx, 1973a, 87). Communism does not abolish property as such. Rather, it will *socialise* it so that it corresponds to the social character of advanced industrial production.

## After capitalism

In 1844 Marx appears to believe that genuine communism can be achieved immediately after the revolutionary overthrow of capitalism. By the time of writing the *Communist Manifesto* in 1847 only a few years later, he has abandoned that view. The creation of a truly communist society will require a transitional stage 'between capitalism and communism' as he later puts it (Marx, 1978c, 538).[23] In this transitional stage the state will not be abolished immediately. Instead, a workers' state will be created, a state in which the working class is the ruling class.[24] Nor will all forms of private property be abolished, but only bourgeois private property, capital, private property in the means of production: this will be taken into state ownership.[25] Payment for work

---

[22]Property relations in this sense are a particular aspect of the relations of production. The relation between these two concepts needs further exploration. When Marx (1978b, 4) says that property is the 'legal expression' of 'the existing relations of production', I take him to be referring to property in the narrow legal sense.

[23]Following Lenin (1969b, 331), this phase is sometimes referred to as 'socialism'. The idea of stages of communism is criticised by Lebowitz (2010, 107) on the grounds that 'Marx described a *single organic system* ... that necessarily emerges initially from capitalism with *defects* ... [and] is in the process of *becoming*'. That is true. Nevertheless, a single organic system (e.g., a plant) can develop through distinct stages.

[24]Marx later calls this the 'dictatorship of the proletariat' (Marx and Engels, 1978a, 220).

[25]'The first step in the revolution by the working class, is to raise the proletariat to the position of ruling class, to win the battle of democracy. The proletariat will use its political supremacy to wrest, by degrees, all capital from the bourgeoisie, to centralise all instruments of production in the hands of the State, i.e., of the proletariat organised as the ruling class; and to increase the total of productive forces as rapidly as possible.' (Marx and Engels, 1978c, 237)

(i.e., wages) and private ownership in the sphere of consumption will continue. Everyone who can will have to work for wages.

In some significant respects this programme is similar to the 'crude' communism denounced by Marx in 1844, in that capital is concentrated in the state and everyone works for wages. Now, and in subsequent works, Marx does not reject such a programme outright, he sees it as a necessary stage towards the creation of full communism.[26] However, this first, transitional phase is not Marx's ideal of communism nor is it its final form. Marx makes this absolutely clear in the 'Critique of the Gotha Programme'.

> What we have to deal with here is a communist society, not as it has *developed* on its own foundations, but, on the contrary just as it *emerges* from capitalist society, which is thus in every respect, economically, morally and intellectually, still stamped with the birth marks of the old society from whose womb it emerges. (Marx, 1978c, 529)

In this work Marx goes into detail about the economic principles involved in this transitional stage. He criticises the Lassallean idea that the 'undiminished proceeds of labour' should be distributed 'equally' to 'all members of society' (Marx, 1978c, 528). Some 'deductions', he insists, must first be made centrally to cover the replacement of means of production, for the development of production and to insure against accidents and other contingencies, etc.. In addition, provision must be made for administration, for 'the common satisfaction of needs, such as schools, health services, etc.', and to provide for those unable to work (the young, the elderly, the sick, etc.).[27]

According to Marx, in the first phase of communism, after such deductions have been made for social expenditure by the state, individuals will be paid according to the amount of work they perform. Distribution is to be governed by the principle: to each according to their work. As Marx observes, this is a principle of equal exchange, an exchange of 'equal values'. In this respect it is similar to the economic principle governing capitalism (Marx calls it a principle of 'bourgeois right'), except for one important difference: in communism it is no

---

[26]Cf. Elster, 1985, 451. This is the sort of programme that was carried out by the Soviet, Chinese and Cuban communists after their revolutions.

[27]The proportion of the social product devoted to social purposes has expanded greatly, even in capitalist societies, with the growth of welfare provision.

longer possible to gain an income merely by owning capital. 'Everyone is a worker', everyone who is capable of doing so must work in order to earn a living. Hence, Marx says, there is an 'advance' in equality (Marx, 1978c, 530).

## Equality

Many recent writers have tried to maintain that Marx advocates communism on the basis of principles of equality and justice. In this passage, in particular, it is often argued, he justifies first phase communism as an 'advance' in equality compared with capitalism, with the supposed implication that 'full' communism will involve an even more equalitarian distribution of wealth.[28] This is a fundamental misunderstanding. This passage should not be interpreted as an endorsement by Marx of first stage communism for its greater equality. Its main purpose, rather, is to point out the 'defects', the *in*equalities, that exist in this form of communism. The principle of equal exchange leads inevitably to inequalities – inequalities that are an inescapable effect of the principle of equal right itself.

> This equal right is still constantly encumbered by a bourgeois limitation. The right of the producers is proportional to the labour they supply; the equality consists in the fact that measurement is made with an equal standard, labour. But one man is superior to another physically, or mentally, and supplies more labour in the same time, or can work for a longer time.... This equal right is an unequal right for unequal labour. It recognises no class differences, because everyone is only a worker like everyone else; but it tacitly recognises unequal individual endowment, and thus productive capacity, as a natural privilege. It is, therefore, a right of inequality, in its content, like every right.... Besides, one worker is married, another is not; one has more children than another, and so on etc., etc.. Thus, with an equal amount of work done, and hence an equal share in the social consumption fund, one will in fact receive more than another, one will be richer than another, and so on. (Marx, 1978c, 530–1)

Even from an egalitarian point of view, in other words, the principle of equal right that prevails in the first stage of communism has 'defects'.

---

[28]Geras, 1985; Cohen, 1988c; Rawls, 2007, 359; etc..

Rawls (2007, 367) questions Marx's view that distribution according to work must inevitably lead to inequalities. 'Why, e.g., can't society, adopting a principle like the Difference Principle[29] impose various taxes etc.. And adjust incentive so that the greater endowments of some work to the advantage of those with fewer endowments?' Of course, a socialist society can take steps to mitigate inequalities – as, indeed, do virtually all capitalist societies through their tax and welfare systems.[30] The 'deductions' that Marx specifies are made for precisely this purpose – for the support of the sick, the elderly and others who cannot work (Graham, 1990). However, in a communist society this support would not be left to the goodwill and voluntary contributions of private 'self-owning' individuals. It is achieved socially by means of the deductions just described.

Moreover, Marx's argument is more radical than Rawls realises. Marx insists that *any* principle of distribution according to equal property rights will generate inequalities. Where people have different needs and responsibilities, equal wages will result in differences of individual wealth, as Marx argues in the passage just quoted. The general point is that *any* system of property right must necessarily result in inequalities, since every right, 'is a right to inequality in its content' (Marx, 1978c, 530). Wood explains the point that Marx is making as follows.

Equal rights, whatever their nature, are always in principle rights to unequal shares of need satisfaction or well being. When I have a right to a certain share of means of consumption, I have a claim on this share against others which, within very broad limits,

---

[29]Rawls' principle that social and economic inequalities are just only if they work to the benefit of the least advantaged members of society.

[30]Rawls appears to be oblivious to this. He thinks he is following Cohen in attributing to Marx an idea of communism based on the universal right of 'self-ownership' (though Cohen does not in fact endorse this interpretation). Interpreted in this way it appears that, 'Marx does not suggest that the better endowed should be required to earn their greater consumption shares in ways that contribute to the well-being of those less well endowed. Beyond respecting everyone's equal right of access to external natural resources, no one owes anything to anyone else, other than what they want to do voluntarily' (Rawls, 2007, 367). This is far distant from anything recognisable as Marx's view. Rawls would have done better to read Marx himself instead of relying so heavily on Cohen.

I may enforce irrespective of the consequences to others of my so doing. This is part of what it means to have a right. (Wood, 1981b, 208)

However, Marx is not arguing for communism on egalitarian grounds. On the contrary, he is criticising the principle of equal right as 'bourgeois', even though he believes it is necessary for the immediate post-capitalist stage of historical development.

These defects are inevitable in the first phase of communist society as it is when it has just emerged after prolonged birth pangs from capitalist society. Right can never be higher than the economic structure of society and its cultural development conditioned thereby. (Marx, 1978c, 569)

To do away with these defects, communism must 'wholly transcend the narrow horizon of bourgeois right'. Its aim is not a more equal distribution of private property,[31] but rather the overcoming of private property altogether.

In present society, quantity of labour is measured both by its duration and intensity: the longer, harder or more skilfully individuals work, the more they are rewarded. Marx (1978c, 530) suggests that similar principles will apply in the first phase of communism. Why not pay people simply according to hours worked and regardless of intensity? Would that not be fairer? That is debatable. In a wages system, people expect to be rewarded for the amount of work they do, measured not only in terms of time but also of intensity, as is presently the case under capitalism. If working harder is not rewarded, people feel that their effort is not being fairly recognised. Moreover there is no material incentive to work harder. The result is likely to be a decrease in productivity that is detrimental to all.[32]

In short, according to Marx, a system of payment according to work is a necessary feature of the first phase of communism in which the wages system remains. This leads inevitably to inequalities. However,

---

[31]Wood (1981b) makes this point cogently.
[32]This was the experience of egalitarian experiments in China during the Cultural Revolution. The system of equal pay according to time without regard to level of performance was called the 'iron rice bowl' (because it was rigidly the same size). It created resentment and a sense of unfairness and was abandoned.

the ultimate aim of communism is not to construct a more equal form of property distribution or a fairer system of wages. It is to abolish private property and wages altogether. This is what is also envisaged in the idea of 'true appropriation', introduced in 1844. It remains Marx's ideal of communism right through to the end of his life.

## 'Full' communism

So far I have been considering the first transitional phase of post-capitalist development. 'Full' communism requires much deeper and more extensive economic, social and human changes. It means not only the abolition of private property in the means of production (capital) – i.e., not only a partial and 'abstract' negation of private property, as Marx puts it in 1844 – but a complete overcoming of private property; and, going along with that, the elimination of all class divisions, the abolition of the state, the overcoming of alienation, and the creation of a free and consciously organised community.

The radical and far reaching character of this vision was not well understood in much of the mainstream Marxist literature of the Soviet period. The abolition of private property in the means of production by the Soviet regime had, it was supposed, removed the material basis for class differences and created the material conditions for communist society. The transition to full communism was then expected to occur more or less spontaneously with the passage of time, as old habits died out and were superseded (Lenin, 1969b; Bukharin and Preobrazhenskii, 1969; Nove, 1983). The ending of all class distinctions and the 'withering away' of the state, it was assumed, would occur automatically and relatively rapidly: in 'twenty or thirty years' was the optimistic estimate of an influential work published in the early years of the Soviet Union (Bukharin and Preobrazhenskii, 1969, 116). Unfortunately, there were no signs of this happening in the Soviet Union – quite the reverse indeed. Nor has there been any discernable movement in this direction in any other of the 'actually existing' communist societies. It seems clear that more is involved in creating communism than the abolition of private property in the means of production (Sayers, 1980; Sayers, 1990a).

Moreover, as I am arguing, a careful reading makes it is clear that Marx believed this too. Communism, for him, means a far fuller and deeper transformation than can be achieved by a change in the property system in its usual narrow legal sense. This theme is central to his earliest communist writings, as we have seen. It is continued throughout his later work, as we will now see, even though the way he talks of communism changes, becoming less abstract and philosophical, and more concrete and specific, both economically and socially.

The essential features of this later account of full communism are presented for the first time in the *Poverty of Philosophy*, but only in hazy outline.

> The working class, in the course of its development, will substitute for the old civil society an association which will exclude classes and their antagonism, and there will be no more political power properly so-called, since political power is precisely the official expression of antagonism in civil society. (Marx, 1978a, 170)

Class distinctions will be eliminated. The state will lose its 'political character' and 'it withers away [*er stirbt ab*]'.[33]

Although Marx's descriptions of full communism become somewhat more detailed as his thought develops, they always remain vague and sketchy. There are some important and suggestive passages in later works dealing with economic and social relations that have been relatively neglected in this context. As these make clear, full communism will also entail a total transformation of economic and social life, of the division of labour and the system of distribution. It will involve entirely new forms of appropriation and economic organisation.

Under capitalism, where there is commodity production and wage labour, individuals work separately and independently in a complex division of labour. The social connection of their activities is established subsequently through economic exchange, and the connection appears to be established by the independent and alien mechanism of the market.

> The social character of activity, as well as the social form of the product, and the share of individuals in production here appear as something alien and objective, confronting the individuals, not as their relation to one another, but as their subordination to relations which subsist independently of them and which arise out

---

[33]Engels, 1962, 385. 'Withers away' was the earlier translation and has achieved a certain familiarity, not to say notoriety; the more recent translation is 'dies out'. There is a similar and slightly fuller account in Marx and Engels, 1978c, 490–1.

of collisions between mutually indifferent individuals. The general exchange of activities and products, which has become a vital condition for each individual – their mutual interconnection here appears as something alien to them, autonomous, as a thing. In exchange value, the social connection between persons is transformed into a social relation between things; personal capacity into objective wealth. (Marx, 1973a, 157)[34]

Communism, by contrast, is a system of communal production in which ownership is social and the social form of production is explicit and presupposed in advance. 'Instead of a division of labour, such as is necessarily created with the exchange of exchange values, there would take place an organization of labour whose consequence would be the participation of the individual in communal consumption' (Marx, 1973a, 172). Relations between individuals are no longer mediated through exchange and exchange values, they are transparent and directly cooperative and social. There is 'free exchange among individuals who are associated on the basis of common appropriation and control of the means of production' (Marx, 1973a, 159). Communism is a consciously planned system: 'a community of free individuals, carrying on their work with the means of production in common, in which the labour power of all the different individuals is consciously applied as the combined labour power of the community' (Marx, 1961a, 78).

In such a system the idea that the individual's labour creates a distinct product that should be rewarded by an individual wage will cease to apply.[35]

> Communality is presupposed as the basis of production. The labour of the individual is posited from the outset as social labour. Thus, whatever the particular material form of the product he creates or helps to create, what he has bought with his labour is not a specific and particular product, but rather a specific share of the communal production. He therefore has no particular product to exchange. His

---

[34]This is what Marx (1961a, chapter 1.4) later calls the 'fetishism of commodities'.

[35]Marx quotes Hodgskin, 'there is no longer anything which we can call the natural reward of individual labour. Each labourer produces only some part of a whole, and each part, having no value or utility in itself, there is nothing on which the labourer can seize, and say: it is my product, this I will keep to myself' (Marx, 1961a, 355n).

product is not an *exchange value*. The product does not first have to be transposed into a particular form in order to attain a general character for the individual. (Marx, 1973a, 172)

Of course, distribution to individuals will still be necessary, and different individuals will appropriate different things – not as their private property, however, but rather as their portion of the common lot.[36]

In short, social relations will no longer be dominated by alien economic forces, they will be clear and transparent. Individuals will be able to reappropriate them and determine their lives consciously and freely. In Engels' words:

> The whole sphere of the conditions of life which environ man, and which have hitherto ruled man, now comes under the dominion and control of man, who for the first time becomes the ... master of his own social organization. The laws of his own social action, hitherto standing face-to-face with man as laws of Nature foreign to, and dominating him, will then be used with full understanding, and so mastered by him. Man's own social organization, hitherto confronting him as a necessity imposed by Nature and history, now becomes the result of his own free action. (Engels, 1958b, 153)

## Equality

This conception of communism is radical and visionary. Although it involves the abolition of private ownership of the means of production, it encompasses a far fuller and deeper economic, social and human transformation than is usually understood by that phrase as I have been stressing.[37] This is only partially understood by recent writers on communism in the analytic tradition, such as Cohen and Rawls.

To illustrate his idea of communism, Cohen uses the example of a camping trip by a group of friends in which equipment is shared col-

---

[36]This is what happens among family or friends. Property is treated as communal and there are shared understandings about the way it is distributed. I get my agreed share, but this is not regarded as private property with which I can do as I please. If I do not want to use or consume my share myself it is there for others. Cf. Cohen's example of a camping trip among friends discussed below and in Chapter 9.

[37]I will be discussing other aspects of the idea of communism in detail in coming chapters.

lectively and activities are organised cooperatively and by mutual agreement. In other words, private property is suspended and treated as communal, and the principles of market exchange cease to operate for the duration and purposes of the trip. When one of the group requires something or needs help, this is given freely, as it is needed, without an accounting of the cost or expectation of payment.

Cohen is concerned mainly with issues of equality and justice (so too is Rawls). This is not a promising starting point for interpreting Marx, since Marx consistently repudiates the idea that communism can be understood in these terms as I have already stressed (Wood, 1981b). Nevertheless, Cohen's camping trip example serves well to bring out some of the essential features of communism that I have been describing. Unfortunately, however, Cohen continually forgets these in his attempt to impose liberal standards of equality and justice that communism transcends, with the result that his account is inconsistent and unsatisfactory.

According to Cohen both the camping trip and communism are governed by two basic principles. One is a principle of community: 'the antimarket principle according to which I serve you not because of what I can get in return by doing so but because you need or want my service, and you, for the same reason, serve me' (Cohen, 2009, 39). This is indeed the fundamental principle governing social relations in communist society, Cohen is right.

However, he also insists that the camping trip and communism are governed by a principle of equality. This claim is more problematic. In some senses, no doubt, communism involves principles of equality, but many different things can be meant by that term. According to Cohen (2009, 13) the crucial principle concerns what he calls 'radical' or 'socialist' equality of opportunity. This 'seeks to correct for all unchosen disadvantages.... When socialist equality of opportunity prevails, differences of outcome reflect nothing but differences of taste and choice, not differences in natural and social capacities and powers.' (Cohen, 2009, 17–18)

As Cohen points out, an important feature of equality of this sort is that it can exist together with large differences. Different individuals will appropriate different things and use different facilities and services according to their preferences.

> Somebody fishes, somebody else prepares the food, and another person cooks it. People who hate cooking but enjoy washing up may do all the washing up, and so on. There are plenty of differences,

but our mutual understanding, and the spirit of the enterprise, ensure that there are no inequalities to which anyone could mount a principled objection. (Cohen, 2009, 4)

Thus everyone's needs or 'preferences' as Cohen calls them are met – there is equality in that sense – but there is no attempt to achieve a quantitatively equal distribution of resources and there is no need for an accounting of resources to ensure this. Cohen does not sufficiently appreciate this. He is worried that 'large inequalities' can arise that are not ruled out by the principles of 'socialist equality of opportunity' but which 'are nevertheless repugnant to socialists when they obtain on a sufficiently large scale, because they then contradict community: community is put under strain when large inequalities obtain. The sway of socialist equality of opportunity must therefore be tempered by a principle of community' (Cohen, 2009, 34). Thus, he argues, 'certain inequalities that cannot be forbidden in the name of socialist equality of opportunity should nevertheless be forbidden, in the name of community' (Cohen, 2009, 37).

He gives the following example. On the camping trip, 'we eat pretty meagerly, but you have your special high-grade fish pond' which you got by means that do not violate the principles of socialist equality of opportunity. 'Even though there is no injustice here, your [possession] cuts you off from our common life, and the ideal of community condemns that.' (Cohen, 2009, 38)

Here Cohen seems to have forgotten that equipment and resources are supposed to be shared on the camping trip. Private property and hence the principles of distributive justice associated with it have been set aside. There are no individually owned fish ponds. In his discussion of the principle of equality that is supposed to operate on the camping trip and under socialism, however, Cohen repeatedly talks of differences of 'income' and inequalities of property, forgetting apparently that money and private property are not operative. The inequalities that he describes are the sort that can arise in the first stage of communism in which the principle of equal exchange still operates, but it is abolished in full communism, where what Cohen calls the 'principle of community' reigns supreme.

With the abolition of private property the differing needs of different individuals will be satisfied in different ways. One person may eat much, another little, one may eat fish, another not (and have no gastronomic interest in Cohen's fish pond), one may play tennis, another football, one may be fit and healthy another chronically ill, etc.. Each will get what they require to satisfy their particular needs. Wood overstates the case when he says that the principle of distribution according to need 'is not in any sense a principle of "equality"'. However, he is quite right to insist that 'it does not treat people alike or equally from any point of view but considers them simply as individuals with their own special needs and faculties' (Wood, 1979, 292).

As Lebowitz points out, even the principle of distribution that operates in the first stage of communism fails to do this. 'Just like the political economy that Marx criticized in his earliest writings, the conception of distribution according to contribution looks at the producer "only as a worker". This was a perspective Marx always rejected.' (Lebowitz, 2010, 72, quoting Marx, 1975e; cf. Marx, 1978c, 530–1)

And Lebowitz goes on to say,

> Indeed, precisely because differences in ability imply no differences in needs, *The German Ideology* argued that 'the false tenet [...] "to each according to his abilities" must be changed [...] into the tenet *"to each according to his need"*; in other words, a *different form* of activity, of labour, does not justify inequality, confers no *privileges* in respect of possession and enjoyment'.[38]

In so far as one can talk of 'equality' here it consists only in the fact that the needs of all are equally respected and served, but communism is no longer concerned to achieve an equal distribution according to quantitative principles, it has moved beyond equality in that sense. Cohen does not grasp this, he cannot relinquish the quantitative idea of equality. Thus he tries to introduce a quantitative measure to show that the evident inequalities that will exist in the distribution of goods and services are only apparent. Although there are differences of 'benefits and burdens' these do not constitute 'inequalities', he argues, because 'there can be no principled objection to differences in people's benefits and burdens that reflect nothing but different preferences, *when* (which is not always) *their satisfaction leads to a comparable aggregate enjoyment of life*' (Cohen, 2009, 19, Cohen's italics).

In a system of distribution according to need, individual needs or preferences may differ greatly: 'equality' exists only in that they are all

---

[38]Lebowitz, 2010, 72, quoting Marx and Engels, 1975b, 557–8. This is an important passage which I have not previously encountered. It can be taken to imply that communism still involves principles of equality, though not of the sort that Cohen is trying to defend.

met. This is a qualitative notion. The quantitative idea of different 'aggregate enjoyments of life' is an unworkable fiction. How can one assess whether meat eaters and vegetarians, the fit and the ill, have 'comparable aggregate enjoyment of life', except in that each has their needs met?[39] This notion is concocted by Cohen only to sustain the idea that a quantitative principle of equality is still operative here, it plays no other role. Distribution according to need supersedes this sort of equality.

## Justice

Is communism also 'beyond justice'? Will property also be transcended in a communist society? It is often thought that Marx believes so, and that he foresees the total elimination of principles of right.[40] In this respect Marx's philosophy is often compared to that of Hume and other utilitarians. Hume argues that property is a social institution which is justified only as a means of maintaining social order and promoting prosperity. Where it does not have these consequences it has no justification and should be dispensed with. Thus Hume argues that the right to private property is not universal or 'natural' but varies according to social conditions. In situations of acute scarcity considerations of property may cease to be justified. If a person is starving, for example, they cannot be expected to refrain from eating surplus food that is at hand because it is not their property (Hume, 1894, section 5; cf. Hegel, 1991, §127A, 155). Similarly, where there is abundance there is no need or justification for property rights. For example, there is no need to treat the air we breathe or sea water as private property.

Marx's views may seem similar in that he maintains that communism will be a society of abundance in which private property will be transcended, and his philosophy is often identified with Hume's in this respect (Buchanan, 1982; Reiman, 1991, 153ff). However, as I have argued, Marx does not hold that there will be no notion of property under communism, nor therefore is communism 'beyond justice' in that sense. It is wrong to assimilate Marx's account of communism to utilitarianism in this way. For Hume, institutions of justice (which Hume equates with private property) are simply means to the end of preserving social order

---

[39]Cohen (2009, 21–2) acknowledges this problem but sets it aside without addressing it.

[40]Buchanan (1982, 92ff) suggests that only 'coercive' justice will be eliminated.

and creating the conditions for prosperity. They have no necessary place in human life, for it is an entirely contingent matter whether or not they have these consequences. As I have been arguing, Marx comes out of the Hegelian philosophical tradition in which justice and property have a deeper and more fundamental role. For Marx, as we have seen, property relations are a necessary feature of all established societies. Communism abolishes bourgeois private property, but it does not abolish property altogether. It creates a new communal form of property and, with this, new communal, principles of justice and right.

Rawls is another writer who thinks that Marx's communism is 'beyond justice' and that it involves the complete elimination of principles of right, but for somewhat different reasons. His understanding of Marx is influenced by his reading – or rather misreading – of Cohen's attempts to assimilate Marxism to left libertarian equalitarian ideas of 'self ownership'.[41] Cohen gives an over-literal reading to Marx's statement that in communism I can act 'just as I have a mind' (Marx and Engels, 1978b, 160), and he appears to have persuaded Rawls that Marx holds that in communist society we will 'act always as we have a mind to act without worrying about or being aware of others' (Rawls, 2007, 372). This is an absurd and untenable reading of Marx (Graham, 1990).[42] Rawls then goes on to criticise Marx and argue that principles of justice are necessary in all societies. 'The absence of concern with justice is undesirable as such, because having a sense of justice is ... part of understanding other people and of recognizing their claims' (Rawls, 2007, 372).

It is true that Marx describes communism as a society in which the state has ceased to exist, and which is governed by voluntary consent and democratic agreement, not by coercively backed laws. And this does indeed mean that legal justice – law and legal authority – has ceased to operate (Pashukanis, 1978). Such views are not unique to Marx: the idea that genuine community must be founded on consent and mutual understanding rather than on legal coercion is at least as old as Plato.[43] However, notions of justice in a broader sense will

---

[41]Cohen acknowledges that this is not in fact Marx's view, his argument is that there is confusion on this among Marxists (Cohen, 1990, 34). Rawls does not appear to realise that this is what Cohen is saying.

[42]See Chapter 8 below, where I argue that the phrase 'just as I have a mind' is inconsistent with the views that Marx generally holds about communism and the division of labour and should be interpreted with caution.

[43]Buchanan, 1982, 178; cf. Sayers, 1999a, 33–5.

continue to exist in that there will still be moral norms of right and wrong governing human relations, and this is the sense intended by Rawls above. Such norms make up what Hegel calls '*Sittlichkeit*' (ethical life) and are a constitutive feature of all human social relations.

Moreover, in common with many others who hold that Marx's communism rejects justice, Rawls denies that the principle 'from each according to his ability, to each according to his needs' is a principle of distributive justice. 'It is simply a descriptive precept or principle that is accurate to what is done and to how things happen in the higher phase of communism' (Rawls, 2007, 370).[44]

This is a strange and untenable view. The principle of distribution according to need is quite clearly normative, it expresses an ideal of communal distribution. For example, to say that the National Health Service in Britain distributes medicines and services according to need is to describe the ideal to which it aspires, though not necessarily how it actually functions. The same is true in the case of communism. Rawls and others are obliged to deny this only because they are committed to the position that Marx's communism does not involve norms of justice. As I have been arguing, this is simply mistaken.[45]

---

[44]Cf. Wood, 1979, 291; Buchanan, 1982, 58; Cohen, 1990, 36; Tucker, 1970, 48; etc..

[45]An earlier draft of this Chapter was presented at a Marx and Philosophy Society 'Work in Progress' seminar, September 2010. I am greatly indebted to Christopher Arthur, Jan Derry, Nick Gray, Geoff Kay, David Marjoribanks, and particularly to Andrew Chitty and Meade McCloughan for their detailed and helpful comments and criticisms.

# 8
# The Division of Labour and Its Overcoming

It is a fundamental element of Marx's philosophy that the division of labour is harmful and that it will be overcome in a future communist society. People will be able to exercise their powers freely in an all-round way and develop as universal beings. What does Marx mean by these ideas? How does he justify them? Are they as utopian and impractical as many have said?

First we need to be clear about what Marx has in mind when he talks of the 'division of labour' and its overcoming. In the enormous literature on the division of labour in economics, sociology, philosophy, etc., the term is used in a surprising number of different ways to describe various features of work and its organisation. Even within the Marxist literature there is considerable variation. On the one hand the term is used to refer in various ways to the differentiation of productive activities. Thus it can refer to the existence of different sectors of production (industry, agriculture, etc.), or to the various operations which make up these sectors (spinning, weaving, sowing, reaping, etc.), or to the way in which each of these operations is further divided into component tasks. 'Division of labour' in this sense refers to the different activities involved in complex productive processes.

On the other hand, the term is also used to refer to the way in which different tasks are distributed to different individuals in a given society: that is, to the way in which labour is organised socially. When this involves occupational specialisation, and individuals are confined to specific and limited types of work, the social organisation of labour takes the form of a (social) division of labour (Weiss, 1976, 104). Some degree of specialisation has been a feature of work in virtually all societies. Even the simplest and earliest communities have a division of labour between the sexes: for example, with the men hunting, and women gathering food and looking after the home. This is what Nove (1983, 46) calls the 'horizontal' division of labour. The social division of labour often also involves a 'vertical' division or social hierarchy, a division of authority and subordination, rulers and ruled.

Marx uses the term to refer both to the division of productive activities (industry, agriculture, etc., Marx and Engels, 1978b, 150), and also to describe the social division of labour or occupational specialisation (Marx and Engels, 1978b, 150, 160), as well as in other ways.[1] However, when he talks of 'overcoming' the division of labour in a future communist society, it is the social division of labour or occupational specialisation that he has in mind (in both its horizontal and vertical forms, I shall henceforth use the term social division of labour to refer to both).

For Marx, the social division of labour is at the basis of class division. The confining of people to particular forms of work (or exempting them from work) is what determines their social class and their relation to the means of production. It is at the basis of property relations: 'the various stages of the division of labour are just so many different forms of ownership' (Marx and Engels, 1978b, 151). It is also a form of alienation and unfreedom in that it is a social restraint which takes the form of something externally and objectively imposed, a 'fixation of social activity ...[a] consolidation of what we ourselves produce into an objective power above us' (Marx and Engels, 1978b, 160).

Communism, as Marx conceives it, means the abolition of class divisions, it involves eliminating private property in the means of production, and overcoming alienation. Communism will thus involve the overcoming of the social division of labour. That is, it will mean the elimination of enforced occupational specialisation and fixed social hierarchy. Of course, the division of labour in the sense of the division of tasks will still remain. All the various operations of social production will still have to be performed, but individuals will not be confined exclusively to particular tasks or functions. 'In a communist society there are no painters but at most people who engage in painting among other activities' (Marx and Engels, 1970b, 109). There will need to be people to direct and lead, to manage and command complex

---

[1]For example, Marx (1961a, 350–3) distinguishes the 'general' division of labour in society between the main sectors (industry, agriculture, etc.), the 'particular' division of these sectors into sub-species, and the 'detail' division of labour within the workshop.

productive and economic activities, but there will not be a fixed and permanent class of managers, commanders or rulers.

## Attitudes to the division of labour

By the time that Marx was writing, in the middle of the nineteenth century, the effects of the capitalist division of labour were evident. Concern about its impact and ideas about its overcoming were widespread, they are not peculiar to Marx. While the capitalist division of labour contributed to a huge economic expansion, it had destructive human effects as well. Even some of its strongest advocates were well aware of these. According to Adam Smith, for example,

> The understandings of the greater part of men are necessarily formed by their ordinary employments. The man whose whole life is spent in performing a few simple operations, of which the effects are ... very nearly the same, has no occasion to exert his understanding or to exercise his invention in finding out expedients for removing difficulties which never occur. He naturally loses, therefore, the habit of such exertion, and generally becomes as stupid and ignorant as it is possible for a human creature to become. (Smith, 1900, 613)

Such concerns are also expressed strongly in the post-Kantian philosophical tradition, the tradition in which Marx's ideas were formed. Writers like Schiller and Hegel deplore the human impact that the division of labour was having, fragmenting the worker's activity and rendering it routine and meaningless,[2] even though they agree with Adam Smith and other economists in acknowledging – indeed applauding – the increase in productivity that the division of labour had brought about. 'Whence this disadvantage among individuals when the species as a whole is at such an advantage?' asks Schiller (2001, 99).

Although all these writers are concerned about the harmful effects of the division of labour as it had developed under capitalism, however, none of them can envisage any way of overcoming it. Despite their criticisms Smith, Schiller and Hegel all regard the modern division of labour as an unavoidable part of modern economic life and as a cost that ultimately needs to be borne for the benefits it brings in terms of

---

[2]Schiller, 2001, letter 6; Hegel, 1975, 260; Hegel, 1991, §198, 232–3; Kain, 1982.

improved productivity, they confine themselves to suggesting ways to mitigate its worst effects.[3] Smith recommends education (but only in what Marx (1961a, 362) describes as 'homeopathic doses'), Schiller advocates 'aesthetic education', neither give any details.

Some of the early socialists were much bolder. Fourier and Owen envisage ideal communities in which the division of labour would be eliminated altogether. Fourier (1973) spells out plans in extraordinary detail for his ideal society (or *phalansterie*) in which individuals were to move from activity to activity throughout the working day. Owen (1970, 237–70) actually introduced plans for overcoming the division of labour by combining education and work into the community he set up at New Lanark.[4]

## Division of labour in *The German Ideology*

In this way Marx inherits ideas about the division of labour and its overcoming from a number of sources: from political economists like Smith, from post-Kantian philosophy, and from earlier socialists (cf. Lenin, 1969a). Throughout his life, moreover, Marx follows socialists like Fourier and Owen in aspiring, not only to ameliorate the impact of the division of labour, but to do away with it altogether. However, he is hazy about precisely how this is to be achieved. He was famously reluctant to spell out his ideas about future society in any detail. One of his fullest accounts is in a well known and much discussed passage in the *German Ideology*.

> The division of labour offers us the first example of how, as long as man remains in natural society ... man's own deed becomes an alien power opposed to him, which enslaves him instead of being controlled by him. For as soon as the distribution of labour comes into being, each man has a particular, exclusive sphere of activity,

---

[3]'In every improved and civilised society, this is the state into which the labouring poor, that is, the great body of the people, must necessarily fall unless government takes some pains to prevent it.' (Smith, 1900, 613)

[4]Marx mentions these experiments appreciatively. 'From the Factory system budded, as Robert Owen has shown us in detail, the germ of the education of the future, an education that will, in the case of every child over a given age, combine productive labour with instruction and gymnastics, not only as one of the methods of adding to the efficiency of production, but as the only method of producing fully developed human beings.' (Marx, 1961a, 483–4)

which is forced upon him and from which he cannot escape. He is a hunter, a fisherman, a herdsman, or a critical critic, and must remain so if he does not want to lose his means of livelihood; while in communist society, where nobody has one exclusive sphere of activity but each can become accomplished in any branch he wishes, society regulates the general production and thus makes it possible for me to do one thing today and another tomorrow, to hunt in the morning, fish in the afternoon, rear cattle in the evening, criticize after dinner, just as I have a mind, without ever becoming hunter, fisherman, herdsman or critic. (Marx and Engels, 1978b, 160)

These words have provoked an enormous flood of controversy and criticism.[5] They pose genuine problems of interpretation. In the light of Marx and Engels' usual ideas about communism, the account in this passage seems puzzling in several important respects. The inclusion of 'critical criticism' is particularly perplexing.[6] Is it meant seriously? Could it not perhaps be some sort of send up?

Carver has recently reported some important research on the original manuscript which, he claims, sheds light on this. According to Carver, in the original manuscript this passage is written mostly in Engels' hand. A few words and phrases have subsequently been inserted by Marx. These include: 'or a critical critic', 'criticise after dinner' and 'or critic'.[7] Carver (1998, 106) surmises that Marx may have added these phrases to the passage 'humorously, in order to send it up'. That seems quite plausible. However, it is not at all clear what exactly is being sent up or why. Carver (1998, 106) suggests that Marx's insertions are intended to 'reject it as a serious draft'. He goes on, 'to me it shows Marx sharply rebuking Engels for straying, perhaps, momentarily, from the serious work of undercutting the fantasies of Utopian socialists'. Carver gives no evidence or arguments in support of these suppositions. They are inherently unlikely. In the first place, the targets of Marx's insertions

---

[5]Althusser, 1969, 36; Avineri, 1968, 231–2; McLellan, 1974, 147–8; Ollman, 1971, 160–1; Plamenatz, 1975, 143–4; Singer, 1980, 60–4 as well as works discussed below. See also Carver, 1998 for further references to some of the recent philosophical literature.

[6]'Critical criticism' is the derisive phrase used by Marx and Engels to refer to the approach of Left Hegelian philosophers like Bruno Bauer and Max Stirner against whom much of the polemic in *The German Ideology* is directed.

[7]Carver, 1998, 117–18n, reporting editorial work on the original manuscript by W. Hiromatsu.

are the Young Hegelian 'critical critics', not the utopian socialists (a quite different group). Second, there is no evidence of a rift between Marx and Engels as regards their attitude to either group.[8]

Besides the references to 'critical criticism' the passage poses other problems of interpretation. Its purports to describe a communist society of the future, yet, as has often been pointed out, the occupations referred to, are 'solitary' (Nove, 1983), and – with the exception of 'critical criticism' – typical of a simple 'bucolic' (Carver, 1998, 99), 'pastoral' (Arthur, 1986, 137), 'traditional' and 'pre-industrial' community (Callinicos, 2003, 175). This jars with Marx and Engels' insistence, elsewhere in *The German Ideology* and throughout their work, that communism is a form of society that can arise only on the foundation of advanced industrial conditions.

Radical schemes for abolishing the division of labour were widespread at the time that the passage was being written. As mentioned above, Fourier and other utopian socialists had devised detailed blueprints for alternative forms of social organisation. A number of commentators have pointed to specific similarities between the occupations mentioned in this passage and Fourier's vision of work in his ideal community.[9] This has led to the suggestion that Marx and Engels may be parodying Fourier in this passage.

Again, however, it is unclear exactly what is being parodied or why. According to Arthur (1986, 137), 'the pastoralism may well be ironical, since Marx had already, in the *1844 Manuscripts*, criticised Fourier for taking agricultural work as exemplary'. However, the main theme of the passage is the division of labour and its overcoming, and there is no reason to believe that Marx would have wished to reject this aspect of Fourier's ideas. Of course, Marx criticises Fourier for conceiving socialism as a fantastic ideal. Equally, however, he acknowledges the importance of Fourier's criticisms of capitalist society, particularly on the topic of the division of labour and its overcoming. For he shares with Fourier the belief that the division of labour is humanly destructive and that a variety of activities is required for a fully realised life.

---

[8]Carver is here repeating his long standing but questionable theme of a radical divergence between the ideas of Marx and Engels (Carver, 1981).

[9]As Furner (2011) shows, there is some congruence between the activities described by Marx and Engels and Fourier's description of the life he envisages in the utopian community described in Fourier, 1973, 110, cf. also Fourier, 1971, 13–14.

Moreover, he recognises Fourier's pioneering importance in understanding this and seeking ways to realise it. As Arthur (1986, 137) says, although the pastoralism of this passage may be ironical, 'what is not ironical, apparently, is the general idea of such a solution to the division of labour'.[10] All this is equally true of Engels: there is no evidence of a rift between him and Marx on these matters.

The need for a variety of activities in a full life and the overcoming of the division of labour that will be required for this is a constant theme of Marx's thought; and Marx explicitly acknowledges Fourier's contribution to developing this idea in various works.[11] One should be wary of the idea that Marx simply dismisses Fourier as a mere 'utopian'. On the contrary. Given how fantastic and absurd Fourier's writings now seem, what is striking is how favourably disposed Marx is towards them.[12] This is true not only in his later works, when his criticisms may perhaps be thought to have softened somewhat, but also in his early writings. Fourier is compared favourably to Bauer in *The Holy Family* (Marx and Engels, 1956, 118), published only a few months before the writing of *The German Ideology*. In this passage, moreover, as Furner (2011) points out, 'hunting' and 'fishing' are used as examples, with no suggestion of ridicule.

Fourier is one of the 'critical utopian socialists' discussed in the *Communist Manifesto*.[13] Although the utopian character of their proposals is criticised, their ideas are not rejected entirely. On the contrary, Marx and Engels endorse, and indeed praise, these writers, particularly for their ideas on the division of labour and its overcoming. Their writings are not purely utopian, Marx and Engels maintain, they also contain an important 'critical element'. They 'attack every principle of existing society. Hence, they are full of the most valuable materials for the enlightenment of the working class.' Marx and Engels (1978c, 498) mention specifically their ideas for 'the abolition of the distinction between town and country', a fundamental aspect of the division of labour.

---

[10]Cf. Callinicos (2003, 175), 'There is a serious point underlying this passage, which is that the development of the productive forces under communism will be such as to free people from their existing role as cogs of the economic machine.' See also Furner, 2011.

[11]So too does Engels (1962, 402–3).

[12]Marx's (1961a) references to Fourier in *Capital*, volume I, are for the most part positive.

[13]Together with Owen and Saint Simon.

In short, there are no grounds for thinking that this passage from *The German Ideology* is purely ironic, or that Marx is dissociating himself from Fourier and/or Engels in it. Indeed, given Marx and Engels' admiration for Fourier's ideas on the topic of the division of labour one might just as well speculate that they are echoing Fourier's words in order to associate themselves with them. However, the fact is that evidence for any of these interpretations is lacking and the passage remains problematic and puzzling in a number of respects.

In view of this it is tempting to try to discount the passage altogether, as Carver (1998, 107), for example, recommends when he writes, 'the relevance of this passage to the issue of a communist division of labour – however it is conceived – is now thoroughly compromised'. This is also a mistake. The passage expresses ideas that are fundamental to the Marxist critique of capitalism and its conception of communist society. The view that specialisation is harmful and that it will be overcome in a future society is Marx's unvarying view, held throughout his work. It is expressed in a number of other passages in *The German Ideology* (Marx and Engels, 1970b, 108–9, 117–18), as well as in other works throughout his life (Marx, 1961a, 483–4; Marx, 1978c, 531, etc.). The same theme is echoed and amplified by Engels (1962, 400–8; 1958c, chapter IX).

It is sometimes argued that Marx's criticisms of the division of labour are confined to the particular form that it takes in what he calls the 'manufacturing' workshop, where it is developed to an extreme pitch. In such workshops, handicraft work is divided into its component operations and each fragment assigned to a 'detail' worker as his or her sole activity. In the famous description of a pin factory with which *The Wealth of Nations* begins, Adam Smith (1900, 4) describes how the worker's activity is deliberately reduced to 'some one simple operation' which was made 'the sole employment of his life' (Smith, 1900, 6). Smith waxes lyrical about the economic benefits of this sort of division of labour, though as we have seen he was also well aware of its detrimental effects. Nevertheless, he regards these as the inevitable price for economic development.

Marx, too, is particularly eloquent in his criticisms of the 'detail' division of labour in the manufacturing workshop. It 'converts the labourer into a crippled monstrosity, by forcing his detail dexterity at the expense of a world of productive capabilities and instincts' (Marx, 1961a, 360), and thus 'attacks the individual at the very roots of his life' (Marx, 1961a, 363). This has led some to argue that Marx's critique of the division of labour is confined exclusively to its manufacturing form (Llorente, 2006; Rattansi, 1982). There is no basis for this view. As we have seen, Marx maintains that the division of labour is at the root of every kind of class division, not only that of the capitalist manufacturing period. Just as Marx criticises all kinds of class divisions and believes that they will eventually be overcome, so too he criticises occupational specialisation in all its forms and maintains that it will be done away with in a future communist society (Hunt, 1984; Hunt, 1986). 'To subdivide a man is to execute him, if he deserves the sentence, to assassinate him if he does not.... The subdivision of labour is the assassination of a people' (Marx, 1961a, 363, quoting Urquhart).

## Overcoming specialisation

Now let us turn to Marx's idea itself, the idea that the social division of labour will be overcome in communist society. What Marx is envisaging is a system of 'job rotation' through which people will no longer be confined to limited and specialised tasks but will be able to move freely from one job to another. Arthur (1986, 137) objects: 'one does not overcome the present fragmentation of production by collating a heap of fragments'. Why not? Different – or if you like fragmentary – tasks need to be performed in every sort of society and all forms of production. How else can the social division of labour be overcome other than by arranging work so that individuals can 'collate' them?

What Marx envisages is that people will no longer be confined to limited and specialised tasks but will be able to engage in a variety of activities and develop in an all-round way. There is a great deal of scepticism both about the feasibility and the desirability of this idea.

First, as regards its feasibility, specialisation is frequently thought to be an indispensably necessary feature of the social organisation of work in all but the simplest sorts of society. Many pre-modern thinkers believed it to have a natural basis. Plato and Aristotle, for example, maintain that there are natural human differences that predetermine the division of labour.[14] Few modern thinkers accept this view. Modern advocates of the division of labour tend to argue for it on the pragmatic grounds of economic efficiency. Adam Smith, for example, makes the case for the division of labour in this way.

---

[14]In Plato's (1987, book III) scheme, some are born to rule, some to be soldiers, others to do manual work. See also Aristotle (1981, book I). Cf. the Confucian saying, 'some are born to rule, others to be ruled', frequently cited and attacked during the Cultural Revolution in China.

Marx questions both of these approaches. The social organisation of labour is not naturally determined, but nor is it simply a matter for pragmatic choice. The division of labour is a fundamental aspect of the system of relations of production and class divisions. At the present stage of economic development, such economic and social relations take on an alien and independent form, they cannot be altered merely at will. Their form corresponds to the level of development of the productive forces. As these develop so the division of labour changes (Marx, 1978a, chapter 2.2). It is destined ultimately to be overcome altogether and specialisation eliminated when the stage of full communism is reached.

This approach is often questioned. The division of labour, in the sense of occupational specialisation, it is argued, is necessary economically in a developed society. According to Adam Smith it is the main means for increasing economic productivity. The very first sentence of *The Wealth of Nations* announces this theme. 'The greatest improvement in the productive powers of labour, and the greater part of the skill, dexterity and judgement with which it is anywhere directed, or applied, seem to have been the effects of the division of labour' (Smith, 1900, 3). The 'separation of different trades and employments from one another', he argues, has great economic advantages (Smith, 1900, 5). Conversely, when the same person performs many different tasks, expertise and productivity suffer. Arguments of this kind are familiar. 'Jack of all trades, master of none', as the saying goes.[15] However, Smith goes far beyond anything that can be justified by general arguments of this sort. He is trying to defend the extreme form of the division of labour involved in the 'detail' work of the manufacturing workshop. He talks of reducing worker's activity to 'some one simple operation and ... making this operation the sole employment of his life' (Smith, 1900, 6).[16]

Up to a point, concentrating on a particular activity leads to an increase of expertise and is necessary for the development of specialised skills. Beyond that point, however, it also results in fatigue and

---

[15]Cf. Hegel (1892, 145) quoting Goethe, 'the man who will do something great must ... limit himself'; and Hegel, 1991, §13A, 47.

[16]Similarly, Hegel (1991, §207, 238) argues that 'the individual attains actuality only by entering into *existence* in general, and hence into *determinate particularity*, he must accordingly limit himself *exclusively* to one of the *particular* spheres of need'.

boredom. Smith gives no good reasons to suppose that people can be effective only if they are confined to one particular sphere of work as their 'sole employment'. Even the most specialised craft worker, scientist or athlete needs other activities for a satisfactory and full life, and all their activities also benefit from such a diversity. The need for such diversity is well recognised in the psychological literature on work (*Work in America*, 1973) even though these other activities are often regarded as 'hobbies', 'leisure' pursuits, etc.. In so far as they contribute productively, however, they should be thought of as aspects of the division of labour.

## Human universality

Fourier and Marx take an even stronger view. They maintain that variety of work is not only better for productivity and hence perfectly feasible, it is inherently beneficial and desirable. This is sometimes questioned. Cohen (1988a, 142), for example, asks, 'why, ideally, should [people] engage in richly various activities? ... What is so bad about a person dedicating himself to one or a small number of lines of activity only?' The case for variety is often made on empirical and psychological grounds. Thus Fourier maintains that human beings have an inherent psychological need for variety of activity. He calls this the 'alternating' or 'butterfly' passion: 'the desire felt by the soul of periodical variety, of changes of scene and occupations, of contrasted situations, of incidents and novelties calculated to excite charm, and to stimulate at the same time the senses and the soul' (Fourier, 1971, 181). Excessive specialisation makes for unhappiness and inefficiency, he maintains. 'Activity and energy in labor are increased by brief periods of repose' and by variation of work (Fourier, 1971, 182).[17]

Marx's ideas have a different foundation. They have an ontological rather than a merely empirical or psychological basis. According to Marx, human beings are 'universal' beings, endowed with universal capacities and powers. To develop fully as human beings they must exercise these capacities and powers in an all-round way. Other animals, by contrast, are governed by particular drives and instincts; they have only limited powers and are capable of engaging only in limited and particular activities for particular purposes.

---

[17]Similar arguments are put forward by other early critics of specialisation such as William Morris (1973a) and by contemporary management advocates of 'job rotation' (*Work in America*, 1973).

These ideas continue and develop a way of thinking about human nature that runs right through the Western philosophical tradition. We are not mere creatures of need and instinct, we are self-conscious and rational beings. Unlike other species, we are capable of acting according to the universal principles of reason, morality and beauty. We can rise above the level of mere instinct and exercise freedom and choice.

The ideas of human universality and all-round development are central to classical German philosophy. In this tradition these ideas are often worked out in the field of aesthetics. There are historical reasons for this. In Kant's metaphysics and ethics – the topics of his first two *Critiques* – the ideal is conceived as a mere 'ought', separated absolutely from what actually 'is'. Kant's philosophy thus results in an impassable divide between the ideal and the actual, value and fact. In the final part of his system, the *Critique of Judgment*, Kant (1987) points to beauty as a way to bridge this divide. For Kant, however, aesthetic judgement remains purely 'reflective' and subjective in character.

Schiller led the way in seeing a much wider application for these ideas (Hegel, 1975, 61–2). Schiller (2001, Letters 1–3) sees Kant's philosophical dualities as mirroring the social divisions that had arisen in the modern world after the French Revolution – and specifically the division of labour which had developed with capitalism. He looks to beauty and to art to heal these actual divisions and restore human wholeness in modern society. For Schiller, 'aesthetic education' thus becomes the means to overcome the divisions and alienation of modern life.

In this way aesthetics plays a central role in social critique in post-Kantian philosophy.[18] For these thinkers beauty is the ideal actualised: it unites value and fact, the ideal and the actual. Artistic creation both conceives the ideal and shows that it can be actualised. It is the prime example of human wholeness in action, the main means to overcome the divisions and alienation of modern life.[19]

---

[18]This is an enduring feature of work in this tradition. It is evident in the thought of subsequent thinkers such as Lukács, Benjamin, Marcuse and Adorno. As Weber (1977, 79) says, 'it is this concern with wholeness that makes the aesthetic a persistent part of critical theory's concerns. For critical theorists have always seen the aesthetic as embodying ... a non-alienated relationship between man and nature, subject and object, and reason and the senses. They have seen the aesthetic both as a model of such an emancipated relationship and as an indication that such a relationship can exist beyond the limits of the aesthetic dimension.'

[19]Cf. Weber, 1977; Kain, 1982; Lukács, 1970; Houlgate, 2005, chapter 9; Taylor, 1975, 36–8.

The influence of these ideas on Marx's work is evident. The idea of human universality is embodied most explicitly in the concept of 'species being' (*Gattungswesen*). This is a term that Marx adopts from Feuerbach and uses for a brief period in 1844. Humans as species beings are distinguished from other animals by their universal – or more universal – form of productive activity.

> The practical creation of an *objective world*, the fashioning of inorganic nature, is proof that man is a conscious species-being.... It is true that animals also produce. They build nests and dwellings, like the bee, the beaver, the ant, etc.. But they produce only their own immediate needs or those of their young; they produce only when immediate physical need compels them to do so, while man produces even when he is free from physical need and truly produces only in freedom from such need; they produce only themselves, while man reproduces the whole of nature. (Marx, 1975e, 329)

Human production is universal in its scope. Its highest ('truest') form is the free creative activity of art.[20] 'Animals produce only according to the standards and needs of the species to which they belong, while man is capable of producing according to the standards of every species and of applying to each object its inherent standard; hence, man also produces in accordance with the laws of beauty.' (Marx, 1975e, 329)

Although Marx had abandoned terms like 'species being' by the time he came to write about being a hunter and a fisher in 1845, the idea that humans are universal beings whose full development involves the use of all their powers continues to provide the basis from which he criticises the division of labour in capitalist society.[21] The specialisation and detail work to which workers are condemned fragments the whole person and narrows them to a limited and hence less than fully human form of activity.

---

[20]In a much discussed later passage, Marx distinguishes economically necessary labour which takes place in the 'realm of necessity', from free creative activity which occurs in the 'realm of freedom' (Marx, 1971b, 820). Much misunderstanding surrounds this passage. I have discussed it at length in Chapter 5 above.

[21]See, for example, the passages from Marx, 1973a and Marx, 1961a, discussed below.

Many classical German philosophers, including Schiller and Hegel, looked to the ancient Greeks for their ideal of all-round activity. Their lives were not divided in this way. They engaged in many different kinds of activity and developed their abilities in an all-round way.[22] According to Schiller, for example,

> The Greeks put us to shame not only by a simplicity to which our age is a stranger; they are at the same time our rivals, indeed often our models in those very excellences with which we are wont to console ourselves for the unnaturalness of our manners. In fullness of form no less than of content, at once philosophical and creative, sensitive and energetic, the Greeks combined the first youth of imagination with the manhood of reason in a glorious manifestation of humanity. (Schiller, 2001, 98)

Schiller contrasts this idealised picture with modern specialisation and uses it to criticise modern society with its narrow and limiting division of labour. A similar picture of ancient Greece and critique of modern life is shared by many other thinkers in this period, including Hegel, particularly in his early work (Kain, 1982, 34–40).

Marx thinks in similar terms. He, too, criticises the modern division of labour by contrasting it with conditions in antiquity, particularly in his early work. In the *Poverty of Philosophy* (1847) he quotes Lemontey with approval as follows.

> We are struck with admiration when we see among the Ancients the same person distinguishing himself to a high degree as philosopher, poet, orator, historian, priest, administrator, general of an army. Our souls are appalled at the sight of so vast a domain. Each one of us plants his hedge and shuts himself up in his enclosure. I do not know whether by this parcellation the field is enlarged, but I do know that man is belittled. (Marx, 1978a, 138)

Marx remains committed to the idea that humans are 'belittled' by the division of labour and to the ideal of all-round activity throughout his work, but he comes to question whether the ancient Greeks embody this ideal in a sufficiently developed form. This is the theme of a remark-

---

[22]Some of them at least: slaves, women, foreigners were excluded.

able passage in the *Grundrisse*.[23] As Marx notes, ancient and modern attitudes to wealth are quite different.

> [Why] do we never find in antiquity an inquiry into which form of landed property etc. is the most productive, creates the greatest wealth? Wealth does not appear as the aim of production.... The question is always which mode of property creates the best citizens.[24] ... Thus the old view, in which the human being appears as the aim of production ... seems to be very lofty when contrasted to the modern world, where production appears as the aim of mankind and wealth as the aim of production. (Marx, 1973a, 487–8)

However, he goes on to question this view and, with it, the idealisation of the ancient world that he had previously endorsed.

> In fact, however, when the limited bourgeois form is stripped away, what is wealth other than the universality of individual needs, capacities, pleasures, productive forces etc., created through universal exchange? The full development of human mastery over the forces of nature, those of so-called nature as well as of humanity's own nature? The absolute working-out of his creative potentialities? (Marx, 1973a, 488)

What Marx argues is that a fuller and a greater development of human powers and capacities in fact occurs under modern capitalism. However, this takes place in an alienated manner in which human powers take on a form that is independent of individuals and even hostile to them. Thus in capitalist society, 'this complete working-out of the human content appears as a complete emptying-out, this universal objectification as total alienation, and the tearing-down of all limited, one-sided aims as sacrifice of the human end-in-itself to an entirely external end. This is why the childish world of antiquity appears ... as loftier.' (Marx, 1973a, 488)

Here we have Marx's response to Schiller's paradox mentioned above: 'whence this disadvantage among individuals when the species

---

[23]See also Marx's (1973a, 110–11) discussion of the modern admiration for ancient Greek mythology.

[24]An attitude beautifully illustrated in Satyajit Ray's film *The Chessplayers* (1977).

as a whole is at such an advantage?' (Schiller, 2001, 99)[25] Marx's argument is that human powers and human development are, in reality, much greater in the modern world than in antiquity. However, because of the division of labour and the capitalist economic relations of which they are a part, our social powers, which are ultimately the united powers of each individual, have taken on an alien form, external and hostile to the individual. This alienation can be overcome and these powers reappropriated by individuals only with the overcoming of capitalism and the division of labour it has involved.

## All-round development

Thus Marx criticises specialisation by appeal to the notion of human universality and the idea of all-round development. With the overcoming of the division of labour the 'full and free development of every individual' (Marx, 1961a, 592) will become a possibility. People will no longer be confined to a narrow range of activities, they will be able to exercise and develop 'all' their powers. What does Marx envisage by these words?

Cohen takes Marx to mean that in the future people will engage in every possible activity. As he rightly says, that is inconceivable.

> Marx wanted the full gamut of each person's capacity to be realised: 'free activity', he said, 'is for the communists the creative manifestation of life arising from the free development of all abilities.' Whether or not that ideal is desirable, it is certainly unrealisable, as you will see if you imagine someone trying to realise it in a single lifetime. (Cohen, 1988a, 142)

Clearly that is not what Marx means. With the present division of labour people are channelled into particular areas and kinds of work and then confined to these for life. Marx is particularly concerned about the larger

---

[25]Cf. the paradox that Marx poses at the beginning of his discussion of 'Estranged Labour' in the *1844 Manuscripts*, and to which alienation is, there too, presented as being the key to resolving – the paradox that 'the worker becomes poorer the more wealth he produces, the more his production increases in power and extent. The worker becomes an ever cheaper commodity the more commodities he produces. The *devaluation* of the human world grows in direct proportion to the *increase in value* of the world of things.' (Marx, 1975a, 323–4)

divisions, between mental and manual labour, town and country occupations, and so on. The idea of overcoming the division of labour must be interpreted in this context. What is envisaged is that we would do both intellectual and manual *kinds* of work. This is what is required in order to overcome these major social divisions, and this is what Marx and others in this tradition praise about life in antiquity. When Marx talks of realising 'all' our powers, as I understand him, he means engaging in an all-round range of *kinds* of activity. As Ware (1982, 61) says, what Marx wants is 'to replace the partially developed individual by the more fully developed individual rather than a totally developed individual'. He makes the point as follows.

> The abilities that we have are much broader than those we wish to develop. For each instrument in the orchestra, I no doubt have the ability to play it with some degree of competence or incompetence, but I surely do not want to develop all of these abilities so that I can play every instrument. After all, one does not have to play every instrument to develop one's musicality. (Ware, 1982, 65)

The idea of human universality implies that virtually all people normally have the ability to do all kinds of work, at least with some level of skill. Everyone has some ability to hunt and fish, to draw and paint, to do philosophy and mathematics, or operate tools and machinery, etc.. With the present division of labour, the opportunity to develop as an artist or philosopher or mechanic varies enormously according to background and upbringing; and, as Marx says, 'the exclusive concentration of artistic talent in particular individuals, and its suppression in the broad mass which is bound with this, is a consequence of the division of labour' (Marx and Engels, 1970b, 109).

However, the idea of human universality does not necessarily imply that we all have *equal* natural abilities in all areas. In particular, Marx does not appear to believe in universal equality of abilities.[26] As he makes clear, he is not claiming that everyone has the same artistic potential, and that with a different division of labour everyone could do the work of a Raphael, but rather 'that anyone in whom there is a potential Raphael should be able to develop without hindrance' (Marx and Engels, 1970b,

---

[26]In 'Critique of the Gotha Programme' Marx (1978c, 530) talks of 'unequal individual endowment' and recognises that these will lead to inequalities in productivity.

108). Marx's main concern is that people should no longer be confined to limited and specialised tasks but should be able to engage in a variety of different kinds of activity and develop as they choose.

These issues are interestingly treated in Lee Hall's (2008) play *The Pitman Painters*. This deals with a group of remarkably talented painters who emerged from an evening class in the Durham mining community of Ashington in the 1930s. The question is raised of whether, with the same opportunities, similar artists would be found in any working class community. In the play one of the painters indignantly rejects that view. He and the other Ashington painters, he insists, have innate talents that are not universally shared – not everyone is a potential Raphael.[27]

## Freedom and specialisation

The implication of the idea of human universality is that people have a universal range of abilities that they will normally want to exercise in an all-round way. To return to Cohen's question: what if a person would prefer to specialise? Why should they not be able to do so? Marx does not argue that people should be forced to vary their activities.[28] On the contrary. Integral to Marx's idea is the view that work should be freely chosen. One of his fundamental criticisms of the division of labour in capitalist society is that it takes the form of an alien and coercive imposition. In future communist society people will for the first time gain control of their social relations and be able organise their work in a conscious and free fashion. And as universal beings, given that freedom, the implication is that they will generally prefer an all-round variety of activities over specialisation.

Cohen questions this. 'What constitutes the *free* development of the individual is never his *full* development', he says, and Marx 'too casually juxtaposes the two' (Cohen, 1988a, 142). As I have been arguing, the way Marx links these ideas is anything but casual, it comes out of a

---

[27]Evidently this exchange is based on real events (Feaver, 1988). A remarkable group of painters also emerged from Huxian, a remote village in China during the Cultural Revolution (Feaver, 1988, 165–8). Again, there is no reason to assume that similarly talented artists are lurking everywhere. Incidentally, I was one of the first foreigners to visit this village in 1974.

[28]In contrast to the way in which city people were forcibly sent to work in the countryside in the Cultural Revolution in China.

systematic philosophical theory which is part of a long tradition of thought about human universality.[29] The idea that a free choice will be for a full variety of activities is based on the idea that human beings are universal beings. However, given that different individuals have different aptitudes for different kinds of activity, what this variety will consist of will no doubt vary from individual to individual. As Ware (1982, 65) says, 'some may even choose to be one-sided or restricted, but I think most will not and will immediately see better alternatives to the capitalist division of labor'.

As regards this freedom, in the passage about hunting and fishing Marx says that in communist society it will be possible 'for me to do one thing today and another tomorrow ... just as I have a mind [*gerade Lust habe*]'.[30] At best this is carelessly phrased. Industrial work in modern society is intrinsically cooperative. It requires the simultaneous activity of many people acting in concert.[31] Individuals cannot simply work 'as they have a mind'.[32] Organisation and coordination under the command of a directing authority are needed. This is not a feature only of capitalism or of class societies, it is a technical necessity in all modes of production. Marx is well aware of this.

> All directly social or communal labour on a large scale requires, to a greater or lesser degree, a directing authority in order to secure the harmonious co-operation of the activities of individual, and to perform the general functions that have their origin in the motion of the total productive organism, as distinguished from the motion of its separate organs. (Marx, 1961a, 330–1)

For example, 'a single violin player is his own conductor: an orchestra requires a separate one' (Marx, 1961a, 331).

Even though authority and direction are required, however, this does not entail that consent and freedom must be lacking. For work can be a

---

[29]The same cannot be said for Cohen's position on this issue which is simply asserted and not spelled out in any detail at all.

[30]Furner (2011) questions the usual translation which I have quoted. He prefers 'just as I so desire'. It is not clear to me that anything of consequence hangs on this.

[31]A defect of the examples of 'hunting' and 'fishing' as they appear to be envisaged in the passage being discussed is that they are solitary (Nove, 1983, 47).

[32]Cohen and Rawls put undue emphasis on this phrase and, as a result, are led astray in their understandings of communism, see p. 131 above.

matter for *collective* decision and deliberate social regulation. This is often the case with an orchestra or band, for example, which can be voluntary cooperative endeavours. Work as Marx ideally envisages it could be like this. At present it is not so, its forms are dictated by the alien requirements of capital and the market.

As regards the division of labour the question is: how are these roles to be distributed? In Nove's words,

> How is the obviously necessary hierarchy of control and co-ordination to be reconciled with the 'overcoming' of the vertical division of labour? How can one avoid the emergence of the equivalent of an 'officer class', a distinction between rulers and ruled? Is it a matter of election, delegation, rotation? If management is to be responsible, then to whom? ... [F]or instance, should railway management be accountable to the railwaymen or to the passengers? (Nove, 1983, 47)

These are indeed important issues, and not only for Marx's ideas about 'full communism': similar issues arise with the running of existing enterprises where the input and consent of those involved is sought. They are tackled in various ways and with varying degrees of success in existing enterprises. Nove gives no good reasons to think that they constitute insuperable obstacles to Marx's ideas.

When Marx says that it will be possible 'for me to do one thing today and another tomorrow ... *just as I have a mind*' (my emphasis), he immediately goes on to say, '*society* regulates the general production'[33] (my emphasis). The two thoughts appear to be in conflict. Marx is often interpreted to be suggesting that people will be able to exercise a purely individual choice over which particular tasks to perform and when to perform them (Nove, 1983, 47; Cohen, 1990, 31–7). This would imply, for example, that a fisherman could choose only to fish but not to help mend the nets, or a teacher only to teach but not to do any marking or administration, or a manager opt not participate in the work being managed. Clearly this is not what Marx has in mind. On the contrary, these are the sorts of divisions that prevail at present. It is precisely this sort of division of fulfilling and unfulfilling work roles that eliminating the division of labour is supposed to overcome.

---

[33]*die Gesellschaft die allgemeine Produktion regelt.*

If I can choose exactly what I will do purely individually, without regard to any wider considerations, then the social regulation of production is not possible. However, what Marx has in mind when he says that 'society regulates the general production' may involve a social ('positive') rather than the purely individual and 'negative' conception of freedom. If individuals choose what to do not as atomistic individuals but as members of the community, democratically, then perhaps a different way of organising labour can be freely chosen and agreed upon (Graham, 1990, 53–4).

The idea that work might be a free cooperative activity gives rise to some familiar objections. Some jobs are intrinsically unpleasant, it is said, people will never do them willingly. Marcuse (1969) argues that in a highly developed society in the future arduous and routine jobs will be automated and the issue of unpleasant work will no longer arise. This is unrealistic. Automatic machinery itself generates routine work, it needs to be supplied with raw materials, it needs to be supervised and repaired, and its products need to be dealt with. Indeed, even the most creative kinds of work involve routine and toilsome tasks: painters must prepare canvases and paints and look after their brushes, musicians must practice, care for their instruments, etc.. And, of course, like everyone, they create mess and waste which has to be dealt with. It is unrealistic to imagine that such tasks can ever be entirely eliminated. Numerous routine, dirty, menial and unpleasant tasks will inevitably continue to exist. If work is made a matter of choice, so the objection goes, these jobs will not get done.

Fourier has an imaginative proposal for dealing with this problem. Since children positively enjoy playing with dirt, he suggests, gangs of children ('little hordes') can be got to do the dirty work (Fourier, 1971, 13–14). That is a charming but absurd idea. Children no more want to do these jobs than adults, as parents who have tried to get their children to help around the home know. Indeed, children tend to be less willing and less disciplined for such work, though perhaps they are more easily coerced.

However, it is wrong to think that free adults will never do unpleasant tasks willingly. When such work needs to be done and is seen to be necessary then people will do it willingly without needing to be externally coerced (Sayers, 1998, chapter 4). Thus, for example, in cooperative groups disagreeable tasks can be organised on a voluntary rota. It is wrong to think that people are motivated solely by narrow self-interest. They can act cooperatively for the common good even when this means sacrificing their own selfish interests.

This is common experience in the family and among friends. Arguments for the possibility of a free cooperative community frequently appeal to this and, it is said, there is no reason to believe that such forms of organisation cannot also function on the larger social scale (Cohen, 2009). But can the experience of small groups be transferred to larger communities? This may well be doubted. For example, Rousseau, one of the main advocates of cooperative organisation, doubts whether it is possible to create a cooperative community that is large in scale. He therefore argues that a cooperative community must remain small and intimate (Rousseau, 1973). This is not Marx's idea. If communism involves industry it will necessarily be large, since industrial production is large in scale. Indeed, for Marx communism will be a global system (Marx and Engels, 1978b, 162).

These arguments go back a long way. In Plato's ideal republic the family is abolished in the hope that family loyalties will no longer be socially divisive but will instead be transferred to the wider community. Aristotle criticises this. He argues that the form of unity of a larger society is different from that of a family or small group, and greater diversity is essential to it (Aristotle, 1981, 1261a–b). Nevertheless, many on the left have followed Plato in wanting to look upon all fellow beings as comrades – as 'brothers' and 'sisters' – and they have insisted that universal fellowship is a valid aspiration. Marx's vision of communism, I am suggesting, is in this tradition (cf. Sayers, 1999a, 87–9).

Nevertheless, in a voluntary cooperative community there will be some who want to enjoy the benefits of communal productive activity without contributing their share to the common effort. Such would-be 'free-riders', it is often argued, present a problem, particularly for a fully cooperative community.

It should first be noted that there are many 'free-riders' in all societies, though it takes a particular way of looking at things to see them as such. In present society, children, the sick, the elderly, the unemployed, for example, consume without contributing their share economically. If Marx's conditions are met, in a communist society, the voluntarily unemployed or under-employed will be added to the list.

Marx envisages that there will be two stages in the development of postcapitalist society. In the first stage, economic life is still governed by a system of exchange according to principles of justice in many respects similar to those of capitalism. There is a system of property which must be enforced. Individuals are rewarded according to the work they do and free-riding by those capable of working is thus discouraged: if you do not work, you are not paid (Marx, 1978c, 530).[34]

The second stage – 'full communism' – will be governed by the principle 'from each according to their abilities, to each according to their needs' (Marx, 1978c, 531). People will produce and consume as they want to. There are no direct economic sanctions to prevent people from consuming without contributing any work. As a precondition for such a society, Marx envisages that work must first have become a pleasure ('life's prime want') not a chore, so that people will positively want to contribute without needing to be forced economically to do so. Marx also envisages a situation of material 'abundance' in which people can consume as much as they wish without creating scarcities. Given these conditions, no doubt, free-riders will not be an insuperable problem.[35]

Marx rejects the assumption that runs through much of mainstream economics, that human beings are motivated solely by material self-interest (Spencer, 2009). Thus he rejects the view that that we all inevitably want to be free-riders. People are capable of acting in a cooperative fashion for the common good when they can see that their own interests and the common good coincide. However, it is extraordinarily optimistic to believe that work can really become our 'prime want' or that a situation of 'abundance' can be achieved. As regards the less attractive and interesting tasks that will need to be performed, it is difficult to conceive that none will be tempted to relax their efforts. No matter how good the morale of the society and the enthusiasm of its members, there are bound to be some free-riders. It is unrealistic to imagine otherwise. Free-riding is bound to remain an issue and it is doubtful that purely moral means are going to be enough to prevent it.[36] However, if a situation of 'abundance' can indeed be achieved, and people will indeed work because they want to, then the problem may not be serious and free-riders tolerated.

---

[34]To simplify matters I am here ignoring unemployment benefit which did not exist when Marx was writing.

[35]These assumptions are, of course, highly problematic. I will return to them at length in Chapter 9 below.

[36]There has been much discussion of this question in the Marxist economic tradition under the heading of material and moral incentives (Lenin, 1969c; Nove, 1983, 50–4).

## The current situation

I have been discussing some of the common objections to Marx's idea
that the division of labour can be overcome in a future society, and
I have presented some of the philosophical reasons for the view that
this is both feasible and desirable. For Marx, however, it is not just
that: it is the direction in which present society is *actually* moving. His
ultimate answer to scepticism about the possibility of overcoming the
division of labour is that this is actually occurring.

Accounts of the development of the division of labour sometimes
suggest that it has steadily intensified as the forces of production have
developed, and that this has led to a continuous increase in the fragmentation and deskilling of work (Braverman, 1974). According to Marx,
however, its development is more complex than this and goes through
a series of different stages (Ware, 1982, 54–7; Sayers, 1998, 83–8).

In precapitalist society, individual handicraft workers are in control of
their tools and of the whole production process (even though they may
work at the behest of another). With the coming of capitalism, handicraft
production is gathered together in a manufacturing workshop under the
control of the capitalist. The work is divided into its component operations and each fragment is given to a 'detail worker' as their sole activity.
Autonomy is removed, control of the work process passes to the workshop organiser; and skilled handicraft work is converted into a series of
fragmented, limited and repetitive 'detail' operations.

The advent of machinery and large scale industry entail new forms of
working. The tool is taken out of the hands of the worker and operated by a
machine, and the worker is thus subordinated to the machine. Detail work is
replaced by industrial forms of labour: the feeding, supervision and maintenance of machines, assembly line work, etc.. In the process, particular and
detailed processes are superseded by more general forms of work. Handicraft
labour requires specific skills and techniques applied to particular materials.
Industrial labour with machinery involves increasingly universal forms.
Instead of being tied for life to a specific trade or craft, workers can transfer
from one area of production to another. Work becomes transitory and
mobile. Workers need to be more flexible, they must acquire 'transferable
skills' which will equip them for a variety of different kinds of work.[37]

---

[37]See Chapter 3 above for a more detailed account of these developments. It should
be noted that there are some important exceptions to these trends. Some branches
of scientific, technical and academic work have become increasingly specialised
(Weiss, 1976).

When Marx was writing these developments had barely begun. They are now quite evident. Some, like Hardt and Negri (2000, 2005), who rely heavily on Marx's work, portray these changes in optimistic terms as if they were ushering in a new 'postindustrial' era. That may be so, but it is clear that this is quite different from the ideal communist society imagined by Marx. Indeed, for the most part these changes mean only greater insecurity, alienation and exploitation for working people.[38] According to Marx's analysis, however, these effects are not caused by any essential features of the division of labour or of the labour process of postindustrial production. On the contrary, these new forms of work could mean a liberation from narrow specialisations. Rather these effects arise because these forms of work have developed within, and are coming into conflict with, the economic framework of capitalism and the market which exercise an alien and coercive power over peoples' lives.

In sum, Marx's account of the division of labour is not vulnerable to much of the scepticism so often directed against it. Actual developments, so far from refuting Marx's analysis, will serve ultimately to confirm it. If the future that Marx envisages is still far from a reality, that is not so much because of errors in his account of the division of labour and its overcoming, but rather because of the continuing domination of capitalism and the free market. Only when these are overcome can human productive life be brought back under human control and organised for the human good.[39]

---

[38]For example, people are forced by economic pressures to move from one sort of work to another, to 'retrain', to do several different jobs at the same time, etc.. For a graphic account of working conditions for the low paid in America, see Ehrenreich, 2002.

[39]A much earlier draft of this Chapter was presented at a Marx and Philosophy Society Work in Progress Seminar. I am very grateful to Christopher Arthur, David Marjoribanks, Meade McCloughan and other participants, and also to James Furner, for their comments.

# 9
# Marx's Concept of Communism

The crisis that capitalism is going through has put the idea of alternatives to it back on the agenda. Marx himself wrote surprising little about this topic, the bulk of his work is focused on capitalism itself. From early on he came to the conclusion that communism cannot be fully established immediately upon the overthrow of capitalism, a two stage process will be necessary. In the first stage the capitalist state, which rules in the interests of capital, will be overthrown and replaced by a state which will rule on behalf of working people. This is what Marx calls the 'dictatorship of the proletariat', and it supersedes the dictatorship of the bourgeoisie of capitalist society. It will take all private property in the means of production (i.e., capital) into common ownership, and operate it for the 'common good' rather than for private profit.[1] But this is not 'full' (i.e., fully developed) or 'true' communism, as Marx conceives of it, it is only a transitional phase 'between capitalism and communism' (Marx, 1978c, 538).[2] A transitional stage is necessary, Marx believed, because the new society will have just emerged from capitalism and will still embody many of its features.

> What we have to deal with here is a communist society, not as it has *developed* on its own foundations, but, on the contrary, just as it *emerges* from capitalist society; which is thus in every respect,

---

[1]In theory at least. This is the sort of society that was created in the USSR, China, Cuba and other 'actually existing' communist societies.

[2]Some, including Lenin, call this first phase 'socialism' to distinguish it from 'communism' properly so-called, but the idea of separating these phases so sharply is also criticised (Lebowitz, 2010, 107–9), cf. Chapter 7 above.

economically, morally, and intellectually, still stamped with the birthmarks of the old society from whose womb it emerges. (Marx, 1978c, 529)

The new society needs time to consolidate itself and create the conditions for a new social and economic order; but as these are formed it will develop into the second stage of full communism. This is Marx's idea of an alternative to capitalism. It is described in a well known passage in the 'Critique of the Gotha Programme' as follows.

In a higher phase of communist society, after the enslaving subordination of the individual to the division of labour, and therewith also the antithesis between mental and physical labour, has vanished; after labour has become not only a means of life but life's prime want; after the productive forces have also increased with the all-around development of the individual, and all the springs of co-operative wealth flow more abundantly – only then can the narrow horizon of bourgeois right be crossed in its entirety and society inscribe on its banners: From each according to his ability, to each according to his needs! (Marx, 1978c, 531)

Brief and sloganistic as this description is, it has given rise to an enormous amount of discussion and controversy. I will focus on it in this chapter.

As Marx envisages it, communism will come about only when the productive forces of capitalism have been developed to their full potential and their further growth is fettered by the capitalist system. The overthrow of this system, the abolition of private property in the means of production and its appropriation by the producers, will then unleash the productive forces and lead to a great acceleration of economic development, and this will occur in the already advanced industrial conditions created by capitalism.

Although communism emerges out of capitalism, it is important to understand how radical the break with it is that Marx envisages. Communism is not simply an amelioration of the injustices and inefficiencies of capitalism but a completely different way of organising economic and social life.[3] The economic development unleashed by the new social order

---

[3]This is not well understood by many recent writers on Marx's ideas in the analytic tradition, like Cohen (2009), Rawls (2007), and Geras (1985), who tend to treat Marxism as a form of liberal egalitarianism.

will lead, in due course, to a situation of 'abundance'. This will create the conditions for distribution according to 'need' rather than via a system of private ownership and economic exchange. Wages will be abolished: people will work (or not) as they want to, rather than because they must in order to earn a living. Private property will be eliminated, the market and the money economy will be entirely transcended. There will be no accounting of what is mine or thine, and no attempt to abide by the principle of equal exchange.

## Distribution according to need

Let us consider the various elements of these ideas in turn. As Marx suggests, if distribution is to be according to need and the market is to be transcended, then conditions of 'abundance' must obtain. 'Need' and 'abundance' are notoriously problematic concepts. I do not have space to embark on a full discussion of them here.[4] In this context, however, what must be stressed is that the kind of 'abundance' required is not an absolute superfluity, so that anything that any individual could possibly desire is on hand for them. Since desires are potentially unlimited that is impractical. Rather it means that whatever a person could reasonably be judged to need is available to them.

Needs must be distinguished from mere arbitrary subjective desires or preferences. They are determined by what is objectively necessary for human flourishing. However, that varies socially and historically. Beyond the bare minimum for survival, our needs now, in this society, are different from those of people in other kinds of societies and in different historical periods. We are social beings and the character of our needs is, in some part, determined socially. Thus what an individual needs is not a matter of subjective individual caprice, it is a matter of shared understandings about what requirements are reasonable in a specific context. If what we need by that standard is plentiful and freely available then there is abundance in the relevant sense. In these circumstances, the distribution of resources can be achieved without serious conflict, and without resort to allocation by price or mandatory means, such as rationing.

Abundance is a function both of what is available and of the level of our needs. There are thus two different routes to attaining it. A society can either produce more, or limit its needs (Sahlins, 1974, chapter 1).

---

[4]For further discussion of the concept of needs see Sayers, 1998.

Marx clearly and emphatically advocates the first course. From his early writings on, he criticises those who would restrict human needs and hence development. There is nothing ascetic about his vision of communism. He envisages it as an advanced industrial society with its abundance resting on high levels of production and consumption.[5]

Nowadays, this is often criticised on environmental grounds. Marx's view that abundance can be reached by developing the productive forces, it is said, ignores the existence of natural, objective and inescapable – environmentally determined – limits to growth. The aim of continued growth is unsustainable. Again this raises large and complex issues which I cannot deal with adequately here.[6] However, it is clear that growth must be achieved in a sustainable way and Marx is fully aware of that. Marxism is a form of materialism, it is quite false to suggest that it is blind to the existence of environmental limits (Grundmann, 1991b). Indeed, communism should be well able to take them into account. For doing so requires the ability to plan and control the economy, and that will be possible only when the anarchy of the market is replaced with the conscious planning and organisation of economic life that will come with communism.

People are sceptical that abundance can be achieved through economic growth for other reasons as well. Needs, it is often said, expand more rapidly than our ability to satisfy them, and they do so indefinitely. We will always want more than we have. Abundance, and hence distribution according to need, can never be attained by increasing production.

Only a few moments reflection are needed to see that this is a highly questionable argument. Abundance is not as inconceivable as it suggests. It is true that human needs have grown continually throughout history with the growth of the productive forces, and no doubt they will continue to do so. However, at any particular historical period, many, indeed, most of our needs are finite and it is quite possible to satisfy them.[7]

---

[5]This is not to deny that 'false' needs are engendered in modern consumer society. However, such needs must be defined historically and relatively. See Sayers (1998, 66–7) for further discussion.

[6]See Cohen, 2000 for a brief presentation of this argument. I do not believe that this criticism is justified for reasons I state briefly in Sayers, 1998, 166–8. See Grundmann, 1991a; Burkett, 1999; Foster, 2000 for full and well argued defences of Marx.

[7]Perhaps only the desire for money as such has no limit, as Aristotle (1981, 1256b) argues, but it is not a true need.

In fact, abundance and distribution according to need *already* exist in many areas. In Britain and many other similar countries many social services and facilities are not directly charged for, but provided according to need: for example, state education, social welfare services, most roads, some public transport (school buses, free travel for the elderly), etc.. Many local services are also distributed according to need, such as street cleaning, rubbish collection, public libraries, entry to museums and art galleries, etc.. In all these cases, distribution can be free because there are sufficient resources to satisfy all reasonable needs.

Moreover, there are many other areas to which distribution according to need could undoubtedly be extended, since needs are not infinite and relative abundance is possible. This is true, for example, of basic foods (bread, milk, vegetables, fruit and other staple goods), and of many other basic goods and services.[8]

Perhaps the most significant example of provision according to need in Britain is the National Health Service (NHS), which provides a dramatic example both of the possibilities of distribution according to need and also of some of its problems. The aim of the NHS is to provide all round healthcare 'free at the point of delivery': that is, according to need rather than ability to pay. The notion of need here is the one that I have been explaining. In a private healthcare system I can get pretty well whatever I want if I can pay for it. In the NHS provision is according to 'need', and what constitute 'needs' must ultimately be determined by the Service itself. In many cases this is straight-forward and clear, but sometimes it raises controversial and difficult issues. These used to be decided by the various units of the service, locally and unaccountably. There is now a body, The National Institute for Clinical Excellence (NICE), which was originally set up to decide, in a more transparent and uniform way, what treatments and drugs are and are not going to be funded by the NHS.[9] To function satisfactorily these decisions must be socially accepted – that is to say, shared understandings are required about what constitutes need. Moreover, the system can function satisfactorily only if there is relative abundance and adequate resources for such needs to be met. Otherwise, the perception will be of generalised want and enforced rationing.

---

[8] Including higher education (as is the case at present in Scotland), this is a particularly controversial issue in Britain as I write. There is an excellent discussion of these issues in Mandel, 1968, chapter 17.

[9] As of December 2010, the Government has plans to change its role to a purely advisory one.

Similar issues arise in other areas. Nove gives the example of the supply of domestic water. Writing in 1983, he argued that water in Britain was plentiful and hence 'it is not necessary to regulate its use through '"rationing by price", it is available in sufficient quantities for all purposes.... There is no competition for water, there are no conflicts over water' (Nove, 1983, 15–16). Of course, as he notes, things are very different in some other parts of the world, where water is scarce and competition for it intense.

Since Nove wrote this, the way water is distributed in Britain has changed. In 1983 it was freely available to domestic users after payment of a fixed water rate;[10] it is now usually metered and charged for partly according to the quantity used. A justification that is often given for this change is that water usage in Britain has increased and rationing by price is needed to restrain demand. Usage has indeed grown, but to respond in this way is a political choice.[11] Water is plentiful in most parts of Britain. Demand for it, although it has increased, is not limitless. It would be quite possible to discourage wastage and increase supply to meet reasonable needs in other ways (for example, by building more publically funded reservoirs). Nove's arguments are still valid, and what they show is that, in a country like Britain, it is possible to have an abundance of water and to distribute it according to need.

No doubt, there are some areas in which distribution according to need could not be introduced at present: for example with expensive and scarce items, such as housing, cars, or luxury goods (Laibman, 2007, 194). Even in these cases, however, this not because needs for these items are infinitely expandable. These needs, too, are inherently limited. Rather it is because such goods cannot readily be produced in sufficient quantities to satisfy them and create a situation of abundance. However, there is no economic or philosophical reason to prevent distribution according to need being adopted much more widely than at present, and gradually extended as conditions allow (Laibman, 2007, 193–4; Mandel, 1968, 664–8). Such 'creeping socialism' has *in fact* steadily occurred over the years even in the most staunchly capitalist countries. Despite the fears of some on the extreme libertarian right, however, it is clear that the result of this is not usually socialism, let alone communism. Communism will be achieved only when the market and monetary

---

[10]The cost of supplying and distributing it was covered by local taxation.
[11]The change in Britain was connected with the privatisation of the water industry and the change from treating the supply of water as an essential public service to a commodity to be marketed.

exchange have ceased to predominate in economic life, and that is still a far distant prospect.

What I have been arguing, in short, is that abundance and distribution according to need are not fantastic and utopian ideas but practical and feasible goals. To repeat, this is not to deny that our needs, even for the most basic items, grow and develop. They have done so continually throughout history with the development of the productive forces, and there is every reason to expect that they will go on doing so. It would be futile to try to curb them; and communism, as I have stressed, does not aim to do so. Marxism is not an ascetic philosophy of the kind advocated by some romantic and environmental thinkers. It does not seek to limit economic development. Quite the contrary, it celebrates the development of the productive forces.

Why does it do so? Greater production creates greater economic wealth, more goods to consume, and that is what is valued in most mainstream economic thought. For Marx, however, neither production nor consumption is an end-in-itself, nor is economic wealth as such, it is not true wealth. Marx's conception of wealth is quite different. The 'wealth and poverty of political economy' must be replaced by the idea of 'the rich man and the wealth of human need' (Marx, 1975e, 356). The development of needs is of value because it goes together with the growth of human productive and creative powers. This is true wealth (Lebowitz, 2010, 42–5). Communism is of value because it will create the conditions for human development. It will lead to:

> The absolute working-out of [man's] creative potentialities, with no presupposition other than the previous historic development, which makes this totality of development, i.e. the development of all human powers as such the end in itself, not as measured on a *predetermined* yardstick. (Marx, 1973a, 488 punctuation amended)

## Unalienated labour

On the other side of the equation, in a communist society people will contribute 'according to their abilities'. They will work because they want to, not just because they are paid to do so. Work will become 'life's prime want',[12] alienated labour will be overcome. How can

---

[12]*das erste Lebensbedürfnis*, i.e., life's prime need.

communism bring this about? What are the causes of such alienation and how can it be overcome?

Its primary cause, according to Marx, is the capitalist system in which ownership of the means of production is concentrated in a few private hands, and the direct producers have been dispossessed of everything but their power to labour, which they are thus forced to sell for wages to the owners of capital. As a result, workers have lost control of their work and its products, the whole process is owned and controlled by capital. In Marx's words, workers are thus alienated both from the 'object' and the 'activity' of labour (Marx, 1975e, 323–7).

The first step towards the overcoming of alienated labour is taken by communism when it abolishes capitalism and takes the means of production into common ownership. This is the momentous step that was taken by actually existing communist societies such as the Soviet Union, China and Cuba. It constitutes the essential precondition for further transformations towards a communist society. More limited forms of common ownership and control of the means of production can be achieved even in capitalist society: for example, in cooperatives and worker owned enterprises.

When workers own and control their means of production, their motivation usually increases: they have a greater involvement in their work and a greater commitment to it. At least in the early period of the Russian Revolution, when enthusiasm for it was still high, many were prepared to work an extra day on Saturday voluntarily (Lenin, 1969c). However, alienation soon returned as estrangement from management and the state became more widespread (Carr, 1979, 133–4).

Even in the best of cases, however, what is accomplished in the first stage of communism – the taking of the means of production into common ownership – is not sufficient to overcome alienated labour. No doubt, in the right circumstances it can lead to increased motivation, but more is required for the overcoming of alienation. The changes involved in full communism are far more radical.

There is an instrumental aspect to all work, for work is undertaken to create a product, to achieve an end. Where this end is internally connected to the work itself, the achievement of the end can be satisfying and self-realising. But in so far as work is done purely to earn a wage, work becomes a means to an end that is external to it. The work activity itself – what it creates and for whom – is indifferent as far as the end of earning a wage is concerned. The worker works simply as a means to satisfy his own needs and interests. What he produces and how becomes arbitrary and irrelevant. In Marx's words,

> *Wage-labour* consists of the following elements: (1) the estrangement of labour from its subject, the labourer, and its arbitrariness from his point of view; (2) the estrangement of labour from its object, its arbitrariness *vis-à-vis* the object; (3) the determination of the labourer by social needs alien to him and which act upon him with compulsive force. He must submit to this force from egoistic need, from necessity ... (4) the labourer regards the maintenance of his individual activity as the aim of his activity, his actual labours serve only as means to this end. (Marx, 1975d, 269)

In this way, wage labour as such is alienating. The abolition of alienation requires its abolition. People will work not because they are forced to by economic necessity but because they want to: out of an inner need. If they do not want to they will not suffer economically.

Is it really possible to organise society on this basis? The very idea, it is often said, is contrary to human nature. A common view is that we work only as a means of gaining a living. That is also what is implied by the hedonist theory of human nature that underlies much mainstream economics and utilitarian moral philosophy. This holds that we are driven solely by the search for pleasure and the avoidance of pain. Work means toil and pain, we do it only in order to meet our needs, we would avoid it if we could.

Common as these views are, the evidence shows that attitudes to work are a great deal more complex and contradictory than they suggest. There are compelling reasons for rejecting them. Human beings are not mere passive consumers. We are active and productive beings. Working to create and produce things can – potentially – be a fulfilling and self-realising activity. This view is at the basis of Marx's conviction that the alienation in so much modern work can be overcome, and that work can become a fulfilling activity that is undertaken not just as a means to an end but as an end in itself.[13]

Even if it is true that people want to be active and productive, there are other aspects of work which appear to be responsible for alienation, and which even the abolition of both capital and wage labour, radical as these changes would be, would not alter. For there are alienating

---

[13]As I have argued in Chapter 2 above and elsewhere (Sayers, 1998, 2005).

aspects of work that appear to have nothing to do with the economic system within which it is performed. A great deal of work, it seems, is *intrinsically* unsatisfying: it is uncreative, unskilled, repetitive, monotonous and soul destroying. A change in the ownership system might perhaps give those who do it a greater sense of involvement in it. It might increase their motivation, but it will not alter the inherently unsatisfying character of such work itself. Further changes are needed if work is to be made into a self-realising activity.

Some argue that the root cause of alienation is modern industry. Industrial work as such, it is said, is inherently alienating: nothing less than a return to handicraft forms of work is needed in order to overcome the alienation of modern forms of work (Ruskin, 1928; Morris, 1973a; Kamenka, 1966). This is not Marx's view. Alienation, he argues, can be overcome *only* with the help of the most advanced industry. Handicraft work limits and constrains creative possibilities. It confines the worker to specific materials, activities and skills. Machinery can and should have a liberating effect on work. It has the potential to lighten the burden of physical labour and make work more intelligent and attractive. It can take over routine and repetitive tasks. Automation can free people and allow work to become more rational, creative and 'worthy of human nature' (Marx, 1971b, 820, see Chapter 3 above).

But it does not usually have this effect. Why not? In handicraft work, the worker controls the tool and is in control of the work process. In industrial work in capitalist conditions, by contrast, the worker becomes subordinated to the machine and controlled by it. But this is not because of the industrial character of the work. Rather it is because of the way work is organised under capitalism, in which the machinery is owned and controlled by capital and not by the producers. Under communism, the producers will reappropriate the means of production and subordinate them to their collective will. Then industry and science will no longer take the form of alien and hostile powers. They will become forces whose creative potentialities can be controlled and exercised by the producers themselves for the common good, and the benefits of automation will be realised.

Automation is not the whole answer to the problem of alienation, however. Even with a high degree of it, much routine and repetitive work will inevitably still remain to be done. Indeed, even the most intelligent and creative kinds of work – like painting, writing or composing music – have repetitive aspects. Repetition in work is ineliminable.

The problem of unsatisfying work concerns not just the nature of the tasks that work involves but also the way in which they are distributed socially. In the present division of labour, many workers are confined to doing only the routine and repetitive tasks that require little skill. They are treated as 'unskilled' and paid correspondingly. A much smaller number of others are trained to do the creative and intelligent work of planners and managers, designers, scientists, artists and writers. Overcoming alienation (and class divisions) in a communist society must also involve overcoming the present division of labour. No one will be forced to spend their whole working life doing mindless and routine tasks, not because such tasks will somehow have been eliminated but because they will be shared and distributed more equally. In a communist society the division of labour will be overcome. In such a society, Marx says,

> nobody has one exclusive sphere of activity but each can become accomplished in any branch he wishes, society regulates the general production and thus makes it possible for me to do one thing today and another tomorrow, to hunt in the morning, fish in the afternoon, rear cattle in the evening, criticize after dinner, just as I have a mind, without ever becoming hunter, fisherman, herdsman or critic. (Marx and Engels, 1978b, 160)

These ideas raise a great wave of scepticism. How can a modern society possibly be run without specialisation and the division of labour? I have dealt with these issues at length above (Chapter 8) and will not return to them here except to reiterate that specialisation of the sort that existed in Marx's time is already being superseded. The division of labour is being transformed and some of the changes that will eventually allow for it to be overcome are occurring already.

Handicraft labour involves specific and limited skills and techniques applied to particular materials. Much industrial labour is very different. The more automated it becomes, the more it involves forms of work that require general skills. Instead of being tied for life to a specific trade or craft, workers can transfer from one area of production to another. Moreover, the pace of technological change means that people are forced to be adaptable and flexible, and continually to acquire new skills. Work becomes more transitory and mobile. People need 'transferable skills' which will equip them for a variety of different kinds of work.[14]

---

[14]There are significant exceptions: some branches of scientific, technical and academic work have become increasingly specialised.

When Marx was writing these developments had barely begun. They are now quite evident. In capitalism they are forced on people by economic pressures and they usually mean only greater insecurity, exploitation and alienation. However, when the alien power of capital and the market is overcome, then it will be possible to use these developments to enrich and broaden people's lives.

## Is communism possible?

Is all this really possible? Is it really possible to create a society in which capital and wage labour, money and the market, are abolished? We are so often told that there is no alternative to capitalism and the free market that many will dismiss these ideas as completely fanciful and utopian. That would be a mistake. Of course there are alternatives to capitalism. Indeed, communal and cooperative social arrangements not governed by private ownership and market exchange are common and we have all experienced them.

Family life and cooperative activities among friends are familiar examples. To explain and defend the idea of communism, Cohen describes a camping trip among a group of friends. As in a family, this involves social relationships not governed by considerations of property and exchange, but rather by what Cohen (2009, 39) calls a principle of community: 'the antimarket principle according to which I serve you not because of what I can get in return by doing so but because you need or want my service, and you, for the same reason, serve me'. Other examples include monastic communities and socialist experiments such as the early *kibbutzim* in Israel. Indeed, the idea of communist community goes back to Plato's *Republic*. Moreover, as Cohen (2009, 54) observes, 'people regularly participate in emergencies like flood or fire on camping trip principles'.

It is important to remember that such non-market social arrangements actually exist because they refute the claim that there is no alternative to capitalism and also because, ever since Plato, they have been used to suggest models of what the alternatives might be like.

However, it will be said that such models are applicable only in small groups or in exceptional situations (and even then one should beware of idealising the family or friendships, which are often full of rivalries and tensions). In any case, what may work on a small scale or in a limited way, it will be argued, could not possibly work for a whole society, let alone on a global scale as Marxism requires. Families or groups of friends can function as they do because their members feel an immediate bond of fellowship, but this cannot be extended to the larger society.[15] Moreover, most people are not sufficiently generous and self-denying for communism. Human beings are ultimately self-interested: this is what will ultimately prevail.

It would be naïve to deny that people are self interested and argue for communism on the grounds that people are cooperative by nature (Kropotkin, 1955). Human nature is a good deal more complicated than either of these extremes suggest. The ideology of self interest has become so prevalent that we are in danger of forgetting the extent to which fellow feeling exists in almost everyone. A great deal of what gets done in society – for example by parents, carers, teachers, nurses, doctors, and many others – is not determined entirely by self interest, it relies on cooperation and generosity (Cohen, 2009, 58–9). The idea that we are driven purely by selfish interest is untenable as an account of the way in which many aspects of society actually function. But so too is the view that, with the advent of communism, people will set aside self interest and be motivated solely by fellow feeling. The possibility of communism can neither be refuted nor proved by arguments about human nature.

Cohen does not properly understand this. One of his main reasons for doubting the feasibility of communism is that 'we do not know how, through appropriate rules and stimuli, to make generosity turn the wheels of the economy' (Cohen, 2009, 55). However, communism is not predicated on that, it does not require people to be specially generous. People tend to act on what they perceive to be their best interests. The question is where do these lie? With abundance and distribution according to need, there will be nothing to be gained by amassing material possessions. Most people will get more from exercising their creative powers and in working with and for others. They are likely to behave accordingly. But if they do not want to be socially productive they need not be so and they will not suffer materially. As I have argued, however, everything we know about human behaviour suggests that few will take this option, particularly when work is made more attractive – not out of motives of generosity but because being unproductive and inactive is not what they will want *for themselves*.

To return to Cohen's doubts about communism: his claim is that we supposedly know how to make an economy run on the basis of

---

[15]Such arguments have a long history, they date back at least to Aristotle's (1981, 1262b) criticisms of Plato's communism, cf. Sayers, 1999a, 88–9.

selfishness, but not in other ways.[16] Shorn of dubious claims about human nature, the argument that Cohen is pointing towards and that is often made is that the market provides the best mechanism for organising production and distribution in a complex economy. Communism abolishes the market and replaces it with a system of 'production by freely associated men ... consciously regulated by them in accordance with a settled plan' (Marx, 1961a, 80). Such central planning and control, it is argued, is inefficient and will not work on a large scale, as the economic record of actually existing communist societies has shown.

The problems of these central planned economies are evident, but that should not be taken as a reason to write off central planning altogether and think that there is no alternative to the free market. The evidence of experience is far more mixed. In the first place, it is important to see that central planning is an essential feature of the internal organisation of all large scale enterprises, and of the attempts by governments to regulate and control the economy, even in capitalism. The idea of pure free market capitalism is a myth. Moreover, the market has not shown itself to be the efficient, self-regulating mechanism – the automatic recipe for successful economic management – that its advocates claim. Quite the contrary. As recent experience has shown all too clearly, the market behaves like an alien system with a life of its own. It does not necessarily lead to growth and prosperity. Rather, it is an uncontrollable and inherently unstable mechanism. It lurches from booms to depressions in which large numbers of people are thrown out of work and deprived of their livelihoods, and useful means of production are wantonly destroyed. It is a dysfunctional and crisis prone, wasteful and irrational, way of organising economic life that has brought the whole global economic system to the brink of catastrophe.

There is no reason in principle to think that a better way of running things cannot be found.[17] Of course there are alternatives. That is what the experience of capitalism really shows. As I have gone out of my way to stress, many of the alternative forms of economic organisation that communism advocates already exist in embryo in present society.

---

[16]'While we know how to make an economic system work on the basis of the development, and, indeed, the hypertrophy of selfishness, we do not know how to make it work by developing and exploiting human generosity' (Cohen, 2009, 58).
[17]It is argued that in a complex economy, feedback through the market is needed to guide production and this cannot be provided in any other way (Nove, 1983, 30–45). I am sceptical of that view, but will not discuss it here.

Thus communism will not arrive as a bolt from the blue, as a sudden and completely unheralded transformation. The ground for it is already being prepared in present society. As Marx (1973a, 159) says, 'if we did not find concealed in society as it is the material conditions of production and the corresponding relations of exchange prerequisite for a classless society, then all attempts to explode it would be quixotic'.

An essential feature of Marxism is that it understands society in historical terms. One of most important insights that comes from this approach is that capitalism is not eternally ordained, either for economic reasons or by any universal features of human nature. It is not the only way of organising economic and social life. It is a particular stage of human historical development. It came into existence at a certain time and in a certain place and it has evolved and developed. Its periodic crises, Marx argues, show that it is becoming incapable of mastering the productive forces that it itself has created (Marx and Engels, 1978c, 478).

Even though this is still a distant prospect, it is reasonable to believe that this system will eventually be superseded by another and different economic and social system, a communist system in which production will be organised not for private profit but for the common good, and the anarchic and uncontrollable mechanism of the market will be replaced by the conscious and rational regulation of economic life.

# Appendix: The 'Uplifting Influence' of Work and Industry

Prokofiev's 'Soviet' ballet *Le pas d'acier* was conceived in 1925 at the height of enthusiasm for the Russian Revolution both in Russia and abroad. Prokofiev intended it to 'show the new life that had come to the Soviet Union, and primarily the construction effort.' He quotes the ballet's designer Yakulov as saying that the ballet would portray 'the uplifting influence of organised labour' (Prokofiev, 1991, 278). In its theme and its staging it is a celebration of industry and labour.

In a delightfully naïve and direct way, the ballet expresses ideas about industry and labour which were fundamental to the Russian revolutionary outlook and to the Marxist philosophy which inspired it. These ideas would have been familiar to the Russian audience at the time for whom the ballet was initially intended. They were incessantly conveyed by all the means of propaganda available to the new revolutionary regime: in slogans and speeches, in posters, in the press, in films, on the radio, etc.. They were less familiar to the audiences at the first production of the ballet in Paris in 1927, and they are still less familiar to audiences today.

At the time of the Revolution in 1917, Russia was still a predominantly agrarian country. The process of industrialisation was only at its beginning. Nevertheless, the industrial working class was proclaimed to be the political vanguard of the Revolution. In this spirit, the main characters of this ballet are a sailor-worker and a woman worker. They are typical heroes of the Workers' Revolution. They are the new dawn, they embody the hopes for the new revolutionary era. It is significant that there is a women worker as well as a man. The emancipation of women from the private domestic sphere through their participation in the public realm of industrial work was high on the revolutionary agenda.

However, there is another main protagonist with a central place in the ballet: modern industry, in the form of the railway and the factory. The 'step of steel' is the process of industrialisation which would transform Russia into a modern society and create the basis for communism.[1]

These two – the workers and modern industry – were the twin forces of the Revolution. Together, they had created the conditions for the overthrow of capitalism in Russia. Henceforth, the Bolsheviks believed, they would lay the foundations for the building of a fully communist society.

In Russia in the nineteenth century, in the period leading up to the revolution, the introduction of the railway had played the leading role in economic modernisation. Just as in the American West, it had opened up remote and isolated regions of Russia's vast lands. It had connected them for the first time to the metropolitan centres; it had brought trade and commerce, and introduced cosmopolitan influences to regions which had never before been exposed to them.

---

[1]The title was devised by Diaghilev. Prokofiev (1991, 278) professed to be puzzled by it.

The arrival of the train was a major event in a remote community. The scene is familiar from numerous Western films. The sleeping town is wakened into life. In the first scene of the ballet, the train brings out a whole gallery of characters typical of the period. This was the time of NEP (New Economic Policy) when for a brief moment the rigours of communism were relaxed and the free market was partially reintroduced in order to get the economy moving.

In Russia, in the nineteenth century, the introduction of industry had hastened the fracturing and dissolution of the old social order. Lenin (1956) had analysed this process in detail in one his first and most substantial works, *The Development of Capitalism in Russia* (1899). Much of his later thinking is anticipated in this book. Its theme is that despite its initially harmful impact, particularly on the peasantry, the effects of industrialisation would ultimately be progressive and beneficial for Russia. Not only would it bring about the death of the old semi-feudal Czarist social order, it would also set Russia on the path towards development and modernisation. Ultimately it would lead to the birth of an industrial proletariat, the class that would become the vanguard of a future revolution.

These ideas became central to the Bolshevik outlook. Industrial development was one of the highest priorities for the leaders of the new revolutionary regime. They believed it was an essential precondition for building a truly communist society. In 1920 Lenin (1972, 78) summed this up in a pithy slogan: 'Communism is Soviet power plus the electrification of the whole country'.

The October Revolution accomplished the first part of this equation by establishing a government of 'workers and peasants'. The next priority was 'electrification', that is, industrialisation. The revolutionaries wanted this not just because it would eradicate poverty and backwardness, not just for its material and economic benefits. Industry was welcomed also for ethical reasons. It was celebrated for what Yakulov calls its 'uplifting' moral and human effects. To understand these views it is necessary to understand the Marxist philosophy which underlies them.

## Work in Marx's philosophy

Many people think of work as an unwanted and unpleasant activity, as something they do only because they have to, a mere means to the end of earning a living. Implicit in this view is the idea that we are primarily creatures of need and desire – consumers – who wish only to satisfy our desires with a minimum of effort and exertion. If we could meet our needs without the effort of working we would gladly do so.

Marx questions these views. We are not only creatures of need and desire, he maintains, we are active, productive and creative beings. We are producers as well as consumers. Productive activity is what Marx calls our 'species activity', by which he means that it is a distinctively human activity. He also describes it as 'man's spiritual essence, his human essence'.[2]

---

[2]Marx, 1975e, 328–9. These ideas are most fully spelled out in Marx's earliest writings which were not published until 1932. Nevertheless the basic ideas are present throughout Marx's work and indeed they are part of the socialist tradition more widely.

Through work we satisfy our needs in a way quite different to other animals, and in the process we establish a specifically human relationship to the natural world. Other animals are purely natural creatures. They are driven by their natural appetites and instincts. They satisfy their needs immediately, by consuming what is directly present in their environment. The object is devoured, and annihilated in the process.

In work, by contrast, the human being is not driven by immediate instinct. In work we do not simply devour and negate the object. On the contrary, we defer gratification in order to create a product for later consumption. By this process we establish a mediated relation to the natural world and to our own natural desires.[3] Through work, moreover, we fashion and shape the object, we 'objectify' our labour in it and give it a human form. We thus give our own shape and form to things; and we come to recognise our powers and capacities, objectified and embodied in our products.

## Alienation

In this way, according to Marx, work can be a fulfilling and self-realising activity. Very often, however, it is not so. Most often it is felt to be an unpleasant but unavoidable necessity. It is experienced as something we are forced to do as a means to earning a livelihood, but which we would avoid if we could.

When work is like this it has become what Marx calls an 'alienated' activity. Alienation in this sense is a widespread and familiar phenomenon, it is the way in which most people experience their work most of the time. This is also the way in which industry is often perceived. There is a great paradox in this which puzzles Marx and many other social commentators.

> There is one great fact, characteristic of this our nineteenth century, a fact which no party dares deny. On the one hand, there have started into life industrial and scientific forces, which no epoch of the former human history had ever suspected. On the other hand, there exist symptoms of decay, far surpassing the horrors recorded of the latter times of the Roman Empire. In our days, everything seems pregnant with its contrary: Machinery, gifted with the wonderful power of shortening and fructifying human labour, we behold starving and overworking it; the newfangled sources of wealth, by some strange weird spell, are turned into sources of want. (Marx, 1978d, 577–8)

The development of large-scale industry has led to a gigantic growth of human productive capacities. It should be experienced as the greatest expression of human creative power. But it is not perceived in this way. Rather it seems to involve a loss of power for the producers themselves. It appears to result not in their enrichment but in their impoverishment.

It is as though our own productive powers have been turned into alien and external forces, hostile influences working against us. Modern industry, says Marx, is like a genie which we ourselves have summoned up, but which 'by

---

[3]Qualifications are needed here. Some animals work in this sense, some humans do not. For more detailed discussion see Chapter 2 above.

some strange weird spell' has now become an alien and hostile force, out of our control and turned against us. The industry and technology which we ourselves have created has become a power which threatens to consume and destroy us, and indeed to poison and destroy the whole planet.

This need not and should not be the way in which we relate to our own products and powers, Marx argues. It is neither necessary nor inevitable that they should be experienced in this way. Such alienation is not the inescapable result of human nature nor of industry as such. Implicit in Marx's account is the idea that alienation can be overcome. Our productive activity – work and industry – can be fulfilling, an expression and confirmation of our creative powers, not simply a means to an end but an end in itself.

## Capitalism and revolution

According to Marx, the main causes of alienation lie in the capitalist system. People are alienated from their work and its products in the simplest and most straightforward fashion. They do not control their own activity, it is at the disposal of the will of another. Moreover, the materials, tools, and the product of their work are all owned and controlled by others. They are used to exploit the producers and to make profits for a separate class of capitalist owners.

The Revolution put an end to this system in Russia. It expropriated the capitalists. It converted privately owned means of production (including factories and industrial plant) into common property. Work and its products were no longer owned privately and deployed for the profit of a few wealthy capitalist owners. They were to be owned by the state and used for the good of working people as a whole.

With this, the revolutionaries believed that they had eliminated the main cause of alienation. The workers in the new society would now be the collective owners of their enterprises and their products. They would no longer be working for another. Instead of being alienated from their work and its products, they would identify with it, and they would work with a new sense of commitment and enthusiasm.

In the early years of the Revolution commitment and enthusiasm were indeed great. When Lenin (1969c) called for workers to work voluntarily and for free on 'Communist Saturdays' (*subbotniks*) the response was impressive (Carr, 1979, 25–7). The ballet is a product of this time. The brief flowering of Constructivism in the arts, of which it is an important example, expresses what Ehrenburg calls the 'romanticism of the first revolutionary years' (Ehrenburg, 1964, 91). Related artistic movements in Europe, such as Futurism, had a similar vision of industry as the promise of the future. Soon, industry itself came. 'Here was Constructivism, not on [the] drawing board but in reality' (Ehrenburg, 1964, 93). The reality was less romantic. Naïve enthusiasm soon cooled.

## Industry and the division of labour

Is Marx right to argue that capitalism is the main cause of alienation? Many believe that its roots lie deeper, in the industrial form of modern work itself. How can such work possibly be fulfilling and self-realising?

This is the starting point for the earlier critique of industrial society developed by writers like Ruskin, Morris and Tolstoy. It is also the basis for their ideas about art. Beauty is the result of work in which the producer takes pride and pleasure. Such satisfaction can be obtained only from work in which skill and technical ability are involved. In industrial work these qualities are systematically removed. Industry destroys the pleasure of work, hence it produces ugly and cheap products, an ugly society, and an ugly world (Morris, 1973b).

Such ideas were highly influential among radical social critics in the nineteenth and early twentieth centuries. They had a particularly strong impact on the pre-Raphaelites, and on members of the Arts and Crafts movement in England and elsewhere, as well as on Tolstoy and his followers. These artists and craft workers rejected everything industrial and advocated a return to the handicraft methods of an earlier age (Ruskin, 1928; Tolstoy, 1930).

Marx rejects such views as a backward looking sort of romanticism. Marx has a forward looking and progressive outlook, and this leads to the modernist and 'constructivist' aesthetic expressed so clearly in *Pas d'acier*. Industry, he insists, is the highest development of human productive activity. It is the fullest expression and realisation of our productive capacities. It can and should be experienced as the greatest fulfilment of human creative powers.

For most workers, however, it does not have this character. Factory work is tedious, repetitive, alienating and stultifying. No one is better aware of this than Marx.

> Owing to the extensive use of machinery, and to division of labour, the work of the proletarians has lost all individual character, and, consequently, all charm for the workman. He becomes an appendage of the machine, and it is only the most simple, most monotonous, and most easily acquired knack, that is required of him. (Marx and Engels, 1978c, 479)

However, Marx questions the view that these features are due to the industrial character of work as such. All work involves repetition and routine. This is not peculiar to industrial work. Indeed, one of the great benefits of machinery is that it has the potential to take over repetitive and routine operations, as well as onerous and backbreaking tasks, and do them for us. The tedious and soul destroying character of so much modern work is not due solely to its industrial character. The problem lies rather in the division of labour, in the way in which the worker is employed.

The inhumanity and misery of industrial work is due primarily to the fact that the production line worker is confined to a single repetitive activity all day. The work of a craftsman is not fragmented and limited in this way. A carpenter, for example, is involved in all phases of the process, from shaping the raw material through to the final product.

We are all acquainted with the image of industrial work presented in films like *Metropolis* and *Modern Times*. We have the picture of the industrial worker as an insignificant unit of the overall productive process, enslaved to the machine, obliged to repeat a limited set of mechanical and repetitive actions, dictated by the machine. However, it is not industry as such that is the cause of this, but rather the way in which labour is distributed and divided. This is an inherent part of the capitalist organisation of production, Marx argues, which seeks to subordinate the worker and make labour as cheap and unskilled as possible (Braverman, 1974).

## Work as a collective activity

Industry is a cooperative activity on a gigantic scale. An industrial enterprise is a huge collective process which encompasses not only work on the production line, but also the work of designing and maintaining the machinery, organising, administering and running the plant, and all the other activities which are involved in running an industrial enterprise. Each individual plays only a small part in the overall process. If each thinks only of their individual role it appears fragmentary and insignificant. However, this purely individual view ignores the collective character of the activity, it is an alienated perspective. Otherwise viewed, each individual worker is contributing collectively to a collective project as an active member and essential part of the whole. When work is experienced in this way it appears in a different light. For example, a player in an orchestra may see themselves as making an essential contribution to the overall collective activity. Though their part is limited, a mere fragment of the whole, it is essential. There is no reason why they should feel alienated from it, or limited by it.

Again, the Marxist view is that it is not simply the industrial character of work which creates alienation and prevents people for getting satisfaction from work, rather it is the way in which work is divided and organised, and people are individualised. If labour was less rigidly organised and divided, if workers were more actively engaged in all aspects of the production process and had more sense of collective purpose in work, it would be a great deal more satisfying and workers would feel more identified with the overall activity that they are involved in.

## Overcoming alienation

To describe our present situation Marx uses a graphic image. 'Modern bourgeois society', he says, 'with its relations of production, of exchange and of property, a society that has conjured up such gigantic means of production and of exchange, is like the sorcerer who is no longer able to control the powers of the nether world whom he has called up by his spells' (Marx and Engels, 1978c, 478). He sees modern industry as a genie which we have summoned up, but which 'by some strange weird spell' has now become an alien and hostile force, out of our control and turned against us. The industry and technology which we ourselves have created has become a power which threatens to consume and destroy us, and indeed to poison and destroy the whole planet.

This need not and should not be the way in which we relate to our own products and powers, Marx argues. Such alienation is not the inescapable result of human nature, nor of industry as such. On the contrary, that it should appear to be so is itself a symptom of alienation and an indictment of contemporary society. This is the critical force of Marx's concept of alienation and his account of capitalist society. For the sorcerer is capitalism and the uncontrolled operation of the free market. We need to reappropriate the forces that we have unleashed, bring them back under our control and use them for human benefit.

This was what the Russian Revolutionaries believed they were doing in 1917. These are the hopes expressed in the ballet. Much has happened since then to make us more sceptical and pessimistic. But the issues of work and alienation raised by the ballet are still with us. If anything they are even more pressing and urgent today. Industry is now an even greater power with a global reach. It has the potential to be an even greater benefit. But instead, it is still a genie out of control and even more of a threat than ever, endangering the very future of life on earth. If the ballet makes us reflect on these issues and consider the possibility that there may be an alternative and better way for us to work and to live then it will have succeeded in its purpose and demonstrated the continuing relevance of its themes.[4]

---

[4]This Chapter was originally written as an article to accompany the DVD of a reconstruction of Prokofiev's ballet, *Le pas d'acier* [The Step of Steel].

# Bibliography

W. Adams (1991) 'Aesthetics: Liberating the Senses', in T. Carver (ed.) *The Cambridge Companion to Marx* (Cambridge: Cambridge University Press), pp. 246–74.

L. Althusser (1969) *For Marx* (London: Allen Lane).

—— (2006) *Philosophy of the Encounter: Later Writings, 1978–1987* (London: Verso).

L. Althusser and E. Balibar (1970) *Reading Capital*, trans. B. Brewster (London: New Left Books).

P.D. Anthony (1978) *The Ideology of Work* (London: Tavistock).

H. Arendt (1958) *The Human Condition* (Chicago: University of Chicago Press).

Aristotle (1981) *The Politics*, trans. T.A. Sinclair and revised by T.J. Saunders, Revised edn (Harmondsworth: Penguin).

C.J. Arthur (1983) 'Hegel's Master-Slave Dialectic and a Myth of Marxology', *New Left Review*, 142, 67–75.

—— (1986) *Dialectics of Labour* (Oxford: Blackwell).

—— (2002) *The New Dialectic and Marx's Capital* (Leiden: Brill).

S. Avineri (1968) *The Social and Political Thought of Karl Marx* (Cambridge: Cambridge University Press).

—— (1996) 'Labor, Alienation, and Social Classes in Hegel's *Realphilosophie*', in J. O'Neill (ed.) *Hegel's Dialectic of Desire and Recognition* (Albany: SUNY Press), pp. 187–208.

S. Benhabib (1996) *The Reluctant Modernism of Hannah Arendt* (Thousand Oaks CA: Sage Publications).

J. Bentham, E. Burke and K. Marx (1987) *'Nonsense Upon Stilts': Bentham, Burke and Marx on the Rights of Man* (London: Methuen).

T. Benton (1989) 'Marxism and Natural Limits: An Ecological Critique and Reconstruction', *New Left Review*, 178, 51–86.

—— (1992) 'Ecology, Socialism and the Mastery of Nature', *New Left Review*, 194, 55–74.

P. Berger (1984) 'On the Obsolescence of the Concept of Honour', in M.J. Sandel (ed.) *Liberalism and Its Critics* (Oxford: Blackwell), pp. 149–58.

R.N. Berki (1979) 'On the Nature and Origins of Marx's Concept of Labour', *Political Theory*, 7, 1, 35–56.

F.H. Bradley (1927) *Ethical Studies*, 2nd edn (Oxford: Oxford University Press).

H. Braverman (1974) *Labour and Monopoly Capital* (New York: Monthly Review Press).

A.E. Buchanan (1982) *Marx and Justice: The Radical Critique of Liberalism* (London: Methuen).

N.I. Bukharin and E.A. Preobrazhenskii (1969) *The ABC of Communism* (Harmondsworth: Penguin).

P. Burkett (1999) *Marx and Nature: A Red and Green Perspective* (New York: St. Martin's Press).

A. Callinicos (2003) *The Revolutionary Ideas of Marx* (London: Bookmarks).

A. Camus (1961) *The Outsider*, trans. S. Gilbert (Harmondsworth: Penguin).

E.H. Carr (1979) *The Russian Revolution. From Lenin to Stalin (1917–1929)* (London: Macmillan).

T. Carver (1981) *Engels* (Oxford: Oxford University Press).

—— (1998) 'Technologies and Utopias: Marx's Communism', in *The Postmodern Marx* (Manchester: Manchester University Press), pp. 87–118.

P. Chattopadhyay (2006) 'Passage to Socialism: The Dialectic of Progress in Marx', *Historical Materialism*, 14, 3, 45–84.

G.A. Cohen (1978) *Karl Marx's Theory of History: A Defence* (Oxford: Clarendon Press).

—— (1988a) 'Reconsidering Historical Materialism', in *History, Labour, and Freedom* (Oxford: Clarendon Press), pp. 132–54.

—— (1988b) 'The Dialectic of Labour in Marx', in *History, Labour, and Freedom* (Oxford: Clarendon Press), pp. 183–208.

—— (1988c) 'Freedom, Justice, and Capitalism', in *History, Labour, and Freedom* (Oxford: Clarendon Press), pp. 286–304.

—— (1990) 'Self-Ownership, Communism and Equality', *Proceedings of the Aristotelian Society, Supplementary Volumes*, 64, 25–44.

—— (2000) *If You're an Egalitarian, How Come You're So Rich?* (Cambridge MA: Harvard University Press).

—— (2009) *Why Not Socialism?* (Princeton: Princeton University Press).

L. Colletti (1975) 'Introduction', in *Karl Marx, Early Writings* (Harmondsworth: Penguin), pp. 7–56.

A. Denis (1999) 'Was Adam Smith an Individualist?', *History of the Human Sciences*, 12, 3, 71–86.

I. Ehrenburg (1964) *Memoirs: 1921–1941*, trans. T. Shebunina and Y. Kapp (Cleveland: The World Publishing Company).

B. Ehrenreich (2002) *Nickel and Dimed: On (Not) Getting by in America* (New York: Henry Holt).

J. Elster (1985) *Making Sense of Marx* (Cambridge: Cambridge University Press).

F. Engels (1958a) 'The Part Played by Labour in the Transition from Ape to Man', in *Marx-Engels Selected Works in Two Volumes*, II (Moscow: Foreign Languages Publishing House), pp. 80–92.

—— (1958b) 'Socialism: Utopian and Scientific', in *Marx-Engels Selected Works in Two Volumes*, II (Moscow: Foreign Languages Publishing House), pp. 93–155.

—— (1958c) 'The Origin of the Family, Private Property and the State', in *Marx-Engels Selected Works in Two Volumes*, II (Moscow: Foreign Languages Publishing House), pp. 170–327.

—— (1958d) 'Ludwig Feuerbach and the End of Classical German Philosophy', in *Marx-Engels Selected Works in Two Volumes*, II (Moscow: Foreign Languages Publishing House), pp. 358–405.

—— (1958e) 'The Housing Question', in *Marx-Engels Selected Works in Two Volumes*, II (Moscow: Foreign Languages Publishing House), pp. 557–635.

—— (1962) *Anti-Dühring* (Moscow: Foreign Languages Publishing House).

—— (1964) 'Outlines of a Critique of Political Economy', in *Karl Marx, Economic and Philosophical Manuscripts of 1844* (New York: International Publishers), pp. 197–226.

W. Feaver (1988) *Pitman Painters: The Ashington Group 1934–1984* (Ashington: Ashington Group Trustees).

J.B. Foster (2000) *Marx's Ecology: Materialism and Nature* (New York: Monthly Review Press).

C. Fourier (1971) *Harmonian Man. Selected Writings of Charles Fourier*, trans. S. Hanson (Garden City NY: Anchor books).

F.M.C. Fourier (1973) *Le nouveau monde industriel et societaire* (Paris: Flammarion).

E. Fromm (1942) *The Fear of Freedom* (London: Routledge and Kegan Paul).

—— (1963) *Marx's Concept of Man* (New York: Frederick Ungar).

J. Furner (2011) 'Marx's Sketch of Communist Society in the *German Ideology* and the Problem of Occupational Confinement and Occupational Identity', *Philosophy and Social Criticism*, 37, 2.

N. Geras (1985) 'The Controversy About Marx and Justice', *New Left Review*, 150, 47–85.

J. Golomb (1995) *In Search of Authenticity* (London: Routledge).

A. Gorz (1982) *Farewell to the Working Class* (London: Pluto Press).

—— (1989) *Critique of Economic Reason* (London: Verso).

C.C. Gould (1978) *Marx's Social Ontology* (Cambridge MA: The MIT Press).

K. Graham (1990) 'Self-Ownership, Communism and Equality: Reply to G.A. Cohen', *Proceedings of the Aristotelian Society, Supplementary Volumes*, 64, 45–61.

T.H. Green (1999) *Lectures on the Principles of Political Obligation* (Kitchener, Ontario: Batoche Books).

R. Grundmann (1991a) *Marxism and Ecology* (Oxford: Clarendon Press).

—— (1991b) 'The Ecological Challenge to Marxism', *New Left Review*, 187, 103–20.

J. Habermas (1972) *Knowledge and Human Interests* (London: Heinemann).

—— (1987) *The Philosophical Discourse of Modernity: Twelve Lectures*, trans. F.G. Lawrence (Cambridge: Polity).

—— (1996) 'Labor and Interaction: Remarks on Hegel's Jena Philosophy of Mind', in J. O'Neill (ed.) *Hegel's Dialectic of Desire and Recognition* (Albany: SUNY Press), pp. 123–48.

L. Hall (2008) *The Pitman Painters* (London: Faber and Faber).

M. Hardt and A. Negri (2000) *Empire* (Cambridge MA: Harvard University Press).

—— (2005) *Multitude: War and Democracy in the Age of Empire* (London: Hamish Hamilton).

F.A. Hayek (1960) *The Constitution of Liberty* (London: Routledge).

G.W.F. Hegel (1892) *Logic*, trans. W. Wallace, 2nd edn (Oxford: Clarendon Press).

—— (1895) *Lectures on the Philosophy of Religion*, trans. E.B. Spiers and J.B. Sanderson (London: Kegan Paul, Trench and Trübner).

—— (1956) *The Philosophy of History*, trans. J. Sibree (New York: Dover Publications).

—— (1969) *Science of Logic*, trans. A.V. Miller (London: Allen and Unwin).

—— (1971) *Vorlesungen über die Ästhetik: Erster und zweiter Teil* (Stuttgart: Philipp Reclam jun.).

—— (1975) *Aesthetics: Lectures on Fine Art*, trans. T.M. Knox (Oxford: Clarendon Press).

—— (1977) *Phenomenology of Spirit*, trans. A.V. Miller (Oxford: Clarendon Press).

—— (1979) *System of Ethical Life (1802/3) and First Philosophy of Spirit (Part III of the System of Speculative Philosophy 1803/4)*, trans. H.S. Harris and T.M. Knox (Albany: SUNY Press).

—— (1983) *Hegel and the Human Spirit*, trans. L. Rauch (Detroit: Wayne State University Press).

—— (1988a) *Introduction to the Philosophy of History*, trans. L. Rauch (Indianapolis: Hackett).

—— (1988b) *Lectures on the Philosophy of Religion. One-Volume Edition. The Lectures of 1827*, trans. R.F. Brown, P.C. Hodgson and J.M. Stewart (Berkeley: University of California Press).

—— (1991) *Elements of the Philosophy of Right*, trans. H.B. Nisbet (Cambridge: Cambridge University Press).

—— (1997) *Lectures on Natural Right and Political Science*, trans. J.M. Stewart and P.C. Hodgson (Berkeley: University of California Press).

M. Heidegger (1962) *Being and Time*, trans. J. Macquarrie and E. Robinson (Oxford: Blackwell).

A. Heller (1976) *The Theory of Need in Marx* (London: Alison and Busby).

T. Hobbes (1985) *Leviathan* (Harmondsworth: Penguin).

E.J. Hobsbawm (1964) *Labouring Men: Studies in the History of Labour* (London: Weidenfeld and Nicolson).

A. Honneth (2007) *Disrespect: The Normative Foundations of Critical Theory* (Cambridge: Polity Press).

—— (2008) *Reification: A New Look at an Old Idea* (Oxford: Oxford University Press).

S. Houlgate (2005) *An Introduction to Hegel: Freedom, Truth and History*, 2nd edn (Oxford: Blackwell).

D. Hume (1894) 'An Enquiry Concerning the Principles of Morals', in L.A. Selby-Bigge (ed.) *Enquiries*, 1st edn (Oxford: Clarendon Press)

E.K. Hunt (1984) 'Was Marx a Utopian Socialist?', *Science & Society*, 48, 1, 90–7.

—— (1986) 'The Putative Defects of Socialist Planning', *Science & Society*, 50, 1, 102–7.

T. Hunt (2010) *The Frock-Coated Communist: The Life and Times of the Original Champagne Socialist* (London: Penguin).

P.J. Kain (1982) *Schiller, Hegel, and Marx. State, Society, and the Aesthetic Ideal of Ancient Greece* (Kingston, Ontario: McGill-Queen's University Press).

E. Kamenka (1966) 'Marxian Humanism and the Crisis in Socialist Ethics', in E. Fromm (ed.) *Socialist Humanism* (Garden City NY: Anchor Books), pp. 118–29.

I. Kant (1963) 'Conjectural Beginning of Human History', in L.W. Beck (ed.) *On History* (Indianapolis: Bobbs-Merrill).

—— (1987) *Critique of Judgment: Including the First Introduction*, trans. W.S. Pluhar (Indianapolis: Hackett).

S. Kierkegaard (1941) *Concluding Unscientific Postscript*, trans. D.F. Swenson and W. Lowrie (Princeton: Princeton University Press).

—— (1962) *The Present Age*, trans. A. Dru (New York: Harper & Row).

J.C. Klagge (1986) 'Marx's Realms of "Freedom" and "Necessity"', *Canadian Journal of Philosophy*, 16, 4, 769–78.

D. Knowles (2002) *Hegel and the Philosophy of Right* (London: Routledge).

P. Kropotkin (1955) *Mutual Aid: A Factor of Evolution* (Boston: Extending Horizons Press).

T.S. Kuhn (1970) *The Structure of Scientific Revolutions* (Chicago: University of Chicago Press).

D. Laibman (2007) *Deep History: A Study in Social Evolution and Human Potential* (Albany: SUNY Press).

M. Lazzarato (1996) 'Immaterial Labor', in P. Virno and M. Hardt (eds) *Radical Thought in Italy: A Potential Politics* (Minneapolis: University of Minnesota Press), pp. 133–47.

M.A. Lebowitz (2010) *The Socialist Alternative: Real Human Development* (New York: Monthly Review Press).

V.I. Lenin (1956) *The Development of Capitalism in Russia* (Moscow: Progress Publishers).

—— (1969a) 'The Three Sources and the Three Component Parts of Marxism', in *Selected Works. A One-Volume Selection of Lenin's Most Essential Writings* (London: Lawrence & Wishart), pp. 20–4.

—— (1969b) 'State and Revolution', in *Selected Works. A One-Volume Selection of Lenin's Most Essential Writings* (London: Lawrence & Wishart), pp. 264–351.

—— (1969c) 'A Great Beginning', in *Selected Works. A One-Volume Selection of Lenin's Most Essential Writings* (London: Lawrence & Wishart), pp. 478–96.

—— (1972) *On the Development of Heavy Industry and Electrification* (Moscow: Progress Publishers).

D. Leopold (2007) *The Young Karl Marx: German Philosophy, Modern Politics, and Human Flourishing* (Cambridge: Cambridge University Press).

M.A. Lifshitz (1973) *The Philosophy of Art of Karl Marx*, trans. R.B. Winn (London: Pluto Press).

R. Llorente (2006) 'Analytical Marxism and the Division of Labor', *Science & Society*, 70, 2, 232–51.

N. Lobkowicz (1967) *Theory and Practice: History of a Concept from Aristotle to Marx* (Notre Dame: University of Notre Dame Press).

J. Locke (1988) *Two Treatises of Government*, 2nd edn (Cambridge: Cambridge University Press).

K. Löwith (1967) *From Hegel to Nietzsche: The Revolution in Nineteenth-Century Thought*, trans. D.E. Green (Garden City NJ: Anchor Books).

M. Löwy (2003) *The Theory of Revolution in the Young Marx* (Leiden: Brill).

G. Lukács (1970) 'The Ideal of the Harmonious Man in Bourgeois Aesthetics', in *Writer and Critic and Other Essays* (London: Merlin Press), pp. 89–102.

—— (1975) *The Young Hegel* (London: Merlin Press).

A. MacIntyre (1985) *After Virtue*, 2nd edn (London: Duckworth).

E. Mandel (1968) *Marxist Economic Theory* (London: Merlin Press).

B. Mandeville (1970) *The Fable of the Bees* (Harmondsworth: Penguin).

Mao Tsetung, [Mao Zedong] (1967) 'Why Is It That Red Political Power Can Exist in China?', in *Selected Works*, 1 (Peking: Foreign Languages Press), pp. 63–72.

H. Marcuse (1955) *Reason and Revolution: Hegel and the Rise of Social Theory*, 2nd edn (London: Routledge and Kegan Paul).

—— (1969) 'The Realm of Necessity and the Realm of Freedom', *Praxis*, 5, 20–5.

K. Marx (1958) 'The Civil War in France', in *Marx-Engels Selected Works in Two Volumes*, I (Moscow: Foreign Languages Publishing House), pp. 473–545.

—— (1961a) *Capital*, I, trans. S. Moore and E. Aveling (Moscow: Foreign Languages Publishing House).

—— (1961b) *Selected Writings in Sociology and Social Philosophy*, 2nd edn (Harmondsworth: Penguin).

—— (1964) *Pre-Capitalist Economic Formations* (London: Lawrence & Wishart).

—— (1971a) *A Contribution to a Critique of Political Economy* (Moscow: Progress).

—— (1971b) *Capital*, III (Moscow: Progress).

—— (1972) *Theories of Surplus Value*, III, trans. J. Cohen (London: Lawrence & Wishart).

—— (1973a) *Grundrisse: Foundations of the Critique of Political Economy (Rough Draft)*, trans. M. Nicolaus (Harmondsworth: Penguin).

—— (1973b) 'The Eighteenth Brumaire of Louis Bonaparte', in *Surveys from Exile* (Harmondsworth: Penguin), pp. 143–249.

—— (1975a) *Early Writings* (Harmondsworth: Penguin).

—— (1975b) 'Letters from the Franco-German Yearbooks', in *Early Writings* (Harmondsworth: Penguin), pp. 199–209.

—— (1975c) 'On the Jewish Question', in *Early Writings* (Harmondsworth: Penguin), pp. 211–41.

—— (1975d) 'Excerpts from James Mill's Elements of Political Economy', in *Early Writings* (Harmondsworth: Penguin), pp. 259–78.

—— (1975e) 'Economic and Philosophical Manuscripts of 1844', in *Early Writings* (Harmondsworth: Penguin), pp. 279–400.

—— (1976) 'The Result of the Immediate Process of Production', in *Capital*, 1 (Harmondsworth: Penguin), pp. 941–1048.

—— (1978a) *The Poverty of Philosophy* (Peking: Foreign Languages Press).

—— (1978b) 'Preface to *a Contribution to the Critique of Political Economy*', in R.C. Tucker (ed.) *The Marx-Engels Reader*, 2nd edn (New York: W.W. Norton), pp. 3–6.

—— (1978c) 'Critique of the Gotha Program', in R.C. Tucker (ed.) *The Marx-Engels Reader*, 2nd edn (New York: W.W. Norton), pp. 525–41.

—— (1978d) 'Speech at the Anniversary of the *People's Paper*', in R.C. Tucker (ed.) *The Marx-Engels Reader*, 2nd edn (New York: W.W. Norton), pp. 577–8.

—— (1978e) 'The Future Results of the British Rule in India', in R.C. Tucker (ed.) *The Marx-Engels Reader*, 2nd edn (New York: W.W. Norton), pp. 659–64.

—— (1988) 'Economic Manuscripts of 1861–3', in *Karl Marx and Frederick Engels Collected Works*, 30 (London: Lawrence & Wishart).

K. Marx and F. Engels (1956) *The Holy Family: Or Critique of Critical Critique*, trans. R. Dixon (Moscow: Foreign Languages Publishing House).

—— (1970a) *Marx/Engels Gesamtausgabe (MEGA)*, Abt. I Band 3 (Glashütten im Taunus: Verlag Detlev Auvermann KG).

—— (1970b) 'Selections from Parts 2 and 3', in C.J. Arthur (ed.) *The German Ideology Part 1* (New York: International Publishers), pp. 97–120.

—— (1975a) *Karl Marx Frederick Engels Collected Works*, 3 (London: Lawrence & Wishart).

—— (1975b) *Karl Marx Frederick Engels Collected Works*, 5 (London: Lawrence & Wishart).

—— (1978a) *The Marx-Engels Reader*, trans. R.C. Tucker, 2nd edn (New York: W.W. Norton).

—— (1978b) 'The German Ideology: Part I', in R.C. Tucker (ed.) *The Marx-Engels Reader*, 2nd edn (New York: W.W. Norton), pp. 146–200.

—— (1978c) 'Manifesto of the Communist Party', in R.C. Tucker (ed.) *The Marx-Engels Reader*, 2nd edn (New York: W.W. Norton), pp. 473–500.

—— (1998) *Ausgewählte Werke. Digitale Bibliothek, Band 11* (Berlin: Directmedia).

J. McCarney (1991) 'The True Realm of Freedom: Marxist Philosophy after Communism', *New Left Review*, 189, 19–38.

D. McLellan (1974) *Karl Marx. His Life and Thought* (London: Macmillan).

J. McMurtry (1978) *The Structure of Marx's World-View* (Princeton: Princeton University Press).

I. Mészáros (1970) *Marx's Theory of Alienation* (London: Merlin Press).

J. S. Mill (1962) 'On Liberty', in M. Warnock (ed.) *Utilitarianism and Other Writings* (London: Fontana).

C. Morris (2004) *Thought for the Day*, BBC Radio 4, 22 March, 2004 (http://www.bbc.co.uk/religion/programmes/thought/)

W. Morris (1973a) 'Art Under Plutocracy', in A.L. Morton (ed.) *Political Writings of William Morris* (London: Lawrence & Wishart), pp. 57–85.

—— (1973b) 'Art and Socialism', in *Political Writings of William Morris* (London: Lawrence & Wishart), pp. 109–33.

F. Nietzsche (1994) *On the Genealogy of Morality*, trans. C. Diethe (Cambridge: Cambridge University Press).

A. Nove (1983) *The Economics of Feasible Socialism* (London: Allen and Unwin).

J. O'Neill (ed.) (1996) *Hegel's Dialectic of Desire and Recognition: Texts and Commentary* (Albany: SUNY Press).

B. Ollman (1971) *Alienation: Marx's Conception of Man in Capitalist Society* (Cambridge: University Press).

R. Owen (1970) *A New View of Society and Report to the County of Lanark* (Harmondsworth: Penguin).

F. Pappenheim (1959) *The Alienation of Modern Man: An Interpretation Based on Marx and Tönnies* (New York: Monthly Review Press).

E.B. Pashukanis (1978) *Law and Marxism: A General Theory*, trans. B. Einhorn (London: Ink Links).

J. Plamenatz (1975) *Karl Marx's Philosophy of Man* (Oxford: Clarendon Press).

Plato (1987) *The Republic*, trans. H.D.P. Lee, 2nd revised edn (Harmondsworth: Penguin).

S.S. Prawer (1976) *Karl Marx and World Literature* (Oxford: Oxford University Press).

S. Prokofiev (1991) *Soviet Diary 1927 and Other Writings*, trans. O. Prokofiev (London: Faber and Faber).

A. Rattansi (1982) *Marx and the Division of Labour* (London: Macmillan).

J. Rawls (2000) *Lectures on the History of Moral Philosophy* (Cambridge MA: Harvard University Press).

—— (2007) *Lectures on the History of Political Philosophy* (Cambridge MA: Belknap Press).

J. Reiman (1991) 'Moral Philosophy: The Critique of Capitalism and the Problem of Ideology', in T. Carver (ed.) *The Cambridge Companion to Marx* (Cambridge: Cambridge University Press), pp. 143–67.

H.A. Reyburn (1921) *The Ethical Theory of Hegel: A Study of the Philosophy of Right* (Oxford: Clarendon Press).

M. Riedel (1984) *Between Tradition and Revolution: The Hegelian Transformation of Political Philosophy* (Cambridge: Cambridge University Press).

M.A. Rose (1984) *Marx's Lost Aesthetic: Karl Marx and the Visual Arts* (Cambridge: Cambridge University Press).

J.J. Rousseau (1973) *The Social Contract and Discourses*, trans. G.D.H. Cole (London: Dent).

J. Ruskin (1928) *The Nature of Gothic: A Chapter from the Stones of Venice* (London: George Allen and Unwin).

M. Sahlins (1974) *Stone Age Economics* (London: Tavistock).

M.J. Sandel (1982) *Liberalism and the Limits of Justice* (Cambridge: Cambridge University Press).

J.-P. Sartre (1957) *Being and Nothingness*, trans. H.E. Barnes (London: Methuen).

—— (1960) *The Problem of Method*, trans. H.E. Barnes (London: Methuen).

S. Sayers (1980) 'Forces of Production and Relations of Production in Socialist Society', *Radical Philosophy*, 24, 19–26.

—— (1990a) 'Marxism and Actually Existing Socialism', in D. McLellan and S. Sayers (eds) *Socialism and Morality* (London: Macmillan), pp. 42–64.

—— (1990b) 'Marxism and the Dialectical Method: A Critique of G.A. Cohen', in S. Sayers and P. Osborne (eds) *Socialism, Feminism and Philosophy: A Radical Philosophy Reader* (London: Routledge), pp. 140–68.

—— (1997) 'Who Are My Peers? The Research Assessment Exercise in Philosophy', *Radical Philosophy*, 83, 2–5.

—— (1998) *Marxism and Human Nature* (London: Routledge).

—— (1999a) *Plato's Republic: An Introduction* (Edinburgh: Edinburgh University Press).

—— (1999b) 'Identity and Community', *Journal of Social Philosophy*, 30, 1, 147–60.

—— (2005) 'Why Work? Marx and Human Nature', *Science & Society*, 69, 4, 606–16.

—— (2011) 'Macintyre and Modernity', in P. Blackledge and K. Knight (eds) *Virtue and Politics: Alasdair Macintyre's Revolutionary Aristotelianism* (Notre Dame: University of Notre Dame Press).

R.L. Schacht (1971) *Alienation* (London: Allen and Unwin).

F. Schiller (2001) 'Letters on the Aesthetic Education of Man', in W. Hinderer and D.O. Dahlstrom (eds) *Essays* (New York: Continuum), pp. 86–178.

P. Singer (1980) *Marx* (Oxford: Oxford University Press).

A. Smith (1900) *An Inquiry into the Nature and Causes of the Wealth of Nations* (London: George Routledge and Son Ltd).

D.A. Spencer (2009) *The Political Economy of Work* (London: Routledge).

P.G. Stillman (1974) 'Hegel's Critique of Liberal Theories of Rights', *American Political Science Review*, 68, 3, 1086–92.

—— (1980a) 'Property, Freedom, and Individuality in Hegel's and Marx's Political Thought', in J.R. Pennock and J.W. Chapman (eds) *Property* (New York: New York University Press)

—— (1980b) 'Person, Property and Civil Society in the *Philosophy of Right*', in D.P. Verene (ed.) *Hegel's Social and Political Thought* (New York: Humanities Press), pp. 103–17.

C. Taylor (1975) *Hegel* (Cambridge: Cambridge University Press).

—— (1985) 'Atomism', in *Philosophy and the Human Sciences* (Cambridge: Cambridge University Press), pp. 187–210.

—— (1991) *The Ethics of Authenticity* (Cambridge MA: Harvard University Press).

L. Tolstoy (1930) *What Is Art?*, trans. A. Maude (London: Oxford University Press).

L. Trilling (1972) *Sincerity and Authenticity* (London: Oxford University Press).

R.C. Tucker (1961) *Philosophy and Myth in Karl Marx* (Cambridge: Cambridge University Press).

—— (1970) *The Marxian Revolutionary Idea* (London: George Allen and Unwin).

P. Van Parijs ed. (1992) *Arguing for Basic Income: Ethical Foundations for a Radical Reform* (London: Verso).

M. Walzer (1990) 'The Communitarian Critique of Liberalism', *Political Theory*, 18, 1, 6–23.

R. Ware (1982) 'Marx, the Division of Labor and Human Nature', *Social Theory and Practice*, 8, 43–72.

M. Weber (1958) *The Protestant Ethic and the Spirit of Capitalism*, trans. T. Parsons (New York: Scribners).

S.M. Weber (1977) 'Aesthetic Experience and Self-Reflection as Emancipatory Processes: Two Complementary Aspects of Critical Theory', in J. O'Neill (ed.) *On Critical Theory* (London: Heinemann Educational Books), pp. 78–103.

D.D. Weiss (1976) 'Marx Versus Smith on the Division of Labor', *Monthly Review*, 28, 3, 104–18.

M. Westphal (1987) *Kierkegaard's Critique of Reason and Society* (Macon GA: Mercer University Press).

A.W. Wood (1979) 'Marx on Right and Justice: A Reply to Husami', *Philosophy and Public Affairs*, 8, 3, 267–95.

—— (1981a) *Karl Marx* (London: Routledge and Kegan Paul).

—— (1981b) 'Marx and Equality', in J. Mepham and D.-H. Ruben (eds) *Issues in Marxist Philosophy*, IV (Sussex: Harvester Press), pp. 195–222.

*Work in America: Report of a Special Task Force to the Secretary of Health Education and Welfare* (1973) (Cambridge MA: The MIT Press).

J.S. Zeisel (1958) 'The Workweek in American Industry 1850–1956', in E. Larrabee and R. Meyersohn (eds) *Mass Leisure* (Glencoe IL: The Free Press), pp. 145–53.

# Index

Since references to 'alienation', 'Hegel' and 'Marx' occur throughout they are not indexed as such.